Chapter 9 – Conclusions concerning Articles 7, 8, 11, 14, 17 and 18 of the Charter and Article 1 of the 1988 Additional Protocol in respect of the Netherlands

Article 7 — The right of children and young persons to protection

Paragraph 1 – Minimum age of admission to employment

The report describes the rules which apply to the employment of children in the Netherlands. Under the Working Hours Act (ATW), which entered into force in 1996, and the Child Labour Regulations, children under the age of 16 years may not be employed, subject to the exceptions listed below.

Children from the age of 12 onwards are allowed to assist with the carrying out of light work of a non-industrial nature within the context of an alternative sanction.

Children between 13 and 15 years of age are permitted:

– on school days to carry out "domestic chores and chores within the neighbourhood" for up to 2 hours a day and 12 hours per week. The tasks permitted are exhaustively listed in the regulations;

– on Saturdays and other free days to assist with the carrying out of light work of a non-industrial nature, for up to 6 hours a day;

– in holiday weeks assist with the carrying out of light work of a non-industrial nature, for up to 7 hours per day and 35 hours per week, and for no more than 4 weeks a year and only for 3 consecutive weeks. The Committee refers in this respect to its observations under Article 7 para 3.

Children between the age of 13 and 15 years may not work on Sundays and may not work for more than 5 days per week; they must have a minimum daily rest of 14 hours, in any event between 7 p.m. and 8 a.m.

Children from the age of 13 years onwards are allowed to assist in family businesses only when it concerns children of shopkeepers or farmers and the business in question is part of or immediately adjacent to the building in which the child is living.

In addition to the various different kinds of work that children are allowed to perform from the age of 13 onwards, children aged 14 or more are allowed to assist with the carrying out of light work of a non-industrial nature within the context of their education. However this is only possible where a work placement agreement has been drawn up or if the Municipal Executive has approved the request for alternative compulsory education. If the child is working within the context of a work placement agreement or alternative compulsory education, he or she is not allowed to perform any other work during the week or weeks in question.

The Labour Inspectorate supervises and enforces the regulations relating to the employment of children through inspections in branches with special risks for children or young persons and in branches which employ children and young persons, and through complaints.

As regards enforcement, the policy is determined in consultation with the Public Prosecutions Department. There is a standard procedure with two phases; the first phase consists of issuing a warning, while the second involves the compilation of a prosecution report which is passed to the public prosecutor. There is also a procedure for serious or repeat offences. Since November 1999, it has also been possible for the Labour Inspectorate to fine employers.

The Committee wishes to receive further information on the work of the Labour Inspectorate, for example the number of inspections carried out, number of breaches detected, number of warnings issued and the number of prosecutions.

The Committee concludes that the situation in the Netherlands is in conformity with Article 7 para. 1 of the Charter.

Paragraph 2 – Higher minimum age in certain occupations

The Committee takes note, in the Dutch report and its appendices, of the provisions of the Working Conditions Decree, which forms part of the Working Conditions Act, that came into effect in July 1997. The Decree sets out special provisions for employees under the age of 18 years. The Committee notes the list of types of work that are completely prohibited to those under 18 years of age, and the list of tasks that may be carried out by those aged 16 or 17 years with expert supervision, as defined by the Decree. In addition, employers are obliged under the legislation to draw up an inventory of all the risks to health, safety and welfare involved in their operation. There is a list of points that require particular attention when drawing up the risk

Eurc

Europ

Concl
Vol. 2

Council of Europe Publishing

French edition:

Charte sociale européenne – Conclusions XV-2, tome 2

ISBN 92-871-4555-5

Council of Europe Publishing
F-67075 Strasbourg Cedex

ISBN 92-871-4556-3

Printed in Germany

inventory and assessment if the employer in question is employing people under 18 years of age.

The Committee asks that the next report supply information on the rate of occupational accidents and diseases among young workers under the age of 18 years.

The Committee concludes that the situation in the Netherlands is in conformity with Article 7 para. 2 of the Charter.

Paragraph 3 – Safeguarding the full benefit of compulsory education

The Committee recalls that it previously considered the situation in the Netherlands not to be in conformity with the Charter because:

– children of compulsory school age and over 15 years could work throughout the school holidays for up to 8 hours a day and 40 hours per week

– children of compulsory school age and over 15 years could deliver newspapers from 6 a.m. onwards on school days.

As regards the first ground, the Committee notes that the Working Hours Act (ATW) and the Child Labour Regulations provide that children aged 13 and 14 years may work for up to 4 weeks per year, but not more than 3 weeks consecutively. Children aged 15 may work for up to 6 weeks per year, but not more than 4 weeks consecutively. School holidays last for eleven weeks.

The Committee considers that the main purpose of school holidays is to let children rest in order to benefit from school after the holidays. It refers to its case-law that the period of rest must at least cover half the holiday period for children still subject to compulsory education. Despite the above-mentioned limitations to the number of weeks children may work annually, the Committee observes that it can exceed half of the holiday period, which is not in conformity with the Charter.

The Committee considers that the hours that may be worked by children aged 15 (8 hours per day, 40 hours per week) are long, but as they only apply during part of the school holidays they do not constitute a violation of Article 7 para 3 of the Charter.

As regards the situation whereby young persons of compulsory school age and over 15 years can deliver newspapers from 6 a.m. onwards on school days, the Committee notes that there has been no change. It considers that 6 a.m. represents a very early start for children, who may work for 2 hours per day before school starts, 5 days per week. The Committee notes from an appendix to the report[1] that the Dutch Ministry of Social Affairs and Employment states that the delivering of newspapers in the mornings is not considered to fall within the legal concept of "light work of an non-industrial nature", since it "can be an arduous task for a child of 15 in view of the fact that it has to be done very early in the morning before school and also due to the fact that it involves lifting heavy bundles of newspapers".[2] The Committee finds in these circumstances that the situation is not compatible with Article 7 para 3.

The Committee concludes that the situation in the Netherlands is not in conformity with Article 7 para. 3 of the Charter

– As the limits on mandatory rest period during school holidays for children aged 15, still subject to compulsory education is not sufficient to ensure they fully benefit from such education;

– As it is possible for children aged 15, still subject to compulsory education, to deliver newspapers from 6 a.m. for up to 2 hours per day, 5 days per week before school.

Paragraph 4 – Working hours for young workers and apprentices

The Committee takes note of the detailed information contained in the Dutch report on the prohibition of child labour and the rules on working hours of children and young people laid down in the new Working Hours Act (ATW) which entered into force in 1997. It asks that the next report contain a copy of the Detailed Child Labour Regulations referred to in the report.

The Committee recalls that children under 16 are subject to compulsory school. However, persons aged 15 who are partially or entirely exempt from compulsory school for various reasons may perform light work of a non-industrial nature for a maximum of 8 hours per day and 40 hours per week. Work on Sundays is only allowed if there are at least 4 free

---

[1] *Child and juvenile labour bound by strict rules*, Ministry of Social Affairs and Employment.

[2] *Ibidem.*

Sundays over a period of 13 weeks and for any Sunday worked Saturday must be free.

Persons aged 15 may also deliver newspapers in the morning. In that case a delivery round agreement must be signed, not only by the employer and the child, but also by the child's parent or guardian. The maximum working time is 2 hours per day and work on Sundays is not allowed.

The Committee considers the working hours permitted for children under sixteen who are exempt from compulsory school – 8 hours per day and 40 hours per week – to be excessive under this provision of the Charter. However, before reaching a conclusion it asks how many children are exempt or partially exempt from compulsory school and have taken up work on an annual basis. It also needs up-dated information on the reasons which may lead to exemptions being granted as well as on the procedures involved in making such decisions.

Finally, with reference to its previous conclusion, the Committee requests clarification as to whether the arrangement, whereby children obliged to follow training for two days per week as a substitute for compulsory education could enter the labour market only with the authorisation of the head of the Regional Labour Inspectorate, is still in force. If so, it repeats its request for information on the number of children concerned.

Pending receipt of all the information requested, the Committee defers its conclusion.

Paragraph 5 – Fair remuneration for young workers and apprentices

The Committee notes the detailed information contained in the Dutch report on the minimum wage and minimum holiday allowance system established by legislation (*Wet minimumloon en minimum-vakantiebijslag*, WML). It also takes into account the information presented during the meeting with the Dutch Government on Article 4 para. 1 which took place on 29 June 1999.

The report states that the statutory minimum wage is applicable to adult workers aged 23-64 years. As of 1 July 2000 the adult minimum wage stood at 2,307.50 Netherlands Guilders (NLG) gross per month (excluding an 8% holiday allowance). For young workers aged 15-22 years a reduced minimum wage rate is derived from the minimum adult wage according to fixed percentages for the various age categories. Thus, for young workers aged 15 years the minimum wage corresponds to 30% (or 692.30 NLG gross per month) of the adult minimum wage, for those aged 16 the rate is 34.5% (or 796.10 NLG) and for those aged 17 the rate is 39.5% (911.50 NLG).

The Committee notes that the minimum wage is adjusted in accordance with the value of the WKA-index (a composite index of contractual wage increases in the private and public sector). The adjustment is only mandatory when the ratio between the number of people claiming social benefits and the number of people in employment is below 82.6. If it is higher, the Government may decide not to apply the linkage. Currently, the ratio is under 75.

The Committee further notes that about 300,000 workers received the minimum wage as of December 1997 of which about 110,700 were aged 15-22 years. 2,800 young workers aged 15 years, 7,900 aged 16 years and 11,900 aged 17 years received the minimum wage.

The Committee does not consider the minima applied to young workers under 18 in the Netherlands to be fair in the meaning of this provision of the Charter. It recalls that it has found the minimum wage of adult workers aged 18-22 to be not adequate under Article 4 para. 1 (Conclusions XIV-2, pp. 547-549). The Committee has held that where the reference wage, i.e. the starting wage or minimum wage of an adult worker, is not sufficient, the wage of a young worker cannot either be considered as fair. The Committee further observes that the minimum wage of a young worker aged 15 amounts to less than 70% of the minimum wage of an adult worker aged 18. The Committee holds, as it has done in the past, that a 30% reduction for a young worker in relation to the adult minimum wage is excessive.

The Dutch Government maintains that the minimum wage for young workers is "quite fair". It refers *inter alia* to the fact that the minimum wage for young workers varies between 67% and 77% of the average wage of all young workers in the age groups concerned. It also states that a higher minimum wage for young workers would worsen the situation of young people in the labour market and that the balance between education and participation is an important consideration: on the one hand there is an interest in keeping young people in school to provide them with good education and on the other hand it should still be attractive for employers to hire inexperienced and low-skilled young workers.

The Committee notes that the relevant reference wage when assessing the fairness of a young worker's wage is not the average wage within the age group concerned, but the starting wage or minimum wage of an adult worker. It recalls that an important objective of Article 7 para. 5 of the Charter is to prevent the exploitation of young workers. Furthermore, the Committee's case-law allows for a significant reduction of young workers' wages which in its opinion is fully compatible with concerns related to keeping young persons in education and to ensuring their integration into the labour market.

As regards apprentices and their wages the report merely states that no figures are available, but in general apprentice wages vary between the statutory minimum wage and the lowest pay scales agreed in collective agreements. The Committee insists that the next report provide all the necessary information in respect of apprentices, if necessary in the form of estimates based on appropriate surveys.

Finally, the Committee wishes to underline that the next report should contain information on the net value of the minimum wages of young workers and apprentices, i.e. after deduction of taxes and social security contributions, as well as on the net value of adult minimum wages. The calculation of net wages should be made for the case of a single worker.

The Committee concludes that the situation in the Netherlands is not in conformity with Article 7 para. 5 of the Charter as the minimum wages of young workers under 18 cannot be considered as fair, within the meaning of this provision of the Charter.

Paragraph 6 – Treatment of the time spent in vocational training as forming part of the working day

The Dutch report states that under the Working Hours Act (ATW) which entered into force in 1996 time spent on vocational training during a normal working day with the consent of the employer is treated as forming part of the working day and is classified as working time by the Labour Inspectorate. Time spent on vocational training in this sense, is paid according to the employment contract. However, the report also emphasises that the Working Hours Act (ATW) makes a distinction between a learning process and a working process. This implies that vocational training taken by workers in an educational institution is not regarded as working time, whereas training taken somewhere else (e.g. in-company training) is regarded as working time.

The Committee notes that only time spent on certain types of vocational training is treated as forming part of the working day for purposes of calculating working hours. Moreover, it notes that whether such time is remunerated will depend on the content of the individual employment contract. Consequently, the Dutch government must, in accordance with Article 33, demonstrate that the great majority of the workers concerned in fact enjoy the benefits guaranteed by Article 7 para. 6 of the Charter on the strength of their employment contracts. Having found no evidence to this effect, the Committee asks that it be contained in the next report.

As regards apprentices the report states that the majority has a part-time contract with the employer that equals the time (including practical training on the job) spent by apprentices in the enterprise, excluding the time spent on theoretical learning in school. It further states that time spent in school is not considered as "training time during normal working hours with the consent of the employer" in the meaning of Article 7 para. 6 because the time spent in school does not form part of the working day of the apprentice. In addition, it is underlined that apprentices are fully paid in the Netherlands unlike in some other countries where they receive lower wages. Having noted under Article 7 para. 5 that the minimum wage applicable to young persons, including apprentices, is only a relatively small percentage of the adult minimum wage, the Committee asks the Government to explain what is meant by "fully paid".

According to the report, and as previously noted by the Committee, about 21% of all apprentices do nevertheless receive remuneration for the time spent in school due to stipulations in collective agreements.

The Committee observes that the Dutch system allows for a situation where young workers and apprentices are not entitled to remuneration for time spent on vocational training with the consent of the employer. It holds that vocational training within the framework of and for the purpose of an apprenticeship should be considered as working time and remunerated as such and it notes that in the Netherlands this is recognised in a number of collective agreements.

Consequently, as the Dutch Government has not demonstrated that the great majority of young workers and notably apprentices benefit from the guarantees of Article 7 para. 6 of the Charter, the Committee can only conclude that the situation in the Netherlands is not in conformity with the Charter.

Paragraph 7 – Annual holiday of young persons under eighteen

The Committee notes the information contained in the Dutch report on additional holidays for young workers provided for in collective agreements. According to a 1999 survey, young workers in the 16-18 age group benefit from an extra three days on average per year.

The Committee recalls that legislation guarantees a minimum of four weeks paid holiday per year and it therefore concludes that the situation in the Netherlands is in conformity with Article 7 para. 7 of the Charter.

Paragraph 8 – Prohibition of night work for young persons under eighteen

The Committee notes from the Dutch report that the definition of night work in the Working Hours Act (ATW) is work between midnight and 6 a.m. Children and juveniles are prohibited from working at night. An exception applies to 16 and 17 year olds working in the merchant navy: for this category of workers work is also allowed between 5 a.m. and 6 a.m. Moreover, work between midnight and 5 a.m. in the merchant navy is allowed, if it takes place in the context of vocational training.

In the light of this information, the Committee concludes that the situation in the Netherlands is in conformity with Article 7 para. 8 of the Charter.

Paragraph 9 – Provision of regular medical control for young workers under eighteen

The Committee notes from the Dutch report that there is no general mandatory medical examination for persons under 18. Moreover, no information is available on the conditions in which and how often medical examinations are made. The report explains that under Section 1.38 of the Working Conditions Decree "employers are required to offer employees under the age of 18 a medical examination, if the risk inventory and assessment shows that there are specific dangers attached to the work to be done."

The Committee requests up-dated information on how and by whom the risk inventory and assessment is made and its insists on receiving information confirming that medical examination is periodical (and not only takes the form of pre-employment examination) and specifying on how often, i.e. with what intervals, the examinations are carried out.

Pending receipt of this information, the Committee defers its conclusion

Paragraph 10 – Special protection for children and young people from physical and moral dangers to which they are exposed.

The Committee notes the information contained in the report of the Netherlands

As regards the protection of working children the Committee refers to its conclusions under Article 7 paras. 2 and 3.

It notes the information contained in the report on young offenders including alcohol related crime and refers in this respect to its conclusion under Article 17.

The Committee wishes to be informed as to whether legislation prohibits the use of children in the sex industry, and to receive information on any supervisory system and sanctions that may accompany this prohibition.

The Committee concludes that the situation in the Netherlands is in conformity with Article 7 para. 10 of the Charter.

Article 8 — The right of employed women to protection

Paragraph 1 – Maternity leave

1. The right to maternity leave

Under Dutch law, all insured female employees are entitled to 16 weeks' compulsory maternity leave, including the 4 weeks before the birth and 8 weeks after it (Labour Act of 1919, as amended).

In its previous conclusion, the Committee found the Netherlands to be in breach of Article 8 para. 1 of the Charter here, inasmuch as employees in private households working for less than 3 days a week are not entitled to maternity benefit nor, consequently, to maternity leave.

The report states in this regard that all female employees are insured from the day they start work. However, certain categories, notably women working in private households and in the public health services for less than 3 days a week, constitute an exception to the rule. Because they are not regarded as employees and therefore are not insured, these women have no entitlement to either maternity leave or maternity benefit.

According to the report, this situation has arisen because the women concerned do not wish to be insured, because the financial burden on their employers would be too great and because making insurance compulsory would reduce the market for this type of work.

The Committee considers that denying the right to maternity leave to a category of workers is not in conformity with Article 8 para. 1 of the Charter.

Moreover, it requests that the next report include information on the penalties for breaches of the law on compulsory maternity leave, as well as notification of any breaches detected by the Labour Inspectorate.

The Committee concludes that the situation in the Netherlands is in breach of Article 8 para. 1 inasmuch as women working in private households and in the public health services for less than three days a week are not regarded as employees and are not insured. This means that they have no entitlement to maternity leave.

2. The right to adequate social security benefits

The Dutch report states that there is no qualifying period for entitlement to maternity benefit and that women other than those in the above-mentioned categories are thus covered from their first day at work.

The level of maternity benefit is equal to 100% of wages, up to a ceiling of 286.84 Netherlands Guilders (NLG) per day (as of 1 January 1994). The report notes that most collective labour agreements provide for employees earning more than the limit to receive a supplement from their employers. This brings the total up to the full level of their wages. The report does not provide information with regard to the number of women earning wages above the ceiling; the spread of earnings above the ceiling; or the average monthly earnings of women in executive positions.

The Committee notes that the material circumstances of employees on maternity leave must be such that they do not need to work and can thus get proper rest. This requirement can be met only by continuing to pay the employee her salary or granting her a benefit equivalent to, or worth not substantially less than, her salary. Nonetheless, the Committee considers that in the case of salaries above the ceiling, a substantial reduction in earnings during maternity leave is not, *per se*, contrary to Article 8 para. 1 of the Charter. In order to assess the situation and satisfy itself that the reduction in earnings in reasonable, the Committee takes various factors into account, including the level of the ceiling, where it lies on the earnings scale and the number of women whose salaries exceed it.

In the Netherlands' case, the Committee regards the ceiling as relatively high and notes that many of the women whose earnings exceed it receive their full salaries under collective agreements. It therefore takes the view that there is no problem of compliance with the Charter in this regard.

Replying to a question asked by the Committee, the report also states that the privatisation of sickness insurance will not affect maternity benefits. All insured female employees are, in fact, entitled to maternity leave and benefits for a period of 16 weeks. If, after that period, a woman is unable to return to work as a result of her pregnancy or the delivery of her child, she is entitled to sickness benefit, equivalent to 100% of her wages, for up to 52 weeks.

The Committee concludes that the maternity benefit situation in the Netherlands is in breach of Article 8 para. 1 inasmuch as women working in private households and in the public health services for less than three days a week are not regarded as employees and are not insured. This means they have no entitlement to maternity benefit.

Paragraph 2 – Illegality of dismissal during maternity leave

The Committee takes note of the information contained in the Dutch report.

Prohibition of dismissal

The Committee notes that female employees in the Netherlands are protected from dismissal during pregnancy and then for six weeks after the end of maternity leave.

Replying to questions by the Committee, the report states that:

– protection from dismissal applies to pregnant women generally even if they have taken leave for reasons of health and safety;

– women working in agricultural undertakings, other than plantations, and in private households are protected during pregnancy by the Dutch Civil Code in the same way as other female workers;

– during the 1997-1998 period there were no cases of an employee on maternity leave being dismissed "on urgent grounds". The Committee notes that, under Section 1639p of the Civil Code, "urgent grounds" can include cases where "[the worker] substantially lacks the ability or aptitude to carry out the work for which she was taken on". It asked whether this provision could be applied to women on maternity leave. The report replies that such a situation would only occur in "exceptional circumstances" and that, in any event, there had been no case of a woman on maternity leave being dismissed. The Committee now asks that each report include information about any cases of dismissal on these grounds. The Committee asks once more that the next report provide information on this matter and give examples of the "exceptional circumstances" mentioned above.

Consequences of unlawful dismissal

The report includes no information on this aspect of Article 8 para. 2.

The Committee points out that reinstatement must be the standard remedy in cases of unlawful dismissal. The aim of Article 8 para. 2 is not only to guarantee financial security for women employees who become pregnant but also to secure their jobs. Payment of compensation is an acceptable remedy only in exceptional cases where reinstatement is not possible (for example because the company has ceased its business) or not wished for by the worker. In such cases, the Committee verifies that the level of compensation is sufficiently dissuasive as far as the employer is concerned and that it affords the employee sufficient reparation.

For these reasons, the Committee asks that the next report review this aspect of the situation.

Conclusion

Pending receipt of the information requested, the Committee defers its conclusion.

Paragraph 3 – Time off for nursing mothers

According to the Dutch report, the Working Hours Act (ATW), which came into force in 1996, explicitly provides for working women to have paid breaks for breastfeeding. The timing of the breaks shall be fixed in consultation with the employer.

The Committee takes note of this improvement and concludes that the situation in the Netherlands is in conformity with Article 8 para. 3 of the Charter.

Paragraph 4 – Regulation of night work and prohibition of dangerous, unhealthy or arduous types of work for women workers

1. Regulation of night work for women in industrial employment (Article 8.4*a*)

The Dutch report states that the Working Hours Act (ATW), including its provisions concerning night work, applies to employees of both genders. It affirms that this legislation does not alter the provisions of the 1919 Labour Act with regard to night work for women in industrial employment.

Night work is defined as work carried out between midnight and 6 a.m. Employees who work shifts may not perform night work on more than

10 occasions in 4 weeks; over a 13-week period the limit is 25 nights, or 28 in exceptional cases.

The Working Hours Act (ATW) requires employers to implement an in-house risk-assessment policy, paying particular attention to specific groups of employees including pregnant women and those who have recently given birth or are breastfeeding.

Accordingly, if night work represents a risk to the health or safety of a pregnant woman who has notified her employer of her pregnancy, or to a worker breastfeeding her baby, the employer must take steps to eliminate or reduce the risk. Failing that, the employer must offer the woman day work. Should this not be feasible, she must be allowed to take leave. Thus, pregnant women and those who have recently given birth or are breastfeeding cannot be obliged to do night work.

The Committee recalls that states are not required, under Article 8 para. 4*a* of the Charter, to prohibit night work for women, but to regulate it. The regulations, which may be general and applicable to both sexes, must strictly stipulate the conditions under which night work is possible, permitting it only where it is justified by specific production requirements and with due regard for the particular circumstances of the workplace and the way the work is organised. They must also set out the conditions under which women may do night work, such as Labour Inspectorate authorisation if necessary; set hours with fixed breaks and rest days after periods of night work; and the right to be transferred to day work should they experience health problems associated with working at night. The Committee further notes that the regulations must address the situation of pregnant women and those who have recently given birth or are breastfeeding.

The Committee considers that the regulations in the Netherlands take adequate account of the situation of pregnant women and those who have recently given birth or are breastfeeding. It also notes that night work is generally regulated inasmuch as it is defined and, in the case of shift workers, restricted, and that employees are entitled to be transferred to day work should night work constitute a threat to their health or safety.

The Committee asks that the next report include a review of the situation with regard to authorised night work (whether or not the Labour Inspectorate is the authorising body and whether night work is introduced under collective agreements at industry or company level) and of the conditions under which it is carried out (e.g. with provision for breaks and rest days after periods of night work).

Pending the information requested, the Committee defers its conclusion as regards Article 8 para. 4*a* of the Charter.

2. Prohibition of the employment of women in certain dangerous, unhealthy or arduous types of work (Article 8 para. 4*b*)

The Committee points out that Article 8 para. 4*b* includes a dual prohibition.

– The employment of women in underground mining must be prohibited by statute: this ban concerns only extractive work in the strict sense.

– Women must be prohibited "as appropriate [from doing] all other work which is unsuitable for them by reason of its dangerous, unhealthy or arduous nature". The stipulation "as appropriate" has been taken to mean that the prohibition should apply only where necessary, such as to protect pregnant women and those who have recently given birth or are breastfeeding.

On the first point, the Committee recalls its conclusion that such a prohibition is irrelevant in the Netherlands because underground mining is no longer carried out there (Conclusions XIII-1, p. 184).

On the second point, the report explains that Dutch law does not prohibit any specific type of work for pregnant women, those who have recently given birth or are breastfeeding but, as indicated with reference to Article 8 para. 4*a*, it requires employers to assess the risks to which such women are exposed. The assessment must cover work hazards including the effects of chemical, physical and biological agents and industrial processes deemed to involve risk, as well as working conditions, including posture or movements that constitute a health risk, and mental and physical fatigue. The risks of exposure to lead, benzene, high temperatures or vibration must also be assessed.

If the results of the assessment show a risk to health or safety, the employer's first, provisional, step must be to alter the working conditions or hours of the employee concerned in order to avoid exposing her to the risk. Failing that, the employer must take the necessary measures to offer the employee an alternative. Should this be impossible, she must be permitted to stop work for as long as necessary in order to protect her health or safety.

The report also states that a system of penalties was introduced under the Working Conditions Act as amended in 1999. The Labour Inspectorate may fine any employer who has not drawn up a risk inventory and assessment covering risks to pregnant women and those who have recently given birth or are breastfeeding, who does not provide the women concerned with information about the potential risks, or who does not offer alternative work if necessary. The Committee requests that the next report state the level of fines and, if possible, the number of offences detected. It also asks whether the Working Conditions Act contains specific provisions on pregnant women and those who have recently given birth or are breastfeeding.

Lastly, replying to a question by the Committee, the report states that, with regard to exposure to ionising radiation, the limit values fixed under Dutch law, particularly in respect of pregnant women, are stricter than those proposed by the International Commission on Radiological Protection (ICRP).

On the basis of all this information, the Committee concludes that the situation in the Netherlands is in conformity with Article 8 para. 4*b* of the Charter.

Article 11 — Right to protection of health

Paragraph 1 – Removal of the causes of ill-health

The Committee takes note of the information provided in the Dutch report on the Charter and its appendices and in the 1997 report submitted to the World Health Organisation (WHO)[1].

State of health of the population – General indicators

Life expectancy and principal causes of death

The Committee notes from OECD data[2] that in 1997 life expectancy at birth was 80.5 years for women, which was lower than the average for European Union and European Economic Area countries (80.9), and 75.2 years for men, which was higher than the European average (74.6).

Diseases of the circulatory system are the main causes of mortality (39%), followed by cancer (28%). The Committee notes from Eurostat data[3] that the death rate from lung cancer among men is one of the two highest in the European Union and European Economic Area countries (96.8 deaths per 100,000 in 1995). As regards morbidity rates, the report states in reply to a question asked in the previous conclusion that the high incidence of cancer, especially breast cancer, stems from earlier diagnosis of the disease following the launch of the screening campaigns in the early 1990s and that the incidence of breast cancer decreased in 1995.

The Committee notes that the number of diagnosed cases of AIDS (morbidity) per year dropped sharply during the reference period from 525 in 1995 (the peak year) to 155 in 1997.

Infant and maternal mortality

According to Eurostat data, the infant mortality rate dropped significantly since the last reference period from 6.3 deaths per 1,000 live births in 1992 to 5 in 1997.

---

[1] *Highlights on Health in the Netherlands* (WHO European Regional Office website: www.who.dk).

[2] OECD, *Health Data*, 1999.

[3] Eurostat Yearbook: *A Statistical Eye on Europe*, 1988-1998.

The Committee notes an increase in the average maternal mortality rate, which stood at 8.9 deaths per 100,000 live births between 1994 and 1996 (as against 7.1 between 1991 and 1993). In reply to a question asked in the previous conclusion on the high maternal mortality rate, the report states that most births traditionally take place at home and that average maternal age at the birth of the first child is rising, which increases the risk of problems at birth.

The Committee emphasises that maternal mortality is an avoidable risk that states must control in order to comply with Article 11 of the Charter. Given the Netherlands' highly developed health care system, it considers that all possible steps must be taken to achieve a result a risk as close as possible to zero. Before reaching a conclusion, it asks the Government what steps it intends to take to improve the situation.

Health care system

Access to health care

The Netherlands' health care system is divided into three categories based on the insurance principle.

Firstly, "high medical risks" such as hospital stays exceeding one year or the placement of people with disabilities are governed by the Exceptional Medical Expenditure Act (AWBZ), which covers everyone living in the Netherlands and provides for funding by social security contributions deducted from income.

Secondly, the "general" scheme (Health Insurance Act, ZFW) based on compulsory insurance for persons below a certain income threshold (64% of the population) and voluntary private insurance (about 30% of the population). There is a special scheme for civil servants. Under the compulsory insurance scheme, insurance funds compete but are obliged to accept all applicants. An income-related social security contribution on all incomes is paid into two national funds, with refunding and compensation for insurers. Each fund then sets a uniform flat-rate premium reflecting the additional costs incurred by the fund in the management of compulsory benefits. Where private insurance is concerned, standard contracts provide for basic protection and maximum contributions are paid.

Thirdly, insured persons can take out complementary insurance, for instance to ensure a more comfortable hospital stay.

In 1997, according to the above-mentioned OECD data, total health care expenditure accounted for 8.5% of GDP and public expenditure for 72.6% of total health care expenditure.

Under the compulsory health insurance scheme, insured persons do not have to advance fees for visits to the doctor. A system under which they bore a share of the cost, with a maximum of 200 Netherlands Guilders (NLG) per year, was introduced in 1997 but abolished in 1999. Where exceptional medical expenses are concerned, insured persons over the age of 18 are required to pay a share of the cost of care in health care establishments. This is not a requirement for hospital stays in lower-grade rooms with authorisation from the fund.[1]

According to the OECD data, the average rate for reimbursement of hospital care in 1997 was 82%, one of the two lowest among the OECD's European member countries. The average rate of reimbursement of out-patient medical care was 64%, also one of the three lowest among the OECD's European member countries.

Under the compulsory health insurance scheme insured persons pay 20% of the cost of pharmaceutical products, while the rest is refunded up to the prescribed limit for alternative products of the same type. The cost of supplements is borne by the insured person.[2] The Committee notes in the OECD data that the average rate of reimbursement of pharmaceutical products dropped sharply from 91.3% in 1992 to 88.8% in 1996 and 63.9% in 1997. It wishes to know the reasons for this trend.

In order to assess whether the cost of health care does not hinder access to care, the Committee asks for the next report to state whether there are measures to prevent health care costs from being an excessive burden on people with low incomes, such as exemption from the requirement to pay a share of the cost. It also asks whether waiting lists exist for access to hospital care.

Health care professionals and equipment

The Committee notes in the OECD data that the total number of hospital beds rose to 175,580 in 1997 (from 172,596 in 1992) and that the ratio of hospital beds per 1,000 inhabitants is among the three highest in the OECD's European member countries (11.3 beds).

---

[1]European Commission, *Social security systems in the states of the European Union: situation on 1 July 1999 and evolution* , Missoc.

[2]*Ibidem.*

The number of general practitioners increased by comparison with the previous reference period to 6,997 in 1997, i.e. about 0.5 doctors per 1,000 inhabitants, which remains the lowest density in the European Union and European Economic Area countries. The same applies to the density of specialists (one per 1,000 inhabitants) and to the density of pharmacists (0.2 per 1,000 inhabitants).

Conclusion

Subject to the information requested, the Committee concludes that the situation in the Netherlands is in conformity with Article 11 para. 1 of the Charter.

Paragraph 2 – Advisory and educational facilities

The Committee takes note of the information provided in the Dutch report.

Development of a sense of individual responsibility

Health education in schools

Health education is a statutory part of primary and secondary school curricula, especially via "life skills" classes in secondary school, and is designed to encourage young people to adopt a healthy lifestyle. Training courses in health education are accordingly organised for teachers. The specific content of teaching and the teaching materials to be used are not prescribed. The report states that since 1991 the Netherlands Institute on Mental Health and Addiction has devised projects aimed at promoting individual health education policies in schools on drugs, alcohol, medication, smoking and gambling. In 1999 about half of the country's schools were systematically running projects of this kind.

Public information and awareness-raising

As it is apparent from previous reports, national information campaigns are regularly conducted on the dangers of smoking, alcohol and drugs and on AIDS prevention. The Committee takes note of the efforts made during the reference period to bring home to young people the dangers of alcohol and drugs. As regards the prevention of drug addiction in particular, campaigns have been carried out on cannabis and ecstasy, as well as a general campaign on "Going out and drugs" designed to put across a strong message using several media (e.g. television, posters, activities) in all the areas that make up young people's world (family, school and leisure).

Counselling and screening

Children and adolescents

Considerable attention is paid to the prevent of health problems among children from birth to the age of 18. Pre-school medical examinations, including vaccinations, are given in specialist child welfare centres which also provide parents with advice on infant health care. Medical examinations are then organised in schools, starting in nursery school, by municipal health care services. A previous report stated that children received six health checks during their school careers, each one including examination of eyesight, hearing, teeth, speech, growth and so on. School medical services comprise doctors and nurses and co-operate with specialist services (including school guidance officers and psychologists).

Rest of the population

The report states that since 1990 women between the ages of 50 and 70 have been screened for breast cancer. Men also receive prostate cancer screening.

Conclusion

The Committee concludes that the situation in Netherlands is in conformity with Article 11 para. 2 of the Charter.

Paragraph 3 – Prevention of diseases

The Committee notes the developments in the Netherlands concerning prevention of health risks generally and prophylactic measures in particular.

Policies on the prevention of avoidable risks

General

The Committee requests that future reports indicate as far as possible the share of the government budget devoted to the main prevention policies listed below.

Reduction of environmental risks

Air pollution – Concerning management of local pollution, the report states that air quality standards for sulphur dioxide, nitrogen dioxide, carbon monoxide, black smoke, lead, and benzene are generally not exceeded except in certain areas of intense activity, and that the situation in such areas is likely to improve as a result of the implementation of European Union standards on car emissions.

Concerning overall control of emissions of these pollutants, the Committee notes in OECD data[1] that emissions of sulphur dioxide, nitrogen dioxide and volatile organic compounds fell significantly over the reference period.

Concerning pollution on a world scale, the Committee notes that in 1993 the Netherlands ratified the United Nations Framework Convention on Climate Change (Rio de Janeiro, 1992) and undertook, *inter alia*, to reduce the 1990 level of emissions of the main greenhouse gases by 6% over the period 2008-2012 in order to help reach the targets set for the European Union following the 1997 Kyoto Conference. The Committee notes from OECD's Environmental Data that in 1995 the control target for anthropic methane emissions had already been met. Major efforts were still necessary, however, to control nitrogen protoxide and carbon dioxide emissions.

Asbestos – In reply to the general question about measures taken to protect the health of people exposed to asbestos (Conclusions XIII-4, pg 116), the report indicates that the use, storage, and consequently marketing and sale of asbestos and any product containing asbestos are banned. The Committee would still like to know whether any measures have been taken to check for the presence of asbestos, particularly in blocks of flats.

Ionising radiation – The Committee notes that approximately 5% of electricity is produced by nuclear power plants in the Netherlands. In reply to the general question in Conclusions XIII-4 about the safety of people living near such plants, the report states that protection against ionising radiation is guaranteed by implementation of European Union and domestic legislation and is based, in accordance with the recommendations of the International Commission on Radiological Protection (ICRP), on three fundamental principles: justification of practices, optimisation of protection, and dose limitations. All activities in this field

---

[1]OECD, *Environmental Data*, Compendium 1999.

come under the Nuclear Energy Act, which provides in particular for a licensing system. The Committee notes in the report under Article 8 para. 4 that the dose limitations fixed by Dutch legislation are at least equal to those recommended by ICRP in 1990. The National Institute for Public Health and the Environment is responsible for monitoring compliance with authorised limits and maintaining emissions at the lowest possible level. There are also special provisions concerning radioactive waste treatment and emergency plans. The task of monitoring compliance with legislation is entrusted to the Environment Inspectorate of the Ministry of Housing, Spatial Planning and the Environment. The Committee considers that the situation in the Netherlands is in conformity with Article 11 para. 3 in this respect.

Noise – The report states that maximum noise levels have been established with respect to homes, schools and hospitals, and that by 1998 70,000 homes were protected against road and rail traffic noise and 4,000 against aircraft noise. All new infrastructure is subject to stricter noise levels, and only a few dwellings per kilometre can be exposed to higher levels. These new rules were applied to the new Brussels-Amsterdam high speed rail link. The report states that according to the results of a 1998 survey, the impact of noise on the population is diminishing except in the case of neighbourhood and aircraft noise. Owing to the high population density in the Netherlands, the Committee is particularly concerned about reducing noise pollution and requests that the next report include information about any measures taken to improve the situation, not least as regards neighbourhood noise.

Food safety

In view of the threat to health represented by diseases related to food and the recent outbreaks of such diseases in particular the new variation of the Creutzfeldt-Jakob disease, as well as the emergence of new food products derived from biotechnology, the Committee has decided to look at food safety measures in all states parties to the Charter. It recalls that under Article 11 states have a responsibility to ensure a high degree of safety in this area for their populations.

Referring in particular to the resolution adopted by the 53rd World Health Assembly in May 2000 on food safety[1] and while recognising the relevance of international strategies, the Committee points out that in order to comply with the Charter in this field, states must set legal

---

[1]WHO Internet site : www.who.int

norms at the national level regarding food hygiene taking into account scientific data, and establish and maintain mechanisms for monitoring compliance with these norms throughout the food chain, develop, implement and up-date systematic prevention measures, notably by way of labelling, as well as monitor the occurrence of food-borne diseases.

The Committee requests that the next report provide up-to-date information on these three aspects (standards, monitoring, prevention) so that the situation can be assessed during the next study of Article 11.

Measures to combat smoking and alcoholism

Smoking – The Committee stresses the importance of measures against smoking in meeting the requirements of Article 11 of the Charter. It wishes to point out that smoking, a major cause of avoidable death in developed countries (in Europe 30% of deaths from cancer are attributable to smoking), is associated with a wide range of diseases (cardiac and circulatory diseases, cancers, pulmonary diseases etc.). Smoking kills one adult in ten throughout the world. The World Health Organisation (WHO) forecasts an increase to up to one in every six deaths by 2030,[1] which is more than the figure for any other cause of death. The Committee also notes that WHO is drawing up a convention on measures to combat smoking and points out that WHO, as part of the Health for All campaign, has set a target for European countries of raising the proportion of non-smokers in the population to at least 80% and protecting non-smokers against involuntary exposure to tobacco smoke.[2]

Under the Dutch Tobacco Act of 1988, smoking is banned in certain public places and tobacco advertising is subject to certain restrictions. The Committee requests that the next report provide more detailed information as well as an update on anti-smoking legislation.

The Committee notes from the Eurostat data that per capita cigarette consumption rose sharply at the beginning of the reference period before dropping to a level well below the average for European Union and European Economic Area countries (1,245 cigarettes per person in 1997 compared with the European average of 1,646).[3]

---

[1]World Health Report 1999.

[2]WHO, *Health Objectives for All – Health Policies in Europe*, September 1991.

[3]Eurostat Yearbook: *A statistical eye on Europe,* 1988-1998 data.

Alcohol – According to the report, there has been a proposal for an update of the Alcohol Licensing and Catering Act and more stringent rules governing the distribution of alcoholic beverages generally, restrictions on alcohol advertising and sponsoring, a limit on the number of points of sale, and proof-of-age requirements for young consumers.

From the Eurostat data, the Committee notes that the level of pure alcohol consumption is stable and lower than the average for European Union and European Economic Area countries (8 litres in 1996 compared to the European average of 9.4 litres).

It requests that the next report contain up-to-date information on legislation aimed at reducing alcohol supply.

Drug-abuse – See conclusion regarding Article 11 para. 2.

Prophylactic measures

Epidemiological monitoring

The report provides up-to-date information to show that the Netherlands has a system of data acquisition and monitoring for communicable and infectious diseases and that in the event of risk of epidemics special measures and selective investigations may be ordered.

Immunisation

Immunisation is not mandatory but the following vaccines are recommended and offered free of charge according to a special immunisation schedule: diphtheria, polio, tetanus, meningitis Hib, whooping cough, pertussis, mumps, measles, rubella. The flu vaccine is offered to people over 64, the BCG vaccine to children at risk and the hepatitis A and B vaccination to specific risk groups.

The Committee notes the coverage rates given in the WHO "Netherlands Immunisation Profile"[1]: in 1998, there was 97% coverage against diphtheria and polio, 96% against meningitis Hib and 96% against measles. According to the report, among the elderly there was 85% coverage against the flu. The Committee asks that the next report contain up-dated information on the coverage rates for all the recommended paediatric vaccinations.

---

[1]who.int/vaccines/surveillance/

Conclusion

The Committee concludes that the situation in the Netherlands is in conformity with Article 11 para. 3 of the Charter.

Article 14 — The right to benefit from social welfare services

Paragraph 1 – Provision or promotion of social welfare services

The Committee takes note of the information contained in the Dutch report on the aims and principles of the 1994 Welfare Act on which it commented in its previous conclusion. The report points out that social services are implemented at the level of the local authorities which in accordance with local needs and priorities fund voluntary organisations, and in certain cases individuals, to perform the actual services under conditions laid down by the 1994 Act. The voluntary organisations employ professionals as paid staff. The role of central government in this decentralised management system is to coordinate the use of resources, to identify and analyse social trends, to initiate new activities and innovative projects of national importance and to develop new policy.

Categories of services

As regards the principal types of social services, the Committee notes the information on elderly welfare, disabled welfare, youth welfare, including childcare, and social emergency care.

The report states that a number of core tasks in the policy for the elderly fall outside the scope of the Welfare Act, such as home care, elderly homes and nursing homes. The Committee asks that information on these aspects of elderly care, including quantitative data, be contained in the next report.

According to the report implementation of services aimed at social inclusion of disabled people is the responsibility of various private sector agencies (organisations of disabled people, voluntary work, support institutions, national organisations and executive agencies). The Committee notes the example given in the report of the Social Pedagogic Services (SPD), an independent organisation providing assistance to people with learning difficulties and special needs based on methods such as early intervention, home-based family support, supported independent living, psycho-social counselling, foster care and group meetings.

The Committee notes that there are various types of social services aimed a young people in the Netherlands. The voluntary youth care sector is concerned with children and young people up to the age of 23 who need special care because of problems and/or shortcomings in their upbringing and growth towards maturity. The term 'voluntary' indicates that children (and occasionally their parents and/or others responsible for them) themselves take the initiative to ask for help and are free to accept or reject (after a certain time) the help offered to them. Youth care under the Youth Services Act comprises preventive care, peripatetic care, day treatment, foster care and residential care.

The report states that there is no legal right to childcare, but the number of childcare places for the 0-12 age group funded from the local authorities, by employers and by parent fees, has risen considerably during the 1990's. At the end of 1998 there were 103,500 childcare places. The Committee notes that a special childcare facility has been introduced in order to enable single parents on benefit to get into employment. In 1998 there were 4,700 such places. It also notes that there are waiting lists for subsidised childcare and asks to receive more information on the nature and extent of this problem.

Social emergency care for those who have left their homes and temporarily cannot look after themselves without help is available at social refuge shelters of which there are currently 48. In addition, there are 38 special shelters for women who have fled their homes because of violence, abuse or other serious problems in their relationships.

The Committee wishes to receive information on social services aimed at certain vulnerable target group not directly addressed by the report such as drug and alcohol addicts, victims of violence and sexual abuse and ethnic minorities.

Access to services

The Committee notes that following amendments to the Youth Services Act which came into effect in 1997, youth care facilities and the institutions for guardianship and fostering must introduce a complaints procedure. Provincial complaints committees where the client can take a complaint in the second instance are also provided for. Moreover, youth care facilities and the institutions for guardianship and fostering must establish a so-called client input procedure and a client council. Executive agencies and institutions may also appoint a confidential client counsellor. The Committee wishes to be informed of the results of this reform.

The Committee requests up-dated information on conditions for being granted the various categories of services, including any applicable residence requirements. Considering the strongly decentralised nature of social services provision in the Netherlands and the number of actors and providers involved, the Committee wishes to receive more precise information on how a reasonable uniformity of treatment regarding access to services is ensured throughout the country.

Supervision and quality of services

The 1994 Welfare Act stipulates that care providers must respect a certain standard of work. With respect to childcare a Quality Rules Interim Decree lays down the minimum requirements for the quality of childcare that local authorities should incorporate in their regulations. In reply to a question posed by the Committee in its previous conclusion, the report states that the women's refuges run by the FIOM (the Dutch Federation of Institutions for the Unmarried Mother and her Child), which have been brought under the umbrella of the Refuge Federation, have defined quality standards that are accepted by the sector as a whole. There is a range of standards for organisation, staffing, accommodation and the process of providing help. An audit procedure has also been drawn up with a view to evaluating the quality standards of the institutions. According to the report the women's refuge sector emerged particularly well from the baseline measurement carried out in 1998.

The Committee requests that the next report contain systematic information on measures and procedures instituted to guarantee and control the quality of all categories of social services. In addition, having noted the information on the number and the qualifications of staff providing certain social services, notably childcare, the Committee asks that such information be contained in each report on this provision of the Charter for all categories of social services.

The Committee notes in reply to its question that the KLIMOP registration system is used by most social services institutions that are affiliated to the Refuge Federation. This system records the number of admissions, age, sex, previous admission, previous address, country of birth and origin, income, training, problems and length of stay. The Committee wishes to know who has access to these data and how it is monitored. It also requests a copy of the figures from this registration system which are made public annually.

Funding of services

The Committee notes that expenditure on childcare services amounts to about 1,5 billion NLG (no year given), however little additional information on this point is contained in the report. It therefore asks that the next report furnish information on total expenditure, public as well as private where appropriate and broken down according to categories of services, for each year of the reference period.

Conclusion

Pending receipt of the information requested, the Committee concludes that the situation in the Netherlands is in conformity with Article 14 para. 1 of the Charter.

Paragraph 2 – Public participation in the establishment and maintenance of social welfare services

The Committee notes that according to the Dutch report the entire social services system rests on the principle set forth by Article 14 para. 2 of encouraging the participation of individuals and voluntary organisations in the setting-up and running of social services: whereas central government is responsible for management and co-ordination and whereas prioritisation and funding take place through the local authorities, the actual provision of services is carried out by a multitude of private sector voluntary and independent organisations, and in some cases also by individuals. The Committee refers to its observations under Article 14 para. 1.

According to the report, the government has put considerable effort over the last decade into making social services provision demand driven rather than supply driven, resulting in individualised combinations of services, tailor-made care and solutions geared to individual needs. This approach emphasises participation and empowerment of citizens and client groups, and the establishment of youth councils and senior citizens councils, users councils, old people's associations, patient organisations and initiatives on neighbourhood management taken by residents' associations are examples of this. The report also states that the general public may, alongside social organisations and professionals, play an active part in identifying and calling attention to social problems. Examples include the position of ethnic minorities, help for illegal immigrants, the victims of sexual abuse and the problem of poverty.

The Committee concludes that the situation in the Netherlands is in conformity with Article 14 para. 2 of the Charter.

Article 17 — The right of mothers and children to social and economic protection.

The Committee notes the information contained in the Dutch report.

Establishment of parentage and adoption

The Committee notes from the report submitted by the Netherlands under the United Nations Convention on the Rights of the Child that the law on parentage was amended in 1998. It notes from the report that the situation as regards the establishment of parentage is satisfactory, nevertheless, in order to fully assess the situation, it wishes to receive a copy of this legislation with the next report.

The situation as regards adoption is in conformity with Article 17.

Children in Public care and Protection from ill-treatment and abuse

A court may make a family supervision order or a divestment of parental responsibility order in respect of children whose mental or physical well-being is at risk. If a family supervision order is made, a family supervision agency is appointed to supervise the parents and children. If parental responsibility is removed then a guardianship agency may be appointed as guardian. Children in these circumstances may be placed in a home, institution or with a foster family.

The Committee wishes to receive information in the next report on the number of families in receipt of assistance and supervision, the number of children removed from their families and placed with a foster family, in a home or in an institution.

The Committee wishes to receive information on the types of institutions that exist.

It also wishes to be informed as to whether there is any body responsible for monitoring care in institutions and whether there is any specific procedure for complaining about the care and treatment in institutions and on the conditions under which an institution may interfere with a child's property and mail, affect personal integrity, as well as the right to meet with persons close to him.

The Committee notes the information contained in the report on the facilities for homeless children.

Child abuse reporting centres were established in 1997 in order to, *inter alia*, receive reports on child abuse, provide counselling, refer to social services, help with investigations, etc. These centres co-operate with the office of the child abuse counsellor in the region, the Childcare Protection Board and the police's juvenile and vice squads.

The Committee wishes to know whether legislation prohibits all forms of corporal punishment of children, in schools, in institutions, in the home and elsewhere.

Children and the law – Young offenders

Criminal responsibility is set at 12 years of age.

Juvenile criminal law applies to children under 18 years of age. However in certain exceptional circumstances (such as the gravity of the offence etc.) a court may direct that adult criminal law be applicable to 16 and 17 years old defendants. The Committee wishes to know how many 16 and 17 years olds are subject to this procedure.

Under juvenile criminal law the principal sentences are youth detention, or a fine or `alternative sanctions'. These may be imposed by the Public Prosecutor or by the courts. Alternative sanctions may be the performance of activities for the general good or participation in an education project or a combination of the two. The alternative sanction may be up to 200 hours or up to 240 hours where the sanction combines an education component and a community service component.

A court may also pass a suspended sentence and impose certain conditions on the offender.

A young offender may avoid prosecution if he takes part in certain projects.

There are two types of judicial juvenile facilities, detention centres and treatment centres. Detention centres are intended for young people who have been placed in pre-trial detention and for young offenders who have been sentenced to a term of imprisonment. Youth detention for 12 to 16 years olds is a maximum of 1 year and for 16 to 18 year olds a maximum of 2 years. Young offenders may also be sentenced to treatment centres for between 2 and 6 years. The Committee wishes to receive further information on this procedure (the criteria for admission to a treatment centre, types of treatment, etc.).

The Committee wishes to be informed as to how many young offenders are in these juvenile facilities. It also wishes to be informed of the progress of the Bill which was introduced into parliament in 1998 concerning the rights of juvenile detainees in these institutions, e.g. the right to complain about their treatment, the right to receive mail etc.

The Committee wishes to know what is the maximum period a minor may be held in police custody or on remand.

Conclusion

The Committee concludes that the situation in the Netherlands is in conformity with Article 17 of the Charter.

Article 18 — The right to engage in a gainful occupation in the territory of other Contracting Parties

Paragraph 1 – Applying existing regulations in a spirit of liberality

Foreign nationals and migratory movement

As of 1 January 1998 the number of foreign nationals in the Netherlands was estimated to be 678,000 in a total population of 15.5 million.[1] The main nationalities were: Moroccans (137,000), Turks (114,000), Germans (53,900), Britons (39,200) and nationals of the former Yugoslavia (28,400). The Committee notes that the number of foreign nationals has considerably dropped from previous years (as of 1 January 1994 the foreign population was estimated to be 780,000). Information from a source other than the report[2] leads the Committee to conclude that this trend is largely attributable to a fairly high rate of naturalisation.

The Committee notes that between 1994 and 1997 there was a significant increase in migratory flows from the European Union and Turkey (an increase of 177% from the European Union and of 200% from Turkey). It also notes that, in practice, family reunion is the only official method of entry into the Netherlands.[3]

The Committee further notes that the rate of unemployment among foreign nationals fell during the reference period (19% in 1994, 16% in 1997) but remains significantly higher than the rate for Dutch nationals (4%), especially for Turkish nationals (36% in 1994, 31% in 1997).[4]

Work permits

Under Dutch legislation there are 2 types of work permit: a temporary, non-renewable work permit granted for 24 weeks and a work permit granted for a maximum of 3 years. The Committee notes that foreign

---

[1]OECD, *Trends in International Migration*, 1999 edition.

[2]*Ibidem.*

[3]European Commission, Employment Observatory – *SYSDEM Trends No. 32.*

[4]C. WITHOL DE WENDEN, *L'immigration en Europe*, La documentation française, 1999.

nationals who hold a residence permit for an unbroken period of 3 years for employment purposes and who do not take up residence outside the Netherlands at the end of that period are no longer required to obtain a work permit.

Relevant statistics

The report provides statistics on the number of permits applied for and granted between 1996 and 1998 to nationals of the Contracting Parties to the Charter which are not members of the European Union or parties to the European Economic Area. The statistics show that during the reference period approximately 90% of such applications were granted (92% in 1996, 90% in 1997 and 94% in 1998) and this corresponds to the levels observed in previous conclusions, with the exception of the 1990-93 period, in which there was a noticeable reduction (Conclusions XIII-2, pp. 171-172).

The Committee observes, however, that the figures do not distinguish between nationals of the different Contracting Parties. In addition, the figures for first applications and renewal applications are too general (all nationals of countries which are not members of the European Economic Area being lumped together) to enable the Committee to assess with any precision how the regulations are applied to nationals of Contracting Parties to the Charter. The Committee therefore insists that the next report contain the necessary data.

Conclusion

Pending receipt of the information requested, the Committee defers its conclusion.

Paragraph 2 – Simplifying existing formalities and reducing dues and taxes

Administrative formalities

Issue of work permits

The Committee notes that application for the work permit has to be made by the employer, who has to give the Public Employment Service five weeks' notice of the application for a work permit for a foreign national. The Committee refers to the observations in its conclusion under Article 18 para. 3 on the employer's duty to show that he has taken appropriate steps to recruit someone from the category of priority worker when filling a vacancy. The Committee asks that the next report explain what this duty involves in terms of administrative formalities.

Self-employment

The Committee wishes to know what the formalities are for obtaining a self-employment permit.

Conditions for renewal

The information provided to the Committee suggests that each application for renewal is examined in the same way as a first application and that, consequently, the same formalities are involved as for the first permit. The Committee would like this information to be confirmed in the next report.

Work permit and residence permit

The procedures for applying for a work permit and a residence permit are interlinked: when the Public Employment Service has issued a work permit the Ministry of Justice will issue a residence permit provided that the statutory conditions applicable to aliens are satisfied. Refusal of a work permit means that a residence permit cannot be issued and, conversely, if the residence permit is not renewed because the person concerned no longer satisfies the conditions, the work permit will be withdrawn in accordance with the 1995 Aliens Employment Act.

Time necessary for obtaining work permits

Under the 1995 Aliens Employment Act a decision on issue of a work permit must be made within five weeks of the application. The Committee asks that the next report provide information on how successfully the time limit is met in practice.

Chancery dues and other charges

As stated in previous reports, no chancery dues or other charges are payable for issue of a work permit.

Conclusion

Pending receipt of the information requested, notably on the obligation of an employer to recruit a “priority worker category” in filling a vacancy, the Committee defers its conclusion.

13th report – reference period 1993-1998

Paragraph 3 – Liberalising regulations

The Committee notes the entry into force of the Aliens Employment Act on 1 September 1995, replacing the 1979 Foreign Workers Employment Act.

It notes that the policy consideration here is to limit the employment of foreign workers in the Netherlands and to promote the integration of those who are permanently resident. As a result the provisions on entry into the Dutch labour market are particularly stringent.

The Committee points out that the statutory provisions apply only to nationals from non-European Union countries. Nationals of the European Union and European Economic Area member states are on the same footing as Dutch nationals and are accordingly treated as categories of priority workers (see below).

Access to the national labour market

The Committee notes firstly that nationals of non-European Union member states or of countries which are not party to the European Economic Area Agreement can obtain employment on the national labour market only when it is not possible, for the vacancy for which an application for a work permit has been made, to find someone from a category of priority worker (Dutch nationals and nationals of the European Union and the European Economic Area). To meet this requirement in practice, an employer who wishes to employ a foreign worker must comply with certain formalities (he must notify the Public Employment Service of the application for a work permit) and further show that he has made sufficient effort to fill the vacancy from a category of priority workers. The Committee refers to the question in its conclusion under Article 18 para. 2.

In addition to the principle of preferential recruitment of certain categories of workers, the Committee notes that under Section 8 of the 1995 Act a work permit may be refused if it is not in the interests of the Netherlands that the vacancy in question be filled by a foreigner. The Committee feels that this provision gives wide discretionary power to the bodies responsible for issuing or refusing work permits. It wishes that the next report indicates how this provision is interpreted in practice.

There are other possible reasons for refusal: where no priority worker is immediately available, reasonable prospect of finding one; lack of suitable accommodation; the permit application's having been made by a person outside the age limits laid down in the ministerial regulations. The Committee asks the Dutch Government to explain the interpretation given to these grounds in practice.

However, the Committee notes that under the 1995 Act the Ministry of Social Affairs can derogate from these requirements in exceptional circumstances or in order to encourage international trade. The Committee asks that some precision on the content of these exceptional circumstances be given in the next report. It finds however, that the overall conditions described above, that must be fulfilled by nationals of Contracting Parties to the Charter, non-nationals of the European Union, before they may access the labour market, do not amount to a liberalisation of the regulations and therefore the situation is not in conformity with Article 18 para. 3 of the Charter.

Exercise of the right to employment

The Committee notes that the work permit is issued for a specific employer but that the foreign national can change his employer provided he obtains another work permit. The report states that another work permit is usually granted if the new employment is similar to the previous. In addition, as mentioned in the Committee's conclusion on Article 18 para. 1, the foreign worker can change jobs without restriction after working in the Netherlands for three years without interruption.

Consequences of job loss

A foreign worker who, while his work permit is still valid, loses his job through no fault of his own is entitled to sign on with the Public Employment Service and to enrol for the training courses on offer.

Conclusion

The Committee concludes that the situation in the Netherlands does not comply with Article 18 para. 3 because of the restrictions which the regulations place on entry to the labour market for nationals of Contracting Parties to the Charter which are not members of the European Union.

Paragraph 4 – The right of nationals to leave the country

As stated in the Committee's previous conclusion, the grounds for passport refusal were made stricter by the Passport Act which entered into force on 1 January 1992.

The present report explains that certain grounds for refusal have been abolished, such as serious reason to believe that the applicant would be involved in activities outside the Kingdom which were a threat to the public order of friendly powers or serious reason to believe that an applicant who had received financial assistance from a diplomatic mission would not repay the debt. In addition, even if a person has been convicted of a criminal offence in the previous 10 years a visa may only be refused if there is serious reason to believe that he will re-offend.

The Committee concludes that the situation in the Netherlands is in conformity with Article 18 para. 4 of the Charter.

Article 1 of the 1988 Additional Protocol — The right to equal opportunities and equal treatment in matters of employment and occupation without discrimination on the grounds of sex

The Committee took note of the information contained in the report of the Netherlands.

Situation in law and practice

The Committee notes that the report of the Netherlands answers the questions raised in its previous conclusion exhaustively. In particular, it notes that Article 7:646 of the Civil Code stipulates that employers in the private sector may not differentiate between men and women in regard to terms and conditions of employment, including remuneration. This Article also lays down that any clause that is contrary to this provision is null and void. Section 1a of the Equal Opportunities Act (WGB) lays down the same principle for public sector employers.

The Equal Treatment Act (AWGB), which covers all areas of discrimination and not just sex discrimination, prohibits (in Section 5) differentiation with regard to terms and conditions of employment in the public and private sectors. As a result of its open wording, this provision applies also to others involved in the terms and conditions of employment, such as the collective bargaining parties. Section 9 of the AWGB stipulates that clauses that are contrary to the Act are null and void.

The report underlines that Article 7:646 of the Civil Code, Section 1a of the WGB and Section 5 of the AWGB prohibit not only differentiation with regard to terms and conditions of employment but also differentiation when entering into an employment contract or upon appointment as a public servant, and with regard to training opportunities, promotion and termination of a contract of employment. Any clause in an individual employment contract or a collective agreement that is contrary to this is null and void in accordance with the above mentioned provisions.

Furthermore, the Committee notes that, pursuant to Section 8 of the AWGB and Article 7: 647 of the Civil Code discriminatory termination of the employment relationship, in both the public and the private sector, is subject to annulment if the employee appeals against it within two months. If the court declares the notice given to be null and void, the employment contract is still valid and there is no need for reinstatement.

The report further states that no "nullity sanction" applies if the employee suffers other disadvantages than dismissal on account of an appeal to the law. Protection is, however, offered in such situations by the general rules of civil law on tort and good faith.

In reply to a question asked by the Committee, the report states that failure to respect the WGB and Article 7:646 of the Civil Code may result in civil as well as criminal sanctions.

With respect to wage comparisons, the report states that Section 9, sub-section 2, of the WGB stipulates that account shall be taken of elements of wages other than cash in accordance with the market value that can be assigned to them.

The Committee observes, moreover, that in Dutch social security legislation no differences exist between men and women in social security matters or as regards unemployment, old age and survivors' benefit.

On 1 November 1996, the Equal Treatment (Working Hours) Act entered into force, providing for equal treatment of employees and public servants who do not have normal working hours. The Act makes it easier for an employee to challenge unequal treatment based on the fact that he or she works part-time as it is no longer requisite to argue that this constitutes indirect sex discrimination.

An amendment to the WGB was made in March 1998 to implement the "Barber Directive" (Community Directive 96/97 of amending Community Directive 86/378 on the implementation of the principle of equal treatment for men and women in occupational social security schemes). Prohibition against discrimination between men and women is now provided in three areas: as regards categories of persons eligible for pension provision, the details of such provision, and the implementation of pension schemes. Article 7:646 of the Civil Code was also amended in that payments and entitlements under pension schemes are now also regarded as "terms of employment".

As regards the employment situation of women, the Committee notes that the percentage of female wage earners in the Dutch labour force increased to 40% in 1998. Unemployment is somewhat higher for women than for men. The proportion of the workforce employed on temporary contracts is 10% (women 14% and men 8%). Women (60%) are also more often working part-time than men (10%).

Figures provided in the report show that in the past few years, there has been a steady increase in the number of women in management jobs in particular in trade, business services, health and welfare, culture and other services.

Research by the Labour Inspectorate in the Netherlands reveals that, on average, women still earn approximately 24% less than men. In all age groups, the average remuneration of women in nearly all economic sectors is lower than that of men. A significant proportion of the difference in pay observed can be explained by differences in job level (40%), part-time/full-time (11%), age (5%), experience (4%), etc. Once these factors have been eliminated there remains a pay difference of approximately 7%.

According to the report one of the explanations for lower pay for women may be that they work part-time more often than men. In the Netherlands, still about 15% of collective labour agreements do not apply to employees working "short part-time" (about less than 12-hours a week). Especially in the trade sector, individuals working part-time are not treated equally with their full-time colleagues. The Committee would like to find some examples in the next report of the differences in treatment that may exist and asks what measures are taken by the Dutch Government to improve the situation.

The Committee takes note of the list, appended to the report, of occupational activities and the training required for them, for which a person's gender may be decisive.

Positive action

As to the measures of positive action undertaken by the Dutch Government during the reference period, the Committee refers to the description in its conclusion under Article 1 para. 2 of the Charter (Addendum to Conclusions XV-1, p. 82).

Conclusion

In the light of the information contained in the report and its appendices, the Committee concludes that the situation in the Netherlands is in conformity with Article 1 of the Additional Protocol.

Chapter 10 – Conclusions concerning Articles 7, 11, 14 and 17 of the Charter and Articles 1 and 4 of the 1988 Additional Protocol in respect of Norway

Article 7 — The right of children and young persons to protection

Paragraph 2 – Higher minimum age in certain occupations

The Norwegian report under this provision indicates that significant amendments were introduced into the Working Environment Act as of 30 April 1998, in order to implement Community Directive 94/33 of 22 June 1994 on the protection of young people at work. Employers must assess the risks faced by young workers, who may not be permitted to perform hazardous or dangerous activities. Whenever a minor is employed, the company safety delegate must be consulted.

The Committee asks that the next report indicate the number of young workers who suffer occupational accidents and diseases.

As regards the presence of children over the age of 14 years on ships for the purpose of education or training, the report stresses that under the Regulations of 3 February 1983, any work assigned to them must not entail a hazard to their health or development. The placement of children on ships is made by an educational institution, and suitable conditions must be ensured on board. The master of the vessel is responsible for supervising children placed on board and ensuring that the work assigned to them is within their capacity and may be performed in safe and secure manner. A special contact person must be appointed.

The Committee concludes that the situation in Norway is in conformity with Article 7 para. 2 of the Charter.

Paragraph 3 – Safeguarding the full benefit of compulsory education

The Committee takes note from the Norwegian report of the amendments made to the Working Environment Act of 1977 to the effect that children under the age of fifteen or subject to compulsory education may not work for more than 2 hours on a school day or 12 hours per week. On days when there is no school, they may work for up to 7 hours, and up to 35 hours per week during school holidays of more than one week's duration. The Committee welcomes this improvement in the situation.

Children may not work between the hours of 8 p.m. and 6 a.m. The Committee recalls that it has previously held that children should not be permitted to do any kind of work before going to school in the morning (Conclusions VIII, p. 108) as such work may deprive them of the full benefit of their compulsory education. However, having noted in the past that Norwegian legislation forbids the employment of children so close to school hours that the child cannot get to school on time and sufficiently rested, the Committee seeks information on the supervision of this rule in practice by the appropriate authorities (labour inspectors, education authorities, social services). It further enquires as to the nature and extent of early morning work performed by children in accordance with Section 35 of the Working Environment Act. Pending clarification of whether the right of school-going children to benefit fully from their compulsory education is implemented in practice, the Committee reserves its position on this matter.

With respect to annual rest, the report recalls that children must be granted four weeks' holidays per year, half of which must take place during school summer holidays. The Committee considers that the main purpose of school holidays is to let children rest in order to benefit from school after the holiday. It has always held that the rest period must cover at least half of the holiday period for children still subject to compulsory education.

This not being the case in Norway, the Committee finds that the situation is not in conformity with this provision of the Charter.

The Committee concludes that the situation in Norway is not in conformity with Article 7 para. 3 of the Charter as the mandatory rest period during school holidays for children still subject to compulsory education is not sufficient to ensure that they benefit from such education.

Paragraph 5 – Fair remuneration for young workers and apprentices

The Committee takes note of the information contained in the Norwegian report.

Young workers

The report provides information on the coverage of collective agreements in different age groups. In the 16-24 age group, 72% of workers are covered by an agreement compared to 77% for all workers as a whole. The report further provides figures on hourly wages for different age groups. In the 16-19 age group, the hourly wage is 71 Norwegian Kroner (NOK) for workers covered by collective agreement and 68 NOK for workers not covered by collective agreement. The corresponding figures in the 20-24 age group are 82 NOK and 79 NOK and in the 24-64 age group 106 NOK and 124 NOK.

These figures, however, are not sufficient as a basis for the Committee's assessment. The figures would appear to represent averages for each age group (although this is not specified in the report) and not the minimum (lowest) wage actually paid in the labour market to young workers. In addition, the figures are gross values. In order to assess the situation the Committee needs information on the net value, i.e. after deduction of any taxes and social security contributions, of the minimum wage paid to young workers under the age of 18 on the one hand and on the starting wages or minimum wages paid to adult workers on the other hand. The Committee insists that this information be contained in the next report.

The Committee recalls that the conclusion in respect of adult workers' wages is deferred pending receipt of the appropriate information (Conclusions XIV-2, p. 591).

Apprentices

As regards apprentices, the report states that in connection with the reform of the upper secondary education system (*Reform* 94*)* the wage level of apprentices was reduced from about 70-80% of that of a skilled worker to about 50% as an average over a two-year training period. The apprentice wage henceforth ranges from about 30% during the first six months of training to about 80% during the last 6 months. According to the report this was accepted by the trade unions in return for a major increase in the number of apprentice places. It would seem to the Committee that the new wage differentials for apprentices still meet the requirements of this provision. However, since the assessment of the adequacy of adult wages is pending, as noted above, it is unable to reach a conclusion at this stage.

Conclusion

Pending receipt of the information requested, the Committee defers its conclusion.

Paragraph 6 – Treatment of the time spent in vocational training as forming part of the working day

The Norwegian report states that the statutory right to three years of upper secondary education encompasses the great majority of young people (about 95% each year). The group of young people between 16 and 18 who has chosen to start working is therefore a small minority.

The Committee acknowledges that the number of young workers concerned may be small, but for the purposes of this provision of the Charter it still needs clarification as to whether at least 80% of these young workers in practice benefit from having time spent on vocational training during normal working hours with the consent of the employer treated as forming part of the working day. It insists that this information be contained in the next report.

The Committee takes note of the information on the reform of the upper secondary education system (*Reform* 94) and on the efforts to integrate young persons not in education and not in employment into the labour market. It recalls that it commented in some detail on *Reform* 94 under Article 10 para. 1 in Conclusions XIV-2 (pp. 599-600) to which it refers.

Pending receipt of the information requested, the Committee concludes that the situation in Norway is in conformity with Article 7 para. 6 of the Charter.

Paragraph 7 – Annual holiday of young persons under eighteen

The Committee notes from the report submitted by Norway that there have been no changes in the situation which it has previously considered to be satisfactory.

It therefore concludes that the situation in Norway is in conformity with Article 7 para. 7 of the Charter.

Paragraph 8 – Prohibition of night work for young persons under eighteen

The Committee recalls that in Norway young people between 15 and 18 years of age are not allowed to work between 10 p.m. and 6 a.m. or 11 p.m. and 7 a.m. pursuant to the Working Environment Act. However, the act also provides that certain types of work are exempted from this prohibition. The exceptions were described in detail in Conclusions XIII-4 (pp. 308-309) to which the Committee refers.

In reply to the Committee's question, the report states that statistical information on the number of persons under 18 engaged in work exempted from the night work prohibition as compared to the total number of young persons below 18 years of age is not available. Nevertheless, the report quotes figures published by the Nordic Council according to which 90% of young workers under eighteen in the Nordic countries (Denmark, Finland, Iceland, Sweden and Norway) do not carry out work before 6 a.m., 4% "work seldom" before 6 a.m. and 6% "do it often". 79% do not work after 10 p.m., 12% work seldom after this hour and 9% do it often.

The Committee observes that the Nordic Council survey only covers young persons between 13 and 17 years of age and not young full-time workers. It asks that the next report contain a more precise estimate of the number of young workers employed in the types of night work concerned.

Finally, the Committee notes that legislation is being prepared which will raise the age limit for night work to cover also 18 year-olds. It wishes to be informed of the new legislation when it has been enacted.

Pending receipt of the information requested, the Committee concludes that the situation in Norway is in conformity with Article 7 para. 8 of the Charter.

Paragraph 10 – Special protection for children and young people from physical and moral dangers to which they are exposed

The Committee noted the information contained in the Norwegian report.

The Committee notes the information provided under Article 7 paras. 2 and 3 on the protection of working children. It therefore refers to its conclusions under these provisions.

As regards measures taken to prevent drug addiction and alcoholism among young people, the Committee refers to its conclusion under Article 11 para. 2.

The Committee wishes to be informed as to whether legislation prohibits the use of children in the sex industry, and to receive information on any supervisory system and sanctions that may accompany this prohibition.

The Committee concludes that the situation in Norway is in conformity with Article 7 para 10 of the Charter.

Article 11 — Right to protection of health

Paragraph 1 – Removal of the causes of ill-health

The Committee takes note of the information contained in Norway's report on the Charter, the 1999 report submitted to the World Health Organisation (WHO)[1] and the 2000 report of the European Observatory on Health Care Systems.[2]

State of health of the population - General indicators

Life expectancy and principal causes of death

The Committee notes that life expectancy increased from 80.3 years in 1992 to 81 years in 1997 for women and from 74.1 years in 1992 to 75.4 years in 1997 for men. However, these increases were smaller than in other European Union and European Economic Area member states.[3]

The main causes of death remain cardio-vascular diseases (45% of all deaths), cancer (22%) and diseases of the respiratory system. The Committee observes that there is a very high rate of ischemic heart disease, which is a major cause of premature death among men, and that the proportion of premature deaths due to lung cancer among women is slightly above the European Union average.

The Committee notes that the total number of suicides fell during the reference period and that Norway now has a suicide rate on par with the average for European Union and European Economic Area countries. However, the rate did not fall among young people aged between 15 and 24, particularly boys, for whom the suicide rate is well above the European average.

The Committee observes that the number of new AIDS diagnoses per year fell during the reference period from 67 in 1995 to 36 in 1998.

---

[1]*Highlights on Health in Norway* (Internet site of the WHO European regional office: www.who.dk).

[2]*Health Care Systems in Transition Profile* (Observatory Internet site: www.observatory.dk).

[3]OECD, *Health Data*, 1999.

Infant and maternal mortality

The infant mortality rate in Norway fell sharply in relation to the previous reference period, from 5.9 deaths per 1,000 live births in 1992 to 4 in 1996. During the previous reference period, the average rate of maternal mortality was very low (3.3 deaths per 100,000 live births). The Committee requests up-to-date information on this subject.

Health care system

Access to health care

The Norwegian health care system covers the whole population.

Primary health care is the responsibility of the municipalities and is carried out in health centres, where doctors usually run group practices. Each county is responsible for the funding, forward planning and management of general and psychiatric hospitals as well as other specialised medical services.

The health care system is publicly funded, mainly through taxes but also through contributions to the national insurance scheme, to which everyone must be affiliated.

In 1997, 7.5% of GDP was devoted to health expenditure. The proportion of health care funded by the state is constantly falling, but remained around 82.2% in 1997.

Patients pay 92 NOK to visit a general practitioner and 185 NOK for a specialist consultation, although nobody should pay more than 1,290 NOK for health care in any one year. This maximum amount includes transport costs to the health centre and patients' contributions to the cost of some pharmaceutical products. The cost of any care or medicines above this figure is covered in full. Care relating to childbirth and the health care for children under 7 years old are also free. Finally, all hospital care is totally free.

According to OECD data, the average reimbursement rate for pharmaceutical products fell slightly to 58% in 1996, which is below average for European OECD countries. The Committee has no standardised figures on which to base a comparison of the average reimbursement rate for out-patient medical care with the rates of other Contracting Parties.

The Committee notes that, there is a waiting list system for access to hospital care. In 1990, in order to combat the persistently long waiting lists for non-emergency treatment, the authorities laid down a set of national standards for priority of admission and set up a national waiting time registration system. A maximum six-month wait was introduced for patients who do not need emergency treatment but who require care if serious complications are to be avoided. The Committee notes that, despite these measures, the number of patients on waiting lists and the number of cases where the maximum wait was not respected rose during the reference period and that 25% of patients had to wait more than three months to be admitted to hospital. Nevertheless, the Committee observes that several provisions introduced outside the reference period are said to have improved the situation, particularly the patient's right to choose a hospital, enshrined in the Act on Patients' Rights which came into force in 2000. It would like to be informed of further developments and resolves to wait until the next report on Article 11 before passing judgment.

Health professionals and equipment

The total number of hospital beds is relatively stable, although it has been falling slowly since the early 1980s, reaching 64,773 in 1997. The number of beds per 1,000 inhabitants (14.7 in 1997) is thus the highest in any European OECD country. However, the proportion of chronic care and psychiatric beds is the lowest, representing 33% and 4.7% of all beds respectively. The few private hospitals account for only 0.1% of beds.

In 1997 the numbers of general and specialist physicians per 1,000 inhabitants were 0.8 and 1.9 respectively. These figures are average for European OECD countries, as is the ratio of dentists, which remains stable (0.9 per 1,000 inhabitants). The density of pharmacists (0.4 per 1,000 inhabitants) is lower than the European average.

Conclusion

Subject to the requested information on waiting lists, the Committee concludes that the situation in Norway is in conformity with Article 11 para. 1 of the Charter.

Paragraph 2 – Advisory and educational facilities

The Committee takes note of the information contained in the current and previous Norwegian reports.

Encouragement of individual responsibility

Health education in schools

The Committee noted from the third report that, as part of a nationwide basic education programme, schoolchildren of all ages receive health education lessons, some of which are compulsory, dealing with the following subjects: healthy living, alcohol, drugs, smoking, sex education, personal and dental hygiene. Teaching materials are provided by the Basic Education Council.

The previous report also stated that a special advisor offers guidance to primary and secondary schools on alcohol and drugs education, while the National Directorate for the Prevention of Drug and Alcohol Problems has developed a special training programme for primary schools.

This information suggests that the situation in Norway is in conformity with Article 11 para. 2 as far as health education in schools is concerned. Nevertheless, the Committee requests that the next report contain an up-to-date summary of the situation and indicate how much funding is devoted to health education in schools.

Public information and awareness-raising

According to previous reports, information campaigns on major public health issues and public awareness programmes designed to promote healthy living are launched regularly. Surveys are carried out to determine the areas in which health promotion needs to be stepped up.

The Committee would like future reports to be more detailed and indicate which partners are involved, what methods are used and how much money is spent on this kind of prevention.

Counselling and screening

Children and adolescents

The municipal authorities are responsible for family health services, which promote children's mental, physical and social well-being (through vaccinations, regular check-ups, health and nutrition appraisals, home visits, etc.). Having noted in its conclusion concerning Article 11 para. 1 that health care for children under seven is totally free, the Committee presumes that access to family health services is also free, but requests confirmation that this is the case.

Family health services also offer antenatal classes, medical check-ups for pregnant women and advice on sexual matters. Specialist medical centres operate within universities.

The municipal authorities are responsible for developing school health programmes and ensuring that appropriate health equipment is available to schools. Schools are regularly visited by school health teams and some have their own clinics. Routine medical examinations are carried out in schools every year or at parents' request.

Rest of the population

The Committee notes from the 2000 report by the European Observatory on Health Care Systems[1] that specific screening programmes for breast, colon and brain cancer are organised.

Conclusion

The Committee concludes that the situation in Norway is in conformity with Article 11 para. 2 of the Charter.

Paragraph 3 – Prevention of diseases

The Committee takes note of developments in Norway concerning the prevention of health risks in general and diseases in particular.

Policies on the prevention of avoidable risks

General

The Committee requests that future reports indicate, as far as possible, how much public funding is devoted to the main prevention policies listed below.

Reduction of environmental risks

Air pollution – The Committee observes from OECD data[2] that Norway has achieved contrasting results in its efforts to control anthropic emissions of traditional pollutants: it has been very successful in

---

[1]*Health Care Systems in Transition Profile* (Observatory Internet site: www.observatory.dk).

[2]OECD, *Environmental Data*, Compendium 1999.

reducing sulphur oxides, with average results for nitrogen oxides and carbon monoxide.

As far as local pollution is concerned, previous reports indicate that air quality targets have been set. The Committee would like to know whether limit values for the concentration of the main pollutants responsible for air quality deterioration have therefore been fixed, and whether an air quality monitoring mechanism is in place.

As far as global pollution is concerned, the Committee notes that Norway ratified the United Nations Framework Convention on Climate Change (Rio de Janeiro, 1992) in 1993 and has been pursuing a highly active policy of reducing the main types of greenhouse gas emission, particularly since the Kyoto Protocol was adopted in 1997. However, it notes from OECD data that the emission control policy is achieving mediocre results and that stronger measures were adopted during the reference period, particularly environmental taxes relating to carbon dioxide emissions.

Asbestos – The Committee notes that asbestos is banned under Norwegian law. Amended Decree No. 235 of 1984 prohibits the importation, production, sale and use of asbestos and asbestos products. While stressing that the total ban on asbestos is in itself vital to the effective implementation of Article 11 para. 3, the Committee would also like to know whether measures are being taken to control asbestos levels in residential blocks and whether companies are under specific obligations with regard to the disposal of asbestos waste.

Ionising radiation – There are two small nuclear power stations in Norway, although they only function for research purposes rather than energy production. A previous report stated that people living nearby are protected by strict limits on radioactive waste and local emergency plans in case of an accident. Numerous preventive and protection measures were also implemented nationally following the Chernobyl disaster. The latest report indicates that radiation protection regulations are currently being reviewed. The Committee therefore requests that the next report contain up-to-date information on standards for the protection of people living near nuclear power stations, dose limits and the monitoring system. With regard to dose limits in particular, the Committee stresses the importance of complying with the maximum values recommended in 1990 by the International Commission on Radiological Protection (ICRP). It asks to be informed of developments in this area in the next report on Article 3 (Supervision Cycle XVI-2).

Noise – The environment and health authorities are jointly responsible for noise abatement and raising awareness of the dangers of noise. Various noise abatement programmes have been implemented in the past. During the reference period, the government issued a white paper on the impact of the various noise abatement standards, highlighting methods of measuring noise and listing the people affected by noise. The Committee would like information on follow-up to the white paper.

Food safety

In view of the threat to health represented by diseases related to food and the recent outbreaks of such diseases, in particular the new variation Creutzfeldt-Jakob disease, as well as the emergence of new food products derived from biotechnology, the Committee has decided to look at food safety measures in all states parties to the Charter. It recalls that under Article 11 states have a responsibility to ensure a high degree of safety in this area for their populations.

Referring in particular to the resolution adopted by the 53rd World Health Assembly in May 2000 on food safety[1] and while recognising the relevance of international strategies, the Committee considers that in order to comply with the Charter in this field, states must set legal norms at the national level regarding food hygiene taking into account scientific data, and establish and maintain mechanisms for monitoring compliance with these norms throughout the food chain, develop, implement and up-date systematic prevention measures, notably by way of labelling, as well as monitor the occurrence of food-borne diseases.

Previous reports show that food safety regulations cover the whole food chain, that strict hygiene rules are in place and that tests are carried out. A central body, the Norwegian Food Safety Authority (*SNT*), is responsible for implementing legislation and coordinating the work of the 82 local food control authorities. During the reference period, extra resources were allocated to the food control programme, which was brought into line with European Union standards. The Committee asks that the next report by Norway provide information on the other aspects set out above so that it can assess the situation on the next occasion that Article 11 is examined.

---

[1]WHO Internet site: www.who.int

Measures to combat smoking and alcoholism

Alcohol – During the reference period, Norway pursued a concerted policy to reduce alcohol consumption by imposing very high taxes on alcohol, introducing broad restrictions on the sale, importation and exportation of alcohol (which was subject to a state monopoly until a licensing system was recently introduced), banning all publicity related to alcohol or alcohol consumption in public places and enforcing a "zero tolerance" approach to drink driving. The Committee observes that the results have been very positive, since pure alcohol consumption is the lowest of any European Union and European Economic Area Agreement country (4 litres per person in 1996 compared to a European average of 9.4).

Smoking – An active anti-smoking policy has also been in place for many years and was strengthened during the reference period by a ban on all direct and indirect advertising, high taxes on retail prices (78% in 1995), a new minimum age for the purchase of cigarettes (18 years), etc. The Committee observes that these measures have also been successful, since the number of cigarettes consumed per person is by far the lowest of any European Union and European Economic Area Agreement country (619 cigarettes compared to a European average of 1,646 in 1997).

Prophylactic measures

Epidemiological monitoring

The Committee notes from previous reports that a system for the collection of data and monitoring of numerous transmittable diseases is in operation in Norway. It also observes that specific measures can be taken and *ad hoc* investigations launched if an epidemic seems likely to break out.

Immunisation

In response to a question in the previous conclusion, the report states that the Government's vaccination programme is optional. The Committee requests that the next report contain more detailed information, indicating the main child vaccination rates (tuberculosis, diphtheria, tetanus, polio, measles) and whether these vaccinations are available free of charge.

Conclusion

Pending receipt of the information requested, particularly concerning vaccinations, the Committee concludes that the situation in Norway is in conformity with Article 11 para. 3 of the Charter.

Article 14 — The right to benefit from social welfare services

Paragraph 1 – Provision or promotion of social welfare services

The Norwegian report contains information on services aimed at drug and alcohol abusers. Following a 1995 amendment to the Social Services Act a pregnant drug or alcohol addict may be placed in an institution without her consent throughout the pregnancy on condition that voluntary treatment is not adequate and it is deemed likely that the abuse will have a harmful effect on the child. The basis for the retention shall be reviewed by the social services every three months. In 1997, a total of 10 pregnant abusers were placed in institutions without their consent by a County Board and a further 18 women were placed in an institution pursuant to an interim decision by the social services. The corresponding figures for 1998 were 17 and 30, respectively.

According to the report considerable emphasis has been put on legal protection and human rights aspects in cases where drug abusers are subjected to compulsory placement. Various new measures in these regards have been adopted outside the reference period. The Committee asks that the next report contain more details on this point and on the development in the total number of compulsory placements. It also asks under which circumstances interim decisions on placement are made by the social services and whether such decisions are subject to confirmation by a County Board.

The Committee's previous conclusion in respect of Article 14 para. 1 was provisionally positive pending receipt of information on the composition of the County Board. The report makes reference to Section 9-10 of the Social Services Act and Royal Decree No. 690 of 1992 according to which the Ministry of Children and Family Affairs shall appoint to the County Board:

– a chairman with legal training and experience and, if necessary, a deputy with similar qualifications;

– a committee of experts;

– a panel of laymen to serve the County Board.

In addition, the chairman of the County Board may call in experts from outside the committee of experts. They shall not, however, take part in the decision-making as such.

The Committee had also asked why there was no right of appeal in respect of County Board decisions. The report emphasises that board decisions can be brought before the City or District Court. It adds that only the municipal social service may bring cases before the County Board and that all cases are carefully prepared in accordance with guidelines issued by the Ministry of Health and Social Services.

Finally, the Committee asks that the next report contain up-dated information on the number of beneficiaries of all categories of social services and on staff levels and expenditure for the various services.

In the light of the information provided, the Committee concludes that the situation in Norway is in conformity with Article 14 para. 1 of the Charter.

Paragraph 2 – Public participation in the establishment and maintenance of social welfare services

In reply to the Committee's question on the implementation of Section 3-3 and Section 8 subsection 4 of the Social Services Act, the Norwegian report states that it is up to the municipalities to decide how these provisions are implemented. The Committee insists that the next report contain specific, practical examples of the involvement of voluntary organisations and individuals in the development and provision of social services. In addition, it repeats its request for specific figures showing the extent of financial aid granted by the state to voluntary organisations for the purposes of this provision of the Charter.

Pending receipt of the information requested, the Committee concludes that the situation in Norway is in conformity with Article 14 para. 2 of the Charter.

Article 17 — The right of mothers and children to social and economic protection

The Committee notes the information contained in the Norwegian report.

Establishment of parentage and adoption

As regards the establishment of parentage and adoption the situation is in conformity with the Charter.

The Committee recalls that a child of 12 years or over must consent to his adoption and that an adopted child has the right to information about his biological parents on attaining the age of 18 years.

Children in public care

Children who are temporarily or permanently deprived of their family environment are the responsibility of the child welfare authorities pursuant to the Child Welfare Act 1992. The decision to transfer care is assigned to the county welfare boards. There is a right of appeal to the courts.

Children, who are placed outside the home, live in foster homes, emergency homes and various types of institutions. 80% of children who are placed outside their biological family homes live in foster homes the remaining 20% are placed in institutions.[1] The number of children placed outside their biological families has decreased in recent years. By the end of 1995, 21,142 children were recipients of child welfare measures. Of these approximately 75% received assistance while remaining in their home. Approximately 25% 5,095 children were placed outside their homes, of which 4,200 were in foster homes, 400 in children's or youth homes and 450 in other types of institutions.

The Committee wishes to receive details on the types of institutions that exist.

The county is responsible for the establishment and operation of institutions that care for children. The county governor is responsible for continuous supervision of the institutions, if necessary with the assistance of a supervisory committee. The Committee wishes to receive

---

[1]Second report of Norway under the United Nations Convention on the Rights of the Child, CRC/C/70 Add. 2, submitted in 1998.

information on the procedures available to children in institutions who wish to complain about the care or treatment in the institution. Further it wishes to receive details on the conditions under which an institution may interfere with a child's property, mail, personal integrity and right to meet with persons close to him.

Protection of children from ill-treatment and abuse

Civil servant and relevant professional groups i.e. doctors, nurses, psychologists, etc. have a duty to report any suspected abuse or ill-treatment of children to the child welfare services.

The municipalities are responsible for protecting children from ill-treatment and abuse. The county social welfare boards have the competence to make decisions in cases involving the possible withdrawal of parental authority.

Child welfare emergency teams have been organised in a number of municipalities, in order to develop a close collaboration between the child welfare services and the police. There also exist confidential help lines that children can ring.

Section 30 of the Children's Act prohibits corporal punishment in connection with child rearing.

Children and the law – Young offenders

The age of criminal responsibility in Norway is 15 years. Child welfare measures are instituted for children under 15 years of age who commit criminal offences.

Criminal proceedings against young persons between the ages of 15 and 18 years are dealt with by the ordinary courts however there are special rules for this group. For example persons under 18 years of age should not be arrested or remanded in custody.

Young offenders between 15 and 18 years of age may be given a suspended sentence, be released on probation, or sentenced to a term of imprisonment. The Committee wishes to be informed of the number of young offenders sentenced to prison and the maximum length of imprisonment. It also wishes to receive information about the conditions of imprisonment, i.e. *inter alia,* whether young offenders are separated from adult prisoners.

The Committee notes from the report that the county welfare board may make an order to place a child, who has shown serious behavioural problems in the form of serious or repeated criminality, in an institution for observation, examination or treatment. The decision may be made without the parent's or child's' consent. An order may be made to place a child in an institution for up to 12 months. The placement shall be periodically reviewed. The Committee wishes to know how many children are the subject of such orders, and whether such orders are imposed on children after conviction of an offence by a court.

Conclusion

The Committee concludes that the situation in Norway is in conformity with Article 17 of the Social Charter.

Article 1 of the 1988 Additional Protocol — The right to equal opportunities and equal treatment in matters of employment and occupation without discrimination on the grounds of sex

The Committee notes the information contained in the Norwegian report.

Situation in law and practice

The Committee deferred its previous conclusion pending receipt of information on the protection of workers against retaliation by their employer in cases of alleged discrimination. The present report merely states that Working Environment 1977 gives workers full protection, also against retaliatory measures that may follow a claim under the Gender Equality Act No. 45 of 1978. The Committee observes that Section 60 of the 1977 Act protects workers from unfair dismissal. This would include dismissal resulting from a claim for equal pay or a claim relating to another form of discrimination based on sex. The Committee has previously asked about protection against other forms of retaliation than dismissal. The previous report answered that alteration of the terms of employment requires a valid reason and thereby limits the employers' access to retaliatory measures; as to measures not concerning the terms of employment it referred to the general comments on the Gender Equality Act.

The Committee wishes to have this last point clarified further. In particular it would like to be informed whether the 1977 Act provides protection also against retaliation other than dismissal and, if so, which provisions cover this issue. If the 1977 Act is not applicable, the Committee wishes to know whether another piece of legislation covers this issue.

The Committee repeats its request for information on the existence of sanctions against employers who discriminate on grounds of gender.

In reply to a question asked by the Committee and to Question F of the Form for Reports, the report states that social security matters, etc. are included in the scope of the Protocol. The Committee therefore asks whether differences exist between men and women in this respect.

The report states that very few occupations are reserved for one sex. It gives the example of fireman, which is only a male occupation and also mentions that shelters for women victims of domestic violence only have female employees.

The Committee notes from report that the Gender Equality Ombudsman deals with 200 grievances per year, whereas the Gender Equality Appeals Board makes final decisions in 10 to 15 cases per year. The cases concern mainly working life, recruitment, promotion, working conditions and pay.

The Committee takes note of the information provided in the report on the measures taken and machinery established to guarantee or promote equality of opportunity and equal treatment in the field of vocational guidance, training and rehabilitation. It notes the improvement in the educational situation for young women; according to the statistics referred to they are in majority at universities and state colleges and approximately 55% of graduate students are women. However, they choose traditionally female education programmes to a large extent. The Ministry of Education is therefore running a programme focusing on stimulating young men and women to choose within a broader range of educational and vocational possibilities to counteract a gender-segregated labour market.

When it comes to higher education, the report states that according to available statistics 35% of all Ph.D. students passing their exams in 1999 and 11% of professors in higher education in 1997 were women. In comparison, the figures for 1990 were 17% and 4% , respectively. Following a White Paper on research submitted in June 1999, the Government intends to take measures to increase the proportion of women in disciplines with few women and to increase the proportion of women in permanent posts, particularly at the level of professor.

As regards the general situation on the labour market the report indicates that 66% of women and 76% of men in the ages 16 to 74 belong to the labour force. The Committee also observes that a sharp rise in employment has boosted the female participation rate,[1] the number of women working full-time is increasing, also as regards women with small children.

According to the report, the fact that Norway has few women in leading positions is a concern of the Government and the Confederation of Business and Industry. The percentage of women in top management is about 7% in the private sector and 20-26% in the public sector. However, there is an increase of women in middle-management jobs,

[1]OECD, Economic surveys, Norway, 1998.

both in the private and the public sector. The report states that the labour market is also less segregated in this respect among the younger employees as opposed to the older ones.

The Committee observes that the over-all wage-gap has been relatively stable, with a difference of approximately 20% in hourly pay between men and women working full time. The report states that structural changes in the labour market and gender segregation of the labour force neutralises the positive effects of a rising educational level among women. Differences in position is an explanation, and a considerable part of the wage differences can be traced back to the wage at the time of appointment. Among women and men with similar backgrounds, women tend to have fewer promotions than men.

The centralised wage negotiations have in recent years had a low-wage and equal-pay profile, in both the private and the public sector. However, in the private sector the effects of local negotiations have to some degree neutralised or even counteracted these positive effects.

An agreement to improve the implementation of the plans for gender equality in enterprises was part of the wage agreement in the private sector in 1996. In the state sector the local negotiations have resulted in a reduced pay gap between men and women.

The Committee notes that the report provides no information on the possible development of a new gender sensitive job evaluation proposed by a Governmental Committee in 1997; it therefore repeats its request on this point.

Positive action

The Committee takes note in particular of the possibility for the regional education authorities to use quotas between the sexes in the intake of students to courses and the distribution of apprentices in cases where there is an insufficient balance. It notes that quota regulations should only be used in cases where the applicants have got the same marks. Applicants belonging to the under-represented sex, shall in such case be given priority until 40% of the available places have been offered to the candidates from the minority group.

Conclusion

Pending receipt of the information requested on other forms of retaliation than dismissal, the Committee concludes that the situation in Norway is in conformity with Article 1 of the Additional Protocol.

3rd report – reference period 1998-1999

Article 4 of the 1988 Additional Protocol — The right of elderly persons to social protection

The Committee takes note of the replies to its questions concerning elderly persons' right to social protection, given in Norway's report and the appendices thereto.

A standard of living enabling elderly persons to remain full members of society for as long as possible (Article 4 para. 1)

The report states that the level of the minimum pension rose considerably in 1998: to 81,360 Norwegian Kroner (NOK) for a single person (compared with 63,000 in 1996) and 140,000 NOK for a married couple. The minimum pension is the sole source of income of about 7% of retired people, and less than 1% of people over 67 years old were dependent on social economic assistance in 1998. The Committee notes that, despite this substantial increase, there is still a significant difference between the amount of the minimum pension and the average net wage (161,736 NOK in 1996). However, it also takes account of the existence of other forms of income, housing allowances and social economic assistance, and the fact that the persons concerned pay only 50 NOK per month as their participation in the cost of home services.

All residents of Norway are entitled to the minimum old-age pension from the age of 67. A three-year residence requirement is imposed for acquisition of entitlement. To receive the full basic pension, a person must have lived in Norway for 40 years. Otherwise, the pension is reduced on a proportional basis. These rules apply irrespective of the beneficiary's nationality. Noting that the minimum pension is non-contributory, within the meaning of the Charter, the Committee considers that the three-year residence requirement for acquisition of entitlement is not excessive and does not violate Article 4 of the Additional Protocol.

Services and facilities allowing elderly persons to lead independent lives in familiar surroundings (Article 4 para. 2)

The four-year plan of action for care of the elderly, mentioned in the previous report, provides for the creation of 6,000 home-service jobs from 1998 to 2001.

Specific protection afforded to elderly persons living in institutions (Article 4 para. 3)

In 1998, 42,406 people lived in institutions - or about 6% of people over 65 years old. Half of these people were between 80-90 years old.

Objectives under the above-mentioned plan of action include building 7,200 new specially adapted housing units, creating 6,000 additional single rooms, and adding 6,400 places to the intake capacity of nursing homes and specially adapted accommodation offering round-the-clock services. Since these objectives are to be met by the end of 2002, the Committee would like the next report to indicate whether they have actually been achieved.

The Committee regrets that the report does not contain the rules governing respect for elderly persons' privacy or the information requested on Senior Citizens Councils and the possible institution of an ombudsman for the elderly. It asks that this information be provided in the next report.

Conclusion

The Committee concludes that the situation in Norway is in conformity with Article 4 of the Additional Protocol.

Chapter 11 – Conclusions concerning Articles 2, 3, 4, 7, 8, 9, 10, 11, 14, 15, 17 and 18 of the Charter in respect of Poland

Article 2 — The right to just conditions of work

Paragraph 1– Reasonable daily and weekly working hours

Article 129 of the Polish Labour Code fixes daily working time at 8 hours and the average working week at 42 hours reckoned over a reference period of 3 months. The distribution of working hours must allow for 39 additional days off work per calendar year,[1] on the understanding that there must be no fewer than 9 such days per 3 month reference period.

Specific rules apply to working time for the following categories:

– persons employed in continuous work: the maximum working time is 12 hours per day and an average of 48 hours per week over a reference period of up to 4 weeks;

– persons working 4 successive shifts: the maximum working time is 8 hours per day and an average of 40 hours per week over a reference period of up to 4 months.

Daily working time may be extended to 9 hours, by way of exception, if the number of additional days off work exceeds 39, to 10 hours for transport vehicle drivers, or to 12 hours where "justified by the kind of work or its organisation".

Hours worked beyond the statutory limits count as overtime. Overtime is permissible in the following circumstances:

– rescue operations required to protect human life or public health, to protect property or to remedy malfunctions;

– particular needs of the enterprise.

The Labour Code stipulates 150 hours per calendar year as the maximum permissible amount of overtime for meeting the particular needs of the enterprise. Overtime is not to exceed 4 hours per day.

---

[1]Additional days off are fixed by the Ministry of Labour and Social Affairs in consultation with the Polish confederations of trade unions.

In addition, since July 1998 collective agreements have provide for 40 hours of work per week in 705 enterprises. Besides these agreements, 54 "above-enterprise level agreements" provide for a reduction of working time for specific categories of employees. According to the report, 75% of employees are now covered by collective agreements stipulating forty hours of work per week.

The Committee recalls that in order to comply with Article 2 para. 1, Contracting Parties must provide for reasonable daily and weekly hours by legislation or regulations, collective agreements or any other obligatory means whose fulfilment is subject to supervision by a competent authority. It takes account of actual working time, i.e. normal hours plus any overtime worked.

In order to asses the situation, the Committee requires the following information:

– the meaning of "additional days off work", and what precise effect they have on the distribution of hours of work;

– the maximum permissible daily working time (absolute limit), inclusive of overtime;

– the maximum permissible weekly working time (absolute limit), inclusive of overtime;

– the penalties which are prescribed for employers infringing statutory rules on hours of work;

– guarantees available to employees in this respect.

Pending receipt of the above information, the Committee defers its conclusion.

Paragraph 3 – Annual holiday with pay

Under Article 152 of the Polish Labour Code, all employees are entitled to receive a certain number of consecutive days of paid annual leave. The terms of this provision do not permit employees to waive their right to leave. Leave entitlements are calculated according to the following rule:

– 18 working days[1] after 1 year of service;

[1]Every day except Sundays and public holidays is regarded as a working day.

– 20 working days after 6 years of service;

– 26 working days after 10 years of service.

Article 166 of the Labour Code provides that periods of absence from work due to illness do not enter into the calculation of leave.

The Committee concludes that the situation in Poland is in conformity with Article 2 para. 3 of the Charter.

Paragraph 4 – Reduced working hours or additional holidays for workers in dangerous or unhealthy occupations

The Polish report lists jobs classified as dangerous or unhealthy and forbidden to women and young people. It also mentions several lists of dangerous or unhealthy occupations, in particular a list of types of work that may pose a particular hazard to health or life and must therefore be performed by at least two persons.

Article 130 of the Labour Code provides that persons employed in dangerous or unhealthy occupations are entitled to rest periods entering into the calculation of working time, or to a reduction thereof.

The report nevertheless indicates that since 12 January 1997 these matters have been settled by collective agreements or by in-plant working regulations. It also states that the official regulations enacted pursuant to Article 130 of the Labour Code remained in force until 1 January 2000.

In order to assess the situation, the Committee asks that the next report provide the list of dangerous or unhealthy occupations with an indication of the issuing authority. It also enquires whether collective agreements continue to prescribe shorter working time or grant extra leave to persons engaged in such occupations. Lastly, it enquires whether penalties are prescribed for employers who infringe the rules in this area.

Pending receipt of the information requested, the Committee defers its conclusion.

Paragraph 5 – Weekly rest period

Article 138 of the Polish Labour Code provides that "Sundays and vacations specified by separate regulations are days off work".

Sunday work is authorised in exceptional cases:

– rescue operations to protect human life or public health, to protect property, or to rectify malfunctions;

– continuous work;

– work organised in four shifts or in a similar form;

– essential repairs;

– transport and communications;

– company fire brigade duty;

– surveillance of premises;

– agriculture and animal husbandry;

– work which is necessary owing to its social utility and fulfilment of the everyday needs of the general public, particularly in shops, service enterprises, catering, the hotel trade, communal establishments, health care and social welfare services and cultural, educational, tourist and recreational facilities.

Employers are required to grant employees working on Sunday another free day in the following week (Article 140 para. 1 of the Labour Code).

In undertakings where Sunday is a working day (see above), employees must have at least one free Sunday every third week. This does not apply to workers whose work is organised in four shifts or in a similar form (Article 140 para. 2 of the Labour Code).

According to the report, employees can inform the labour inspectorate of any breach of the Labour Code and can also bring a case before the labour courts.

The Committee recalls that the purpose of Article 2 para. 5 is to protect workers' health and safety by guaranteeing them a weekly rest period that coincides as far as possible with the day recognised by tradition or custom as a day of rest. It is permissible for such rest not to be taken on Sunday, either when the nature of the activity so requires or owing to the characteristics of the economy. In all such cases, employees must be allowed to rest on another day of the week.

In the light of the above information, the Committee considers that the situation in Poland is in conformity with Article 2 para. 5 of the Charter.

It nevertheless asks whether the 39 additional days off work mentioned in the report under Article 2 para. 1 affect the weekly rest period.

1st report – reference period 1997-1999

Article 3 — The right to safe and healthy working conditions

Paragraph 1 – Issue of safety and health regulations

The Committee notes that general responsibility for safe and healthy working conditions rests with the Ministry of Labour and Social Policy, while the Ministry of Transport and Shipping and the National Mining Authority have specific responsibilities.

Regulations on health and safety at work

The legal framework for the protection of occupational health and safety consists of Section X of the Labour Code as amended by the Act of 2 February 1996 and numerous executive orders, legislation guaranteeing the rights of trade unions and powers of plant-based voluntary labour inspectors and laws defining the powers of bodies responsible for monitoring and supervising working conditions (labour inspectorate, occupational health authority, etc.). The Committee notes that Poland has incorporated Framework Directive 89/391/EEC on the introduction of measures to encourage improvements in the safety and health of workers at work into domestic law.

Section X of the Labour Code sets out the general obligations of employers, particularly their duty not to use materials or technological processes without first assessing the risks involved, the rights and duties of workers and specific obligations relating to the safety of buildings and workplaces, machinery and other technical devices, chemical substances and work procedures that are particularly harmful to health.

The Committee gathers from ILO data[1] that all these legal texts contain provisions on prevention and protection of workers against the main hazards linked to dangerous agents and substances and the working environments and equipment mentioned in the General introduction to Conclusions XIV-2 (pp. 39 and 40). However, it requests that the next report contain a full, up-to-date list of regulatory acts governing all areas of industry, including agriculture.

With regard to the regulations and hazards to which the Committee decided to pay particular attention in relation to Article 3, the Committee

---

[1]www.natlex.ilo.org.

stresses the importance of aligning these provisions with the very latest standards of international law. It also makes the following observations:

– Protection of workers against asbestos: in addition to the general obligations on employers set out in the Labour Code, particularly the need to replace carcinogenic substances or agents with less harmful ones or to take other measures to limit the risks involved, the Committee notes from the report on Article 11 that the Act of 19 June 1997 bans the use of asbestos products. The Committee requests that the next report indicate the scope of the asbestos ban, restrictions on the use of asbestos in the workplace and specific protection standards for asbestos removal. It should also state whether maximum exposure values have been fixed in accordance with Community Directive 83/477 as amended by Community Directive 91/382.

– Protection against ionising radiation: the Committee requests that the next report describe measures taken to ensure that workers are effectively protected from ionising radiation and state whether maximum doses have been set in conformity with the recommendations adopted in 1990 by the International Commission on Radiological Protection.

Personal scope of the regulations

The Labour Code states that specific regulations apply to all employees, i.e. "all persons employed on the basis of a contract of employment, an appointment, an election, a nomination, or a cooperative contract of employment" (Article 2), and all employers, i.e. "any organisational unit even if it has no legal personality, and any legal person if they engage employees" (Article 3). The report explains that the decisive factor is that the work is carried out for an employer, whether on a permanent basis or not. Consequently, virtually all workers are covered, including students, apprentices and persons working for a family business.

Before deciding on the conformity of the situation, the Committee would like to see more detailed information on the protection of self-employed workers, particularly those working on their own account.

Conclusion

Pending receipt of the information requested, the Committee defers its conclusion.

Paragraph 2 – Provision for the enforcement of safety and health regulations by measures of supervision

The Committee takes note of the information contained in Poland's report.

Industrial accidents and occupational diseases

According to the report, the total number of industrial accidents (excluding those on private farms) during the reference period was 111,119 (including 647 fatal accidents) in 1996, 120,897 (702 fatal) in 1997 and 117,503 (651 fatal) in 1998. The mining sector was the worst affected, with more than three times as many accidents as other sectors, closely followed by industry (twice as many).

The Committee notes, with reference to data submitted to the United Nations for the period 1991-1994,[1] that the number of accidents remains stable, while that of fatal accidents has fallen since the beginning of the 1990s, representing 0.5% of all accidents during the reference period.

The main causes of industrial accidents are falls and crushing, followed by contact with toxic substances.

The law defines an industrial accident as a chance event resulting in injury caused by an external agent to a worker carrying out his normal duties on the order of his superiors or in the interest of his employer (even on his own initiative) and which happens during working hours or on the journey between home and the workplace or anywhere else provided the worker was carrying out duties linked to his employment.

In order to obtain a more complete picture of the situation, the Committee requests that the next report contain information on industrial accidents in the agricultural sector and on the procedure for declaring and registering industrial accidents in general.

The Council of Ministers decree of 18 November 1983 on occupational diseases contains a list of twenty recognised groups of occupational diseases. The Committee notes that the number of occupational disease sufferers is constantly rising and increased from 9,326 in 1990 to 12,017 in 1998. It would like to know which diseases are included on

[1]Third report submitted to the United Nations Economic and Social Council on the application of the International Covenant on Economic, Social and Cultural Rights, E/1994/104/Add. 13.

the aforementioned list and what proof is required to show that a worker is suffering from an occupational disease.

Activities of the labour inspectorate

The Committee takes note of the powers and means of action of the main bodies responsible for supervising and monitoring working conditions. The National Labour Inspectorate is accountable to Parliament while the occupational health services operate under the auspices of the Ministry of Health and Social Welfare.

The Labour Inspectorate is responsible under the terms of the Act of 6 March 1981 for enforcing labour legislation in general and health and safety regulations in particular. Labour inspectors are entitled to monitor workplaces by carrying out site visits, requesting information on relevant issues and consulting all documentation that must be kept by law. If they find an infringement, they can order the company manager to remedy the situation by removing the causes of the offence, temporarily closing all or part of the site if workers' lives or health are at risk, allocating new tasks to employees working in illegal, unhealthy or dangerous conditions, etc. They can also impose fines if they find a breach of Articles 281, 282 or 283 of the Labour Code or of the Penal Code. Fines range from 10 Polish Zloty (PLZ) to 5,000 PLZ. As part of their preventive role, labour inspectors assess newly built or renovated work establishments.

The Labour Inspectorate monitors all workers (see conclusion concerning Article 3 para.1) and all establishments, although restrictions apply to private farms, where the 1981 Act nevertheless recognises its right to carry out investigations, and activities related to national defence and state security.

The occupational health services are responsible, under the Act of 14 March 1985, for ensuring that health regulations are complied with, particularly those connected to occupational health. Their inspectors visit workplaces, including changing rooms and sanitary installations, and measure the level of harmful substances in the environment, with the help of approved environmental analysis laboratories, which operate under their instructions. Their supervisory role includes drawing up occupational disease prevention strategies. They can also order the partial or complete closure of an establishment if an offence cannot immediately be put right, and recommend that fines be imposed on offending establishments and company managers (fines range from 5,000 PLZ to 25,000 PLZ).

In addition to being fined, offenders can be sent to prison. The Committee asks whether fines are proportionate to the number of workers affected by the offence.

The Committee takes note of the information contained in the report on monitoring activities in 1998. Labour inspectors carried out 81,495 inspections in 61,242 establishments, while occupational health inspectors carried out 125,929 inspections in 66,721 establishments, thus covering between 70 and 75% of all business establishments on the occupational health department register. In order to help it assess the effectiveness of these inspections, the Committee requests that the next report indicate the proportion of workers covered by the visits and state the number of inspectors involved.

Conclusion

Pending receipt of the information requested, the Committee concludes that the situation in Poland is in conformity with Article 3 para. 2 of the Charter.

Paragraph 3 – Consultation with employers' and workers' organisations on questions of safety and health

The Committee takes note of the information contained in the Polish report.

With regard to consultation at *national* level, the report states that two Acts of 23 May 1991 make provision for consultation of employers' and workers' organisations concerning safe and healthy working conditions. It explains that national inter-union organisations and the trade union representing employees of most plants are entitled to give their opinion on guidelines and draft legislation or regulations on matters related to trade unions' tasks. Employers' federations and confederations enjoy the same rights. The Committee refers to the questions on this subject posed in its conclusion concerning Article 5.

The Labour Protection Council, comprising representatives of trade unions, employers and the government, is consulted with regard to statutory texts in the field of safe and healthy working conditions and supervises the work of the National Labour Inspectorate. The report states that the number of employers' representatives in the Council is rather ambiguous and that measures are in the pipeline to ensure that it is a truly tripartite body.

The Committee requests that the next report provide sufficient information to enable it to assess whether the public authorities must provide for consultation "as appropriate", i.e. "whenever the need arises."[1] The Committee previously pointed out that "the rapid development of techniques and its consequences on security require a constant updating of health and safety regulations, which cannot be achieved without regular consultations with employers' and workers' organisations."[2]

The Committee noted from the report on Article 6 para.1 that there is no institutionalised form of *regional* consultation, but that such talks are held whenever necessary. It asks what the situation is with regard to matters covered by Article 3 para.3.

At *company* level, Section X of the Labour Code stipulates that employers of more than 50 workers must set up a work safety and hygiene commission. These bodies are composed of members of the occupational health and safety authority, the company doctor, the plant-based voluntary labour inspector and representatives elected by the company trade union or, if there is no such body, by the workers. They are advisory bodies responsible for reviewing working conditions, giving opinions on measures taken by employers to prevent industrial accidents and occupational diseases, suggesting how to improve working conditions and co-operating with employers in the fulfilment of their obligations as regards safe and healthy working conditions. The commissions can request the assistance or opinion of outside experts with the agreement and at the expense of the employer. They meet during working hours.

The Committee asks how Article 3 para. 3 is applied regarding companies with fewer than 50 workers.

Pending receipt of the information requested, the Committee defers its conclusion.

---

[1]Conclusions I, pp. 24 and 174.

[2]See in particular Conclusions V, p. 23 and Conclusions VII, p. xvii.

Article 4 — The right to a fair remuneration

Paragraph 2 – Increased rate of remuneration for overtime work

The Committee notes that under Article 134 of the Labour Code of Poland, workers are entitled to a wage supplement of 50% for the first two hours of overtime and 100% for all subsequent hours, as well as work performed at night, on a Sunday or statutory holiday.

Certain categories of workers are excluded from these rules under Article 135 of the Labour Code. Since those excluded occupy senior positions, this arrangement is not contrary to the Charter. The Committee notes that some of these workers are eligible for overtime supplements if they work on a Sunday or statutory holiday (Article 135(2)).

The Committee further notes that pursuant to Article 143 of the Labour Code, an employee may opt for a rest period in consideration of overtime work instead of pay. In such cases, the rest period granted is of the same length as the period of overtime work. Article 4 para. 1 of the Charter allows the replacement of a higher rate of pay by a rest period only where the latter corresponds to the former, i.e. is longer than the period of overtime work. This not being the case in Poland, the situation is not in conformity with the Charter.

Civil servants are subject to a different legal regime. The report refers to two statutes which were in force during the reference period (the Act of 16 September 1982 and the Act of 5 July 1996), but have since been replaced by the Act of 18 December 1998, which entered into force on 1 July 1999, outside the reference period. The Committee notes that the 1982 Act allowed employees to choose between payment and time off in respect of overtime work, although the report does not indicate whether the amount of time off equalled or exceeded the period of overtime work. The 1996 Act merely provided for the normal rate of pay for overtime work. An arrangement of this nature is not in conformity with the Charter. In the case of overtime work performed at night, on Sundays or statutory holidays, the act provided for time off.

The Committee notes that the new act on the civil service of 18 December 1998 does not provide for overtime pay, but for time off work. According to Section 92.4 of the Act, overtime work entitles the official to the same number of hours off work. Overtime work performed at night leads to the same recompense – Section 92.6. This regime is clearly inconsistent with Article 4 para. 4 of the Charter.

The Committee concludes that the situation in Poland is not in conformity with Article 4 para. 2 of the Charter since:

– for workers covered by the Labour Code, it is permissible for overtime work to be compensated by a rest period which merely equals the period of overtime and therefore does not correspond to a higher rate of pay;

– the rules which applied during the reference period governing overtime work by civil servants were not in conformity with this provision of the Charter, since they did not provide for a higher rate of pay or a corresponding period of rest. The situation is the same in the new legislation.

Paragraph 3 – Non-discrimination between men and women workers with respect to remuneration

Article 33 of the Polish Constitution of 1997 guarantees, *inter alia,* the right of men and women workers to equal pay for work of equal value. Paragraph 2 of Article 33 provides: "Men and women shall have equal rights in particular, regarding education, employment and promotion, and shall have the right to equal compensation for work of similar value."

Article 11-2 of the Labour Code provides "Employees shall have equal rights resulting from the equal performance of duties of identical value, this shall apply in particular to the equal treatment of men and women in the area of work."

The report states that in practice there remains certain "extra-legal inequality" in wages between men and women, with women tending to work in sectors of the economy which are lower paid. New criteria for job evaluation are currently being developed. The Committee wishes to receive information on these and on the extent to which job comparisons are carried out in the next report.

In this respect it recalls that job evaluation systems must consider the features of the posts in question rather than the personal characteristics of the workers. Criteria such as willingness to work overtime or the emphasis on muscular effort alone to the exclusion of factors that put pressure on workers such as mental strain and stress can prove discriminatory in practice.

The Committee asks to be informed in the next report of the manner in which job comparisons may be made, and whether they are limited to the same workplace.

According to the report, an employee who believes that he or she has been discriminated against in terms of remuneration may, pursuant to Article 242 of the Labour Code, take a case to the Labour Court. If the Court finds that there has been discrimination, i.e. the principle of equal pay has not been respected, it will make an order remedying the situation, order compensation and/or oblige the employer to make up for the harm done.

The Committee wishes to know whether clauses of collective agreements or individual contracts which contravene the principle of equal pay for work of equal value are rendered null and void.

According to the Charter, a worker claiming equal pay must be protected against retaliatory measures. The Committee requests information on any such safeguards, such as sanctions or remedies. In cases where wage discrimination is proven, the Committee asks about the adequacy of compensation, i.e. whether minimum or maximum awards are laid down in law. Information on court practice on this point should also be included in the next report.

Lastly, the Committee wishes to receive information on the difference between men and women's earnings in practice.

Pending receipt of the information requested above, the Committee defers its conclusion.

Paragraph 4 – Reasonable notice of termination of employment

The Polish Labour Code stipulates the minimum notice periods for termination of employment. The length of the minimum period of notice depends on the type of employment contract. The period may be lengthened by collective agreements or the individual employment contract.

For a contract of employment of indeterminate length, Article 36 of the Labour Code stipulates:

– 2 weeks if the employee was employed for less than 6 months
– 1 month if the employee was employed for at least 6 months

– 3 months if the employee was employed for at least 3 years.

The Committee recalls that in the interpretation of this provision it has refrained from defining in absolute terms the notion of reasonableness. It assesses each situation on a case by case basis. It considers that the abovementioned periods are in conformity with Article 4 para. 4 of the Charter.

Where the notice period is three months, this may be shortened if the reason for the termination is the employer's bankruptcy or liquidation. However, the period must be at least one month and the employee must receive compensation for the remaining period of notice. This situation is in conformity with the Charter, as monetary payments *in lieu* may partially or totally replace the notice period (Conclusions X-1, pp. 64- 65).

The Labour Code provides that during the notice period an employee shall be entitled to time off in order to seek new employment; 2 days off where the notice period does not exceed 1 month and 3 days where the notice period is 3 months (Article 37).

Article 34 of the Labour Code stipulates the minimum periods of notice for contracts of employment for a trial period:

– 3 days if the trial period does not exceed 2 weeks
– 1 week if the trial period is longer than 2 weeks
– 2 weeks if the trial period is 3 months.

The Committee considers that these minimum periods are in conformity with the Charter.

As regards fixed term contracts, Article 33 of the Labour Code stipulates that if the fixed term contract is for more than 6 months it may be terminated by a 2 week notice period provided that the parties include this in the contract itself.

The Committee considers that 2 weeks notice for an employee with 6 months or less service is acceptable, however for an employee with a longer period of service it would not be reasonable.

According to the report, periods of notice for certain categories of employees are specified in separate regulations. A 3 month notice period is required for civil servants and nominated state officers.

The Committee wishes to receive information on any other categories of employees not covered by the Labour Code.

The Committee concludes that the situation Poland is not in conformity with Article 4 para. 4 of the Charter as Article 33 of the Labour Code provides that a fixed term contract of more than 6 months' duration may be terminated by a two week notice period.

Paragraph 5 – Limitation of deduction from wages

Article 87 para. 1 of the Polish Labour Code provides that after the deduction of income tax only the following items may be deducted from wages:

– amounts due in respect of court ordered maintenance payments (up to three fifths of the wage),

– amounts (other than maintenance payments) due following a court order (up to one half of the wage),

– cash advances paid to the employee (up to one half of the wage),

– fines imposed in accordance with Article 108 of the Labour Code for breaches of work rules, safety and hygiene provisions or fire prevention rules (for one infringement up to one day's wage; the total amount due for fines may not exceed one tenth of the wage.).

Total deductions in respect of sums due, (other than maintenance payments) and cash advances may not exceed half the wage, and together with sums deducted for maintenance payments may not exceed three-fifths of the wage. After these deductions, up to one-tenth of the wage may be deducted in respect of fines. Articles 108-113 of the Labour code set out the procedure to be followed before a fine may be imposed, including the possibility for the employee to appeal against the imposition of a fine.

The Committee notes that Article 87 para. 6 of the Labour Code states that the Council of Ministers will specify through regulations the amount of the wage to be protected from deductions. The Committee wishes to receive more information on these regulations, prior to concluding whether the above mentioned limitations to wage deductions are reasonable. It recalls that after all deductions are made a worker must be assured of an income which assures subsistence for them and their dependants.

The Committee further wishes to receive information on Article 88 of the Labour Code which permits an employer to deduct maintenance payments from wages without a court order.

The Committee notes that by virtue of Article 91 of the Labour Code deductions other than those permitted by Article 87 and 108 may only be made with the employee's written consent. It wishes to be informed if in these circumstances regulations protect a fraction of the wage from deductions.

Pending receipt of the information requested the Committee defers its conclusion.

Article 7 — The right of children and young persons to protection

Paragraph 2 – Higher minimum age in certain occupations

The Committee takes note of the information in the report and the appendices. The minimum age for employment in Poland is 15 years – Article 190.2 of the Labour Code. Article 204 of the Labour Code prohibits the employment of juveniles for scheduled tasks, although workers over the age of 16 may be authorised to perform some of these tasks if this is required by their vocational training.

The list of prohibited tasks is set out in the Ordinance by the Council of Ministers of 1 December 1996 on the Specification of Works Prohibited to Juveniles, under twelve headings. The Committee takes note of the detailed regulations concerning risks and hazards under each of the headings concerned. In many cases, juveniles may be employed under stated conditions. Generally, the age limit in such cases decreases to 16 years. Certain prohibitions are, however, absolute, such as exposure to carcinogenic substances, psychotropic drugs and work that might constitute an excessive psychological burden. It appears to the Committee that the relevant national regulations are sufficiently complete to comply with the requirements of Article 7 para. 2 of the Charter.

The report states that the employer is legally responsible for the instruction of juvenile workers in the observation of health and safety rules and the use of personal protection equipment.

Under the Regulation of the Council of Ministers of 28 July 1959 on the employment of juveniles for light, seasonal and casual work, young persons who have reached the age of 16 may be employed in such work on condition, *inter alia*, that it is not prohibited by the above regulations. According to the report, the Ministry of Agriculture and Food Industry is in the process of compiling a schedule of tasks to which young persons may be assigned. The Committee wishes to receive this list with the next report.

With respect to the situation in practice, the Committee notes from the additional information supplied by the Polish Government that there were 1015 recorded accidents involving young workers in 1998. These occurred mainly in manufacturing (495), trade and repairs (238), food processing (215) and construction (98). The Committee asks to receive updated information in the next report under this provision, and for information on the number of accidents involving young workers in agriculture. The Committee takes note of the information provided on the activities of labour inspectors in 1999, who carried out "targeted inspections" to monitor compliance with the abovementioned Council of Ministers Ordinance. The Committee asks to receive similar data covering the subsequent reference period in the next report under this provision.

The Committee concludes that the situation in Poland is in conformity with Article 7 para. 2 of the Charter.

Paragraph 4 – Working hours for young workers and apprentices

The Committee notes from the Polish report that pursuant to Article 202 para. 1 of the Labour Code, working hours of young workers under the age of 16 must not exceed 6 hours per day. According to the report, this regulation is of a universal nature applicable to all employment relationships involving young workers in the age group concerned. No exceptions are provided by law to the limitation on working hours. Overtime work is prohibited pursuant to Article 203 para. 1 of the Labour Code.

The report states that the regulation covers both time spent working and time spent on vocational training. The Committee recalls in this connection that employment of young people between 15 and 18 years old may only take place for the purpose of vocational training (see the conclusion under Article 7 para. 6). However, it also notes that according to Article 202 para. 3 of the Labour Code, time spent on vocational training is taken into account when calculating working time, but only up to a maximum of 18 hours per week. According to information provided in the report under Article 7 para. 6, the time devoted to training should not exceed 18 hours per week. Given the wording of the abovementioned Article 202 para. 3, the Committee requests confirmation that this is in fact the case.

The Committee also wishes to know how the limitation on working hours of young workers under 16 years old is implemented and monitored and whether any problems have been encountered in practice.

On the basis of the available information and pending receipt of the information requested, the Committee concludes that the situation in Poland is in conformity with Article 7 para. 4 of the Charter.

Paragraph 6 – Treatment of the time spent in vocational training as forming part of the working day

The Committee notes that under Polish legislation, young persons are obliged to continue their general education and vocational training until the age of 18 (Article 197, para. 1 of the Labour Code). Young workers are obliged to supplement their education at the level of primary school, if they have not completed primary school and to up-grade their occupational qualification through vocational training or supplement their general education at the level of secondary school.

To enable young workers to fulfill this obligation, employers are in turn obliged to release them for the time necessary to allow for participation in the training concerned (Article 198 of the Labour Code). As stated in the report, young workers are in effect entitled to leave of absence for vocational training without having to seek the consent of the employer.

The report further states that time spent on vocational training forms part of the working day, irrespective of whether the training takes place during normal working hours or outside these hours, and is paid as normal working hours. Finally, the report states that the rules are universal and apply to all categories of young workers.

The Committee asks how the implementation of these rules is monitored and whether any problems have been encountered in practice.

On the basis of the available information and pending receipt of the information requested, the Committee concludes that the situation in Poland is in conformity with Article 7 para. 6 of the Charter.

Paragraph 7 – Annual holiday of young persons under eighteen

As regards the minimum duration of annual holiday with pay for young workers under the age of 18 in Poland, the Committee notes that under Article 205 of the Labour Code young workers are entitled to 12 days leave with pay after 6 months of employment and after one year of employment the entitlement increases to 26 days. In the calendar year in which a young person reaches the age of 18, he/she has a right to 20 days leave, if the entitlement has been acquired before reaching the age of 18.

Under Article 205 para. 3 of the Labour Code, a young worker attending school classes should be granted the leave of absence during school holidays. Moreover, on the application of a young worker attending a school for workers, an employer must grant leave without pay not exceeding, together with the paid holiday, a period of 2 months (Article 205, para. 4).

The report states that the above rules are applicable to all categories of workers under 18 years of age. The right to leave cannot be waived (Article 152 para. 2).

The Committee asks how the implementation of these rules is monitored and whether any problems have been encountered in practice.

On the basis of the available information and pending receipt of the information requested, the Committee concludes that the situation in Poland is in conformity with Article 7 para. 7 of the Charter.

Paragraph 8 – Prohibition of night work for young persons under eighteen

The Polish report states that under Article 137 para. 1 of the Labour Code the term "night work" applies to the 8 hour period falling between 9 p.m. and 7 a.m. The Labour Code further stipulates that a young person under the age of 18 cannot be employed in night work. The daily rest period (including the night period) for young workers should be at least 14 hours (Article 203). According to the report these rules are absolutely binding and apply to all categories of workers under the age of 18.

The Committee asks how the implementation of these rules is monitored and whether any problems have been encountered in practice.

On the basis of the available information and pending receipt of the information requested, the Committee concludes that the situation in Poland is in conformity with Article 7 para. 8 of the Charter.

Paragraph 9 – Provision of regular medical control for young workers under eighteen

The Committee notes from the Polish report that young persons under the age of 18 may only be admitted to employment if they present a medical certificate attesting that the type of work in question is not harmful to their health (Article 191 para. 1 of the Labour Code).

The report states that under Article 201 of the Labour Code, employers are obliged to organise so-called work-entry examinations of young workers prior to their employment and to have them medically examined on a periodical basis, or occasionally as medical clearance examinations, during the course of their employment. Work-entry medical examinations are also required when a young worker is transferred to another workplace. The report further states that the examinations should, if possible, be carried out during normal working hours. Expenses for examinations and any travel involved for the worker in this respect are borne by the employer.

According to the report, the frequency of periodic examinations depends on the kind of harmful or arduous conditions in question. Young workers exposed to noise, for instance, must undergo an examination at least once a year whereas a young worker exposed to ultrasonic noise must be examined at least every two years. The Committee notes that the scope and minimum frequency of medical examinations is specified in Annex 1 to the Regulation of the Minister of Health and Social Welfare of 30 May 1996 on conducting medical examinations of employees and it asks that a copy of this regulation be contained in the next report. It also asks to find more information on the medical services responsible for carrying out the examinations. It recalls that it is essential "that precise guidelines and instructions are expressly given to the bodies responsible for carrying out medical examinations of worker, so that, when such examinations concern young workers, prevention and protection of their health be taken into account." (Conclusions VIII, p. 119).

The Committee notes the distinction between periodic examinations and so-called clearance examinations. The latter term applies to examinations carried out when a worker returns to work after a prolonged absence due to illness (more than 30 days). The aim of such an examination is to assess the state of health and to establish whether the worker is still able to carry out the work after the long illness. If, upon periodical or clearance examination, the physician decides that a given task is harmful to the young worker's health, the employer must seek to find more suitable employment in the enterprise, or, if this is not possible, he must terminate the employment contract and pay compensation equivalent to the amount of remuneration due for the period of notice (Article 201 para. 2 of the Labour Code).

The Committee notes that the rules described above are applicable to employment in general. It also notes that young persons under 18 may not be admitted to employment in certain hazardous and dangerous occupations. However, workers over the age of 16 (in some cases 17) may under certain circumstances be admitted to employment which are in principle prohibited to them (see the conclusion under Article 7 para. 2). In such cases special health and safety protection is foreseen pursuant to Regulation of the Council of Ministers of 1 December 1990. However, the Committee notes that this does not include provision for more frequent and thorough medical control.

On the basis of the available information and pending receipt of the information requested, the Committee concludes that the situation in Poland is in conformity with Article 7 para. 9 of the Charter.

Paragraph 10 – Special protection for children and young people from physical and moral dangers to which they are exposed

The Committee notes the information contained in the Polish report.

As regards the protection of young persons in employment it refers to its conclusion under Article 7 para. 2.

The Committee notes some of the measures taken by the authorities in order to tackle drug addiction, in particular the measures developed under the National Programme for Counteracting Drug Addiction (1993-1998). Such measures included educating children and youth in different areas so as to try to reduce the demand for stimulants, educating parents to recognise the signs of drug addiction, providing support for children at risk etc. The Committee wishes to be informed of the progress of this initiative.

In addition to preventative measures, a number of measures were taken in the area of rehabilitation of drug addicts.

A state agency for the solution of alcohol-related problems was established in 1993. This agency launched several campaigns on alcohol and alcohol abuse aimed at young persons, which covered 800,000 school children. It also launched a programme for counteracting violence in alcoholic families, "Safety in the family". This had as its objectives the reduction of violence in families, increasing the assistance available to victims of alcohol-related violence and deterring the perpetrators of violence. The Committee wishes to be informed of all measures taken in this field.

The Committee asks whether legislation prohibits the use of children in the sex industry, and to receive information on any supervisory system and sanctions that may accompany this prohibition.

Conclusion

The Committee concludes that the situation in Poland is in conformity with this provision of the Charter.

Article 8 — The right of employed women to protection

Paragraph 1 – Maternity leave

1. The right to maternity leave

The Polish report states that under existing legislation, all women in employment are guaranteed 16 weeks' maternity leave when their first child is born, 18 weeks for any subsequent births and 26 weeks in the event of a multiple birth (Chapter 8 of the Labour Code). The Committee requests information on the situation of domestic staff and employees working from home.

Maternity leave must be taken for 2 weeks before the expected date of confinement and for at least 12 weeks after the birth if the mother is entitled to 16 weeks' leave; 14 weeks after the birth if the mother is entitled to 18 weeks' leave; and 22 weeks after the birth if the mother is entitled to 26 weeks' leave. Any maternity leave not taken before the birth is entitled to be taken after the birth.

Post-natal leave cannot be less than 8 weeks under any circumstances. In addition, women may not forego, either in full or in part, their maternity leave entitlement, in particular the 8 weeks' post-natal leave.

The report also states that any employer breaching the relevant provisions of the Labour Code is liable to a fine of between 20 zlotys (PLZ) and 5,000 PLZ.

The Committee observes that the minimum fine for an infringement is not very high. In this connection, it notes from another source[1] submitted by Poland under the United Nations International Covenant on Economic, Social and Cultural Rights that "in Poland cases of violation of women's labour protection provisions, confirmed by the State Labour Inspectorate, are not very frequent. For a total number of 63,000 offences against workers' rights (in small and large establishments, in the public and private sector) less than 5% concerned the protection of women workers or juveniles or the termination of employment contracts in serious violation of labour law provisions." The Committee therefore requests that the next report include comments on this information and

---

[1]Third report 1994/104/Add.13.

indicate, as far as possible, the number of breaches of legislation on maternity protection during the next reference period.

The Committee points out that under Article 8 para. 1 of the Charter, all women in gainful employment must be entitled to maternity leave for a minimum of 12 weeks, including 6 weeks' compulsory post-natal leave.

Pending receipt of the information requested, the Committee therefore concludes that the situation in Poland is in conformity with Article 8 para. 1 of the Charter in this respect.

2. Right to adequate benefits

The Polish report states that all women receive maternity benefits throughout their maternity leave, pursuant to the Act of 17 December 1974 on cash benefits in case of sickness and maternity (standard text: *Dziennik Ustaw* of 1983, No. 30, item 143, with subsequent amendments). This right is not subject to any conditions regarding working hours or length of employment.

The allowance is equal to 100% of the worker's average monthly wage in the six months prior to the period of leave.

The Committee points out that under Article 8, paragraph 1 of the Charter, maternity leave must be remunerated in the form of adequate social security benefits or public funds covering the entire period of leave. The benefits awarded must be as near as possible to the worker's previous wage so that she is not forced to work during this period.

The Committee notes that the situation, as outlined above, does not pose any problems regarding compliance with the Charter. However, in order to have an overview and to make a proper assessment of the situation, the Committee requires the following information:

– are maternity benefits subject to a minimum level below which they are not awarded, and a maximum level above which the amount awarded is reduced?

– if so, what are these levels and do the women concerned receive any form of compensation?

Pending receipt of this information, the Committee concludes that the situation in Poland is in conformity with Article 8 para. 1 of the Charter in this respect.

Paragraph 2 – Illegality of dismissal during maternity leave

Prohibition of dismissal

The Polish report states that employers may not dismiss a woman who is pregnant or on maternity leave (Article 177 of the Labour Code). This applies to all women in an employment relationship, apart from those employed for a trial period of less than one month.

The prohibition is not absolute and may be lifted in the following cases:

– in case of misconduct by the employee in breach of her contractual obligations (Article 177 para. 1 of the Labour Code); in such cases, the consent of the establishment's trade union representing the employee is required;

– if the employer goes bankrupt or the firm goes into liquidation (Article 177 para. 4 of the Labour Code).

The Committee observes that these cases are in keeping with the situations in which it allows dismissal. However, it asks whether a breach of contractual obligations arising out of pregnancy may justify dismissal. It also asks what is the situation in enterprises without a trade union.

The report goes on to mention other cases in which employees' contracts may be terminated while they are pregnant or on maternity leave:

– if the employment relationship is based on an appointment which is subsequently annulled. In such cases, the appointing body is required to offer the employee another post corresponding to her occupational qualifications. If she refuses this post, her contract is terminated at the end of the notice period;

– if the terms of the employee's contract change for reasons "related to the enterprise", the employee rejects these terms and the employer is consequently unable to maintain her contract (Section 6, sub-section 1 of the Act of 28 December 1989);

– by the employee herself or by mutual consent, provided that the employee is aware that she is pregnant and knows her rights. Otherwise, the declaration requesting termination of her contract is deemed null and void.

The Committee observes that the above cases exceed the circumstances which it accepts under this provision of the Charter. It asks whether the workers concerned are protected against pressure from their employer.

The report also states that any fixed-term contracts or contracts for a specific task or a trial period of over one month which would otherwise have been terminated after the third month of pregnancy are extended until the date of confinement.

Consequences of unlawful dismissal

The Polish report fails to provide any information on the consequences of unlawful dismissal.

The Committee points out in this connection that reinstatement should be the norm in cases of unlawful dismissal, the purpose of Article 8 para. 2 being not only to ensure financial security for workers in the event of childbirth, but also to safeguard their jobs. Payment of compensation is only acceptable in exceptional cases, where reinstatement is impossible (e.g. if the business closes down) or the employee does not wish it. The Committee then checks whether the level of compensation is sufficient to discourage employers and to make good the damage suffered by employees.

The Committee therefore requests that the next report indicate whether provision is made for reinstatement in the event of unlawful dismissal. It also wishes to know how the compensation payable to employees in exceptional cases is calculated and what amount is paid.

Pending receipt of the information requested, the Committee defers its conclusion.

Paragraph 3 – Time off for nursing mothers

The Polish report states that all employees who are breastfeeding are entitled to two half-hour breaks per day, which are included in the calculation of working hours and, accordingly, are paid (Article 187 of the Labour Code).

The Committee therefore concludes that the situation in Poland is in conformity with Article 8 para. 3 of the Charter.

Paragraph 4 – Regulation of night work and prohibition of dangerous, unhealthy or arduous types of work for women workers

1. Regulation of night work for women in industry (Article 8, para. 4a)

The Polish report states that the term "night work" applies to work carried out between 9 p.m. and 7 a.m. Night workers are entitled to additional pay at a rate of 20% of the hourly minimum wage (Article 137 of the Labour Code).

The report states that night work is prohibited for pregnant women. In addition, women with a child under 4 years of age may only work at night with their consent (Article 178 of the Labour Code).

This ban entails an obligation on the part of the employer to transfer a pregnant employee to daytime work. Such work must, as far as possible, match the employee's qualifications and current wages. If not, she is entitled to a compensatory allowance.

The Committee points out that Article 8 para. 4*a* of the Charter does not require states to prohibit night work by women but to regulate it. Regulations may be general and apply to employees of both sexes, but must severely restrict the possibilities for night work, permitting it only where it is justified by specific production requirements, with due regard for appropriate working conditions and organisational procedures. They must also lay down conditions governing night work by women, such as permission from the Labour Inspectorate where necessary, working hours, breaks, rest days following periods of night work, and the right to be transferred to daytime work if night work causes health problems. The Committee also points out that such regulations must cater for the situation of women who are pregnant, have recently given birth or are breastfeeding.

In Poland's case, the Committee considers that the situation of pregnant women and women who have recently given birth or are breastfeeding is adequately catered for by the regulations in force. However, it observes that regulations on night work do not appear sufficient. Merely setting out what constitutes night work is not an adequate means of lessening the negative effects of night work on employees' health and family life or avoiding abuses. The Committee therefore requests that the next report specify the circumstances in which night work is permitted and the conditions governing it (whether permission is required from the Labour Inspectorate, regular medical check-ups, the right to be transferred to daytime work if night work causes health problems, etc.).

Pending receipt of the information requested, the Committee defers its conclusion in respect of Article 8 para. 4*a* of the Charter.

2. Prohibition of the employment of women in certain dangerous, unhealthy or arduous types of work (Article 8, para. *4b*)

The Committee considers that Article 8, para. 4*b* provides for two distinct bans:

– a ban, by means of legislation, on employing women in underground mining; this applies only to mining activities in the strict sense of the term;

– a ban on employing women "as appropriate, on all other work which is unsuitable for them by reason of its dangerous, unhealthy, or arduous nature". The expression "as appropriate" is taken to mean that the ban applies only in cases where it is necessary, such as to protect women who are pregnant, have recently given birth or are breastfeeding.

With regard to the first aspect, the Polish report states that, in accordance with the Charter, women are prohibited from underground mining. Penalties in the event of an infringement are the same as for breaches of the regulations on maternity leave. The Committee requests that the next report indicate, if possible, the number of infringements recorded by labour inspectors.

With regard to the second aspect, the report states that the ban does not only apply to women who are pregnant, have recently given birth or are breastfeeding, but applies to all women (Article 176 of the Labour Code). A Council of Ministers regulation lists dangerous, unhealthy or arduous types of work that are prohibited for women. The regulation of 10 September 1996 lists the following types of work:

– work involving strenuous effort and transport of heavy loads;

– work in an environment with a low, high or changeable temperature;

– work in an environment subject to noise and vibrations;

– work exposing employees to electromagnetic fields, ionising and ultra-violet radiation, and work at monitor screens (check);

– underground work;

– work in conditions of low or high air pressure;

– work exposing employees to harmful biological agents;

– work exposing employees to harmful chemical substances;

– works exposing employees to serious physical or mental injury.

The report adds that firms' work regulations may include a list of other dangerous types of work that are prohibited for women.

On the basis of all this information, the Committee concludes that the situation in Poland is in conformity with Article 8 para. 4*b* of the Charter.

Article 9 — Right to vocational guidance

The Committee takes note of the detailed information contained in the Polish report on vocational guidance in the labour market. It asks the Government to include in the next report information on vocational guidance within the education system.

According to the report, an obligation to organise and support vocational guidance follows from Article 65 para. 5 of the Polish Constitution. The provision of vocational guidance takes place on the basis of Act of 14 December 1994 on employment and counteracting unemployment, as amended, and Regulation of the Ministry of Labour and Social Policy of 16 June 1995 which contains detailed rules on employment services, vocational guidance, etc.

Vocational guidance services are implemented under the responsibility of the Minister of Labour and Social Policy by the public employment services comprising the National Labour Office, 16 regional labour offices (voivodship level) with 33 branches and 322 district labour offices (local level). According to the report, the district offices are located so as to be easily accessible by bus and train transport. The Committee notes the existence of 13 mobile centres for vocational information which may be deployed where a special need arises, especially in rural areas.

The Committee notes the definition of vocational guidance given in Section 17 of the 1994 Act: "Vocational guidance consists in provision of assistance to the unemployed and other job-seekers in the area of choice of the adequate job and place of employment and in provision of assistance to employers in the area of selection of candidates for positions requiring particular mental and physical predisposition." Section 17 further states the basic principles applicable to vocational guidance as offered by the public employment services:

- it is free of charge;
- it is available to all unemployed and job-seeking persons;
- use of the service is voluntary;
- equality of access is ensured regardless of nationality, gender, religion, membership of political and social organisations and other circumstances;
- it guarantees freedom of choice of the job and place of employment;

– confidentiality and protection of personal data of persons taking advantage of services.

The Committee requests confirmation that equal treatment in access to vocational guidance is thereby guaranteed for all nationals of the other Contracting Parties to the Charter lawfully resident or working regularly in Poland. The Committee is also interested to know whether there have been any problems in practice as regards the access of foreigners to vocational guidance.

The Committee takes note of the measures taken to improve vocational guidance services targeting new organisational solutions, new methods and tools of work and upgrading the qualifications of guidance counsellors. In this respect, efforts are also made to bring the services to the notice of potential users and their parents: in addition to such specific tools as occupational information publications and job-presenting films, the report mentions the close co-operation between labour offices and the school system, comprising information meetings at schools and so-called "job fairs" and "information fairs" organised by the labour offices. As regards special measures to assist disabled persons, the Committee refers to its conclusion under Article 15.

The report states that a total of 600,000 adults and about 200,000 young persons at school received either individual or group vocational guidance assistance in 1998. To perform these services, the labour offices employed a total of 582 career counsellors with higher education, primarily pedagogues, psychologists and sociologists. Of these, 517 were full-time employees and 65 were part-time employees. The Committee asks that the next report contain a more detailed breakdown of the beneficiaries, indicating if possible age, sex and educational background. Furthermore, it requests that the next report provide information concerning vocational guidance schemes under the auspices of educational authorities and on any collaboration or cooperation between such authorities and those under the responsibility of the Ministry of Labour and Social Policy.

Finally, the report states that pursuant to Section 57 para. 1 of the 1994 Act, resources shall be allocated from the Welfare Fund to finance the development and dissemination of vocational information as well as equipment necessary to provide guidance services. In the period 1997-1999 about 5,405,000 PLZ were allocated from the Welfare Fund for this purpose. The Committee wishes to continue to be informed of total expenditure on vocational guidance. It asks in this respect also that the next report indicate the amount of expenditure as a proportion of total GDP. It further wishes to receive the government's assessment as to whether the staffing of labour offices and the resources available are sufficient to meet the demand for vocational guidance. Pending receipt of the information requested, the Committee defers its conclusion.

Article 10 — The right to vocational training

Paragraph 1 – Promotion of technical and vocational training and the granting of facilities for access to higher technical and university education

The Committee takes note of the information provided in the Polish report, which concerns primarily vocational training for unemployed persons provided under the responsibility of the Ministry of Labour and Social Policy. It points out, however, that training for the unemployed does not come within the scope of Article 10 para. 1. As stated in the General introduction to Conclusions XIV-2 under this provision, the Committee "examines the general vocational training policies and the overall structure of the training system following compulsory schooling, including the role of the social partners in developing and implementing training. It addresses in particular the topic of initial vocational training at school..." (p. 60). Retraining activities for unemployed persons, including labour market training for young persons, come within the scope of Article 10 para. 3 (p. 61).[1]

The Committee therefore asks that the next report under Article 10 para. 1 include a comprehensive overview of the vocational training system, its various levels, "pathways" and activities, focusing on initial vocational training and supported by relevant statistical data. Moreover, the Committee requests information on access to higher education in order to ascertain that such access is based solely on individual aptitude. Finally, the next report should also specifically address the question of how equal treatment of nationals of other Contracting Parties is guaranteed in law and in practice as regards access to vocational education and training.

The Committee notes from an appended source (*Information on the execution of the program "Promotion of Vocational Activity of Young People"*) that the system of vocational education and training under the Ministry of National Education underwent significant reform during the 1990s, both as regards its structure and content. Furthermore, it notes from figures given in the report that 2,011,448 pupils (of which 313,333 adults) were enrolled in vocational schools in the school year 1998/1999. In the same year there were about 90,000 full-time teach-

---

[1]Poland has not accepted Article 10 para. 3 of the Charter.

ers, 48,000 part-time teachers and about 4,000 instructors in practical training in schools at primary and secondary vocational level.

Pending receipt of the information requested, the Committee defers its conclusion.

Paragraph 2 – Promotion of apprenticeship

The Committee notes from the Polish report that pursuant to Article 191 of the Labour Code, young persons between the age of 15 and 18 without a vocational qualification may be admitted to employment only for the purposes of vocational training. According to the report, exceptions from this rule are granted very rarely.

On the basis of the examination of the report, it appears to the Committee that two further legal texts are of immediate relevance to this provision of the Charter: firstly, Regulation of the Council of Ministers of 11 December 1992 on apprenticeship training and, secondly, Regulation of the Council of Ministers of 28 May 1996 on in-work vocational training for young persons.

The 1992 Regulation concerns the organisation and financing of apprenticeship, and the rights and obligations of apprentices and entities organising the training. It applies to students in public primary and secondary vocational schools for young people and adults who undergo vocational training in school workshops, or with particular enterprises on the basis of a contract between the school and the employer. A person undergoing such training retains his status as a student, and there is no formal employment relationship and no entitlement to remuneration.

The 1996 Regulation applies to young workers who on the basis of an employment contract concluded for vocational training purposes receive on-the-job training for a duration of three years with a view to becoming skilled workers. Pursuant to the 1996 Regulation, vocational training for young persons can be effected either through the teaching of an occupation or teaching to perform specific work. The training may be carried out by the employer, a person employed by the employer, or a person managing the plant on behalf of the employer, provided they meet specified vocational and pedagogical requirements.

The occupations in which training can be effected under employment contract for the purpose of a vocational education, the duration of the training, as well as the nature and the scope of skills taught, are defined in teaching plans and curricula drawn up on the basis of the classification of jobs and vocational education. The duration of vocational training is set at up to 36 months, but not less than 33 months (Article 6 para. 1). The employer employing a young person for the purpose of vocational training is obliged to implement the curricula-related minimum requirements for vocational education as laid down for primary vocational schools and included in programme documentation for a given occupation.

In the case of teaching to perform specific work, the duration of training as well as its scope and teaching curricula are set out by employers. Training for a young person to perform specific work can take between 3 and 6 months. In relation to young participants in the Vocational Labour Corps scheme set up under Regulation of the Council of Ministers of 23 May 1995, this period may be extended until the time of the completion of primary education, but not by more than 12 months and its total duration may not exceed 18 months.

During their period of apprenticeship, apprentices are eligible for remuneration calculated as a percentage of an average salary in the national economy in the previous quarter of the year. This percentage cannot amount to less than 4% in the first year of apprenticeship, not less than 5% in the second year, and not less than 6% in the third year of apprenticeship. The Committee notes the information on expenditure from the Labour Fund for the refunding of remuneration and social insurance contributions.

The Committee notes that in 1996, the number of young persons employed for the purposes of vocational training was 407,869, of which 348,118 were employed in the private sector and 59,751 in the public sector.

Finally, the Committee takes note of the information on apprenticeships organised and financed by the Labour Offices for unemployed school graduates. Such apprenticeships take place on the basis of an employment contract and their duration may not exceed 12 months.

The Committee asks that the next report provide further details on apprenticeship training and other forms of vocational training within the scope of Article 10 para. 2, notably as regards the following aspects:

– the availability of training places/"internships" for all interested applicants, including figures showing the number of applicants and the number of apprenticeships actually initiated;

– whether and how equal treatment of nationals of other Contracting Parties is guaranteed with respect to access to apprenticeships;

– the financing of apprenticeship training, including relevant figures;

– the extent to which representatives of workers' and employers' organisations are involved in decision making for apprenticeship training and its implementation.

Pending receipt of the information requested, the Committee defers its conclusion.

Article 11 — Right to protection of health

Paragraph 1 – Removal of the causes of ill-health

The Committee takes note of the information contained in the first Polish report on the application of the Charter, in the third report submitted to the United Nations Economic and Social Council on the application of the International Covenant on Economic, Social and Cultural Rights[1] and in the 1999 report of the European Observatory on Health Care Systems.[2]

State of health of the population - General indicators

Life expectancy and principal causes of death

The Committee takes note of the general indicators of the state of health of the Polish population. It notes that life expectancy for women is rising slightly each year, increasing from 75.7 years in 1992 to 76.8 years in 1996. However, men's life expectancy has remained stable since the end of the 1960's (67.8 years in 1998). Life expectancy in Poland is among the shortest in European OECD countries[3] and the difference between male and female death rates 60% greater than in West European countries.[4]

The report states that the main causes of death remain, as they have for many years, cardio-vascular diseases (50% of all deaths in 1996), followed by cancer (21%) and accidents and poisoning (7%).

The Committee observes that the number of deaths caused by cardio-vascular diseases (502 per 100,000 people in 1996, mainly men) is particularly high in relation to other European OECD countries.

The death and sickness rates caused by malignant tumours are rising steadily, among men as well as women. Over the last 20 years, the sickness rate has increased by 60% and the death rate by 25%.

---

[1]E/1994/104/Add.13.

[2]*Health Care Systems in Transition Profile* (Observatory Internet site: www.observatory.dk).

[3]*OECD Health Data*, 1999.

[4]Internet site of the National Institute of Hygiene (www.medstat.waw.pl).

Selective surveys carried out in areas across the country where the environment is particularly threatened showed a strong correlation between environmental deterioration and the death rate, especially from cancer and cardio-vascular diseases.

The Committee notes that AIDS is fairly rare compared to the other Contracting Parties, but that Poland is unusual in that the number of new cases is rising.

Infant and maternal mortality

The Committee observes that the infant mortality rate in Poland is of the second highest of all European OECD countries. The rate was 12.3 per 1,000 live births in 1996, compared to rates varying between 3.7 and 7.9 in the other Contracting Parties that are also OECD members. The high rate of premature births is a major reason for this.

Since the beginning of the 1990s, including during the reference period, the maternal death rate has fallen. Whereas in 1992 there were 9.9 deaths per 100,000 births, for example, the rate was down to 4.9 in 1996, below average for a European OECD country.

The Committee considers that the state of mother and child health is a key indicator as to whether the health system as a whole is functioning well or badly and that a particularly high infant mortality rate raises a problem over conformity with Article 11 of the Charter (Conclusions XIII-3, Turkey, pp.357-8). It therefore stresses that a fall in the infant mortality rate will be decisive in its assessment of Poland's conformity with Article 11 para. 1.

Health care system

Access to health care

The Ministry of Health and Social Welfare (*MZiOS*) is responsible for health policy and for the funding and supervision of highly specialised medical care. The voivodships, with 400 health centres, are responsible for basic and specialised health care.

The health care system is publicly funded. In 1997, 5.2% of GDP was devoted to health expenditure, almost 20% more than in 1994. More than 90% of all health care was funded by the state in 1997.

Health care (medical consultations, hospital visits, operations, etc.) is provided free of charge by the National Health Service for public and private sector workers, provided they visit an officially appointed doctor in the appropriate health centre or hospital. However, the Committee notes that 70% of doctors and 90% of dentists are private or semi-private and that patients must pay for all private health care. In this connection, it observes that some private clinics, offering a range of services from consultations to hospital treatment, have set up a health care scheme with different types of subscription for policy-holders and their families, varying in price from 100 PLZ for ten consultations per year to 2,000 PLZ for a year's comprehensive care.

Medicines are free for disabled ex-servicemen, some blood donors and the seriously and chronically ill. Otherwise, only medicines prescribed and administered in hospital are totally free. So-called basic medicines, considered vital for a person's recovery or survival, are sold at a fixed price, currently 1.50 PLZ Patients must also pay 30% of the price of other medicines available on prescription.

In the light of this information, the Committee detects some serious shortcomings, particularly concerning the cost and availability of health care for the unemployed.

However, due to the lack of standardised statistics enabling it to compare the average reimbursement rate in Poland with that of other Contracting Parties, and since the health care system was seriously overhauled outside the reference period, the Committee decides not to assess the conformity of the situation, at this time, concerning the accessibility of health care.

Health professionals and equipment

The report indicates that there were 5.4 hospital beds per 1,000 inhabitants in 1997, a relatively low figure compared to other European OECD countries. Around 15% of these were in psychiatric institutions. Private hospitals accounted for only 0.2% of hospital beds in 1997 and 0.4% in 1998.

The Committee notes that the density of general practitioners and pharmacists (2.3 and 0.5 per 1,000 inhabitants respectively in 1997) is below average for a European OECD country. On the other hand, Poland has an above-average density of specialists, 1.7 per 1,000 inhabitants. In 1997, there were 0.5 dentists per 1,000 inhabitants, a figure around the European average.

Conclusion

The Committee notes that the situation in Poland with regard to Article 11 para. 1 of the Charter is poor in several respects relating to the people's state of health and the health care system. However, it resolves to wait until the next examination of Article 11 before assessing the situation and, meanwhile, defers its conclusion.

Paragraph 2 – Advisory and educational facilities

The Committee takes note of the information contained in Poland's report.

Encouragement of individual responsibility

The Committee notes that health education is among the priorities of the 1996-2005 national health programme.

Health education in schools

The report states that significant efforts are being made to promote health education in schools. Until recently, there was no national health education programme. Now, however, all primary schools are targeted by a programme designed to develop a sense of responsibility among young people with regard to their health.

Initiatives to promote a healthy diet and personal and oral hygiene were also launched in schools during the reference period.

The Committee points out that prevention through health education in the sense of Article 11 para. 2 must also cover the prevention of smoking and alcohol abuse and sex education, especially the prevention of sexually transmitted diseases and AIDS. It asks whether these subjects are automatically tackled as part of the normal curriculum or separately.

Public information and awareness-raising

A variety of measures have been taken recently in order to establish a high-quality public information mechanism designed to raise people's awareness of major public health issues in Poland. For example, the scientific and educational foundations of the general health education and promotion campaigns have been strengthened, health institution staff responsible for public health education have been introduced to new health education techniques and the Ministry of Health assistance granted to local authorities and non-governmental organisations has been improved and increased.

Campaigns to reduce smoking, prevent domestic accidents and disseminate information on contagious diseases such as hepatitis B were organised during the reference period, particularly under the auspices of the National Institute of Hygiene.

In order to assess fully whether the situation in Poland conforms with this provision, the Committee requires a more detailed list of the bodies, both public and private, responsible for health education in schools on the one hand and for public information and awareness-raising on the other, as well as the resources available to them (staff and budget).

Counselling and screening

Children and adolescents

Since 1992 all children and teenagers have had access to free prevention, care and rehabilitation services, including hospital treatment. The Committee asks whether specialised mother and child welfare services are available nationwide.

Routine medical examinations are carried out at birth, ages 2, 4, 6 and 10, during a child's final year at primary school and during secondary education.

Prophylactic monitoring of schoolchildren is carried out in each school by the school nurse (hygienist) and the doctor responsible for primary health care in the area in which the child lives. All primary, secondary and post-secondary pupils are monitored in this way. Examinations mainly consist of screening for physical development and psychomotor deficiencies as well as hearing and sight defects and incorrect posture. An oral health campaign has been in operation since 1991.

The Committee requests information on the resources devoted to school health (staff and budget).

Rest of the population

Since the report contains no information on screening services or screening campaigns, the Committee requests that the next report cover this question in full.

Conclusion

Pending receipt of the information requested, the Committee defers its conclusion.

1st report – reference period 1997-1999

Paragraph 3 – Prevention of diseases

The Committee takes note of the information contained in Poland's report concerning the prevention of health risks in general and diseases in particular.

Policies on the prevention of avoidable risks

Reduction of environmental risks

The Committee notes that environmental deterioration is a major problem in Poland. Two of Europe's most polluted regions - Upper Silesia and the Black Triangle - are in southern Poland.

It observes that investment in the environment (1.3% of GDP) is the highest in the region and is average for European OECD countries.

Since 1989, environment protection bodies have been established, while local and regional authorities have also become more heavily involved in environmental issues. The Ministry of Environmental Protection, Natural Resources and Forests, the Public Environmental Protection Supervisory Authority and, through the National Institute of Hygiene, the Ministry of Health and Social Welfare all share responsibility for ensuring a healthy environment.

Air pollution – The Committee notes that atmospheric pollution levels are very high, particularly that of sulphur dioxide, since Poland is heavily dependent on coal for its energy (75% of all energy generated). It observes, however, that emissions of the main harmful gases have fallen since 1989, mainly as a result of the slowdown in economic activity in the early 1990s and the closure of unprofitable, highly polluting factories.

The Committee notes that there is very little legislation in this field. In this connection, it observes from the European Commission's 1999 regular report on Poland's progress towards accession to the European Union that the Large Combustion Plant Directive has been partially transposed into domestic law, but that very little progress has otherwise been made to improve air quality. The aforementioned report also indicates that infrastructures for monitoring atmospheric pollution and equipment levels in industry for the reduction of harmful gas emissions are inadequate. Moreover, the Committee has no information on whether the Polish authorities have set targets for the control of emissions of the main pollutants, even though Poland ratified the

United Nations Framework Convention on Climate Change (Rio de Janeiro, 1992) in 1994.

Water pollution – The Committee notes that water quality monitoring has improved thanks to the establishment of a network of warning and monitoring stations along the whole length of the River Vistula, which is particularly affected by pollution. This system should protect the main drinking water production plants that use river water from accidental pollution. It appears to the Committee from the information at its disposal, that there is little legislation in this field. It notes from the aforementioned European Commission report that European standards concerning waste water and nitrates have been partially transposed into Polish law, but that the 1974 Water Act has yet to be amended in order to incorporate the provisions of the European Union Framework Directive on Water.

Ionising radiation – The Committee has no information on safety standards relating to radiation protection. It is only aware that no progress has been made towards transposing European Union directives on the subject into domestic law (see aforementioned report). Bearing in mind the presence of several working uranium mines and Poland's future energy plans, it insists that the next report contain information on this subject, except in connection with protection in the workplace (dealt with under Article 3 of the Charter) and radiotherapy.

In the light of all this information, the Committee considers that Poland has achieved mixed success in reducing environmental hazards. Bearing in mind the known impact that pollution has had on the health of the Polish people and the poor health indicators mentioned above, particularly in polluted areas (see conclusion concerning Article 11 para. 1), a more ambitious strategy to combat pollution will be central to the Committee's assessment of conformity with Article 11 para. 3. The Committee therefore expects Poland to make sustained efforts and to achieve significant progress, particularly by strengthening its legislative framework through the transposition of environment-related Framework Directives into domestic law.

Asbestos – The report merely states that this area is governed by the Act of 19 June 1997 banning the use of asbestos products. The Committee therefore requests that the next report explain the scope of the ban (use, manufacture, importation, fibres concerned, etc.) and indicate whether any measures are in place to monitor asbestos levels in residential blocks and whether businesses are under any specific obligations regarding the disposal of asbestos waste.

Measures to combat smoking and alcoholism

Smoking – The Committee stresses the importance of measures against smoking in meeting the requirements of Article 11 of the Charter. It recalls that smoking, a major cause of avoidable death in developed countries (in Europe 30% of deaths from cancer are attributable to smoking), is associated with a wide range of diseases (cardiac and circulatory diseases, cancers, pulmonary diseases etc.). Smoking kills one adult in ten throughout the world. The World Health Organisation (WHO) forecasts an increase to up to one in every six deaths by 2030,[1] which is more than the figure for any other cause of death. The Committee also notes that WHO is drawing up a convention on measures to combat smoking and points out that WHO, as part of the Health for All campaign, has set a target for European countries of raising the proportion of non-smokers in the population to at least 80% and protecting non-smokers against involuntary exposure to tobacco smoke.[2]

The Committee takes note of Polish anti-smoking legislation. The first anti-smoking regulations were introduced in 1974 to restrict smoking in health institutions. An Act was then adopted in 1991, limiting tar and nicotine levels in cigarettes sold in Poland. In 1996, on the basis of World Health Organisation (WHO) recommendations, a general Act on Health Protection and the Fight against Smoking was adopted, banning the advertisement and promotion of tobacco products. The main aim of this Act is to protect people of all ages from tobacco products and smoke, to limit the effects of smoking on health and to promote a healthy lifestyle, particularly among the young. In the same year, a regulation requiring health warnings to be carried on cigarette packets also entered into force.

Alcohol – The Committee would like information on measures taken to curb alcohol abuse.

Health and safety in the home

The Committee notes that a programme to prevent lead poisoning among children has been established in the Katowice and Legnica voivodships, using a method developed by the USA's Centre for Disease Control.

---

[1]World Health Report 1999.

[2]WHO, *Health Objectives for All – Health Policies in Europe,* September 1991.

Other remarks

The Committee requests that the next report contain information on steps taken to combat noise pollution and to control foodstuffs. The Committee draws the Polish authorities' attention to the fact that, owing to the high ranking of poisoning among causes of death, it will attach great importance to food safety standards in Poland.

Prophylactic measures

Epidemiological monitoring

The main body responsible for epidemiological monitoring is the Public Health Control Office, which collates, analyses and disseminates information on the number of people contracting contagious diseases, deaths caused by such illnesses and external factors that facilitate their spread. The aim is to acquire the information needed to combat and prevent epidemics.

Local action plans are drawn up by the health monitoring and epidemiological centres established in each voivodship. They are based on an appraisal of the local situation and on Department of Public Health directives issued under the authority of the Chief Health Inspector. General guidelines concerning national issues are regularly drawn up by the National Institute of Hygiene's Epidemiology Department on the basis of the results of inspections carried out by the aforementioned centres.

Between 1992 and 1994, the main epidemiological problems were infections carried in the blood, hospital infections, food poisoning and the risk of epidemics originating in the countries of the former Soviet Union. Huge importance was attached to sterilisation in an effort to prevent infections carried in the blood and hospital infections. The Committee notes that emergency measures can be taken if an epidemic seems likely to break out. For example, it observes from the third report submitted by Poland to the United Nations Economic and Social Council on the application of the International Covenant on Economic, Social and Cultural Rights[1] that, in order to prevent cholera and diphtheria, special measures to carry out health checks at border posts and vaccinate high-risk groups (border guards, railway employees, health officials) have been introduced in voivodships in north-eastern

[1] E/1994/104/Add.13.

Poland. The Ministry of Health keeps emergency serum and vaccine supplies in addition to disinfecting agents.

Immunisation

The Committee takes note of several vaccination rates mentioned in the aforementioned report to the United Nations: in 1994, 95.1% of children were vaccinated against diphtheria and tetanus, 77.1% against measles, 95% against polio and 94.6% against whooping cough. These vaccinations are compulsory for all Polish children. The report states that these rates remained high throughout the reference period. The Committee observes that hepatitis B vaccinations have become widely available. It requests up-to-date information on the next reference period.

Conclusion

The Committee notes that the situation in Poland with regard to Article 11 para. 3 of the Charter is poor in several respects, particularly where environment-related legislation is concerned. However, it resolves to wait until the next examination of Article 11 before assessing the situation and, in the meantime, defers its conclusion.

Article 14 — The right to benefit from social welfare services

Paragraph 1 – Provision or promotion of social welfare services

The Polish report contains a detailed overview of the social assistance services provided for by the Act on Social Assistance of 29 November 1990 as amended. The Committee recalls in this regard that social assistance in the form of material benefits based on a criterion of individual need comes within the scope of Article 13 of the Charter. It has held that "what a state must do, in order to conform to the provisions of Article 14 is to promote the establishment of services providing advice and individual help rather than to encourage the granting of material assistance" (Conclusions I, p. 69).

Pursuant to Section 1 of the 1990 Act, organisation of social assistance in Poland is the responsibility of the organs of the central government administration and local self-government in cooperation with social organisations, the Catholic Church, other churches, denominational groups, foundations and societies as well as natural and legal persons. Observations on the network of municipal social assistance centres throughout the country and the division of responsibilities between the various levels of government are contained in the conclusion under Article 13 para. 3.

Still according to Section 1 of the 1990 Act, every person in a difficult situation has free access to social assistance. Social services are granted to individuals and families, in particular by reason of orphanage, homelessness, the need for maternity protection, unemployment, disability, long-lasting illness, problems in matters relating to care and education and household management, especially in broken-up or large families, alcoholism, drug addiction, difficulties in post-penitentiary social readjustment, natural or ecological disasters. Assistance for refugees and for families in crisis is also foreseen under the 1990 Act.

From information provided in the report under Article 13, the Committee notes that there were 39,700 employees in social assistance centres in 1998, of which 14,072 were social workers who served a total of 3,776,445 beneficiaries. The Committee wishes to be informed in each report of the number of beneficiaries of social services in the meaning of Article 14, if possible broken down by category of service (e.g. childcare, elderly-care, etc.).

The 1990 Act stipulates that the municipal social assistance centres should employ social workers proportionate to the population in the ratio of 1:2,000. The Committee asks whether this goal has been achieved in all parts of the country.

The Committee also notes the information on the qualifications of social workers, who must have appropriate professional qualifications or hold a diploma in social work or be a higher school graduate in social work, social policy, social rehabilitation, sociology, pedagogy or psychology. A person who has a higher school degree in subjects other than those mentioned above can retain or acquire a license for performing the job of a social worker, provided that he/she had finished or started specialization in social work and organization of social assistance prior to the enactment of the present law (Section 49, paras. 1 and 2 of the 1990 Act). The report states that a system of training and upgrading the professional qualifications of social workers has been established. To further these educational objectives, relevant specialisations have been introduced into the school curricula concerned.

The report mentions that, in addition to the general social assistance services available through assistance offices at regional and local level, there are different establishments providing social assistance services to specific categories of persons. These are, for example, centres for the homeless, single-mother homes, day-care centres and other community assistance centres as well as residential social assistance homes and care-giving/educational establishments for children and young persons deprived of the care of their natural families. The Committee asks that the next report contain more information on these establishments, notably as regards their scope, funding and the number of beneficiaries they serve.

The Committee notes that assessment of the quality and effectiveness of social assistance is the task of the voivodship authorities, which ensure that services provided by social assistance centres and care-giving/educational establishments meet the required standards, and are responsible for the acceptance and evaluation of reform programmes in social assistance homes, and the granting or revocation of permits or conditional permits for running social assistance homes. The Committee requests information on the main types of problems identified by the authorities through these supervision and evaluation activities.

Funding for social services comes from the state budget and the budgets of the local self-governments. The report explains the general principle that the state budget finances tasks commissioned by the central government administration under the 1990 Act, whereas the budgets of local governments (county or municipality) finance those tasks directly assigned to them by the act. The state budget also contributes to the financing of certain tasks assigned to counties or municipalities (such as providing meals for children and youth in schools or assisting foster parents). The Committee emphasises that each report should contain information on total expenditure on social services, if possible broken down according to category of service, to permit assessment of whether Poland is in conformity with Article 14 of the Charter.

The Committee notes that the granting of a social assistance benefit upon application by the person concerned is an administrative decision which is subject to the provisions of the Code of Administrative Procedure, pursuant to which an appeal against decisions may be lodged. It also notes, however, that social assistance in the form of counselling and help from social workers does not require a formal decision (Section 43 para. 2 of the 1990 Act). It asks whether a denial of social services may be appealed against.

Finally, the Committee requests confirmation in the next report that equal treatment of nationals of other Contracting Parties to the Charter lawfully resident or working regularly in Poland is guaranteed in respect of social services.

Pending receipt of the information requested, the Committee defers its conclusion.

Article 15 — The right of physically or mentally disabled persons to vocational training, rehabilitation and social settlement

Paragraph 1 – Vocational training arrangements for the disabled

General remarks

The most important piece of Polish legislation on the vocational rehabilitation of the disabled is the Act of 27 August 1997 on the vocational rehabilitation, social resettlement and employment of disabled persons, repealing the Act of 9 May 1991 on the employment and vocational rehabilitation of disabled persons. This Act covers all rights to vocational training and employment for disabled people.

The 1997 Act defines vocational rehabilitation as any activity which aims, with the active involvement of the persons concerned, to develop the skills of disabled people, improve their quality of life and promote their social integration. The Committee observes that the general purpose of the Act is to promote the social integration of disabled people.

In accordance with the changes introduced by the 1998 Act on the powers of public administrative bodies, the 1997 Act is no longer implemented by the specialised departments of local and regional employment offices, but by the general offices of the employment bureaux run by the decentralised administrative authorities. These bodies are therefore responsible for organising the training and rehabilitation of disabled people. Under the 1997 Act, the National Advisory Council for Disabled Persons was created, bringing together representatives of the relevant administrative bodies, non-governmental organisations and employers. This advisory body acts as a link between the various partners involved in the training and employment of disabled people.

The Committee notes that, under the terms of Article 1 of the 1997 Act, disabled people are defined as persons whose physical, mental or intellectual deficiencies restrict, either temporarily or permanently, their role in society, particularly their ability to work. In order to be recognised as such, a person must possess a medical certificate indicating the degree of their disability in accordance with a classification system laid down by law.

Statistics on the disabled population made available to the Committee are based on a survey carried out by the National Statistics Office in 1996. According to the survey, there were an estimated 446,200 disabled people in Poland, 303,100 of whom were of working age. The Committee requests that the next report provide up-to-date figures on this subject.

Assessing the vocational skills of disabled people

The 1997 Act stipulates a disabled person's occupational skills should be assessed before they embark on a vocational rehabilitation programme. In addition to a medical and psychological examination, this entails an appraisal of the person's qualifications, experience, interests and abilities. The Committee requests that the next report contain further information on how this assessment is carried out in practice, which bodies perform such assessments and, finally, how often and to what extent the disabled person is involved in the process.

Vocational training

The report states that the special education system is currently being reformed, with the aim of improving access to vocational training and, ultimately, employment. To this end, measures have been taken to enhance educational guidance services, adapt jobs to the capabilities of young disabled people, diversify education through the establishment of multidisciplinary training courses and ensure companies are closely involved in the training process by means of work placements. School curricula have been restructured along these lines since 1999. The Committee requests that the next report explain whether special education in Poland is provided in separate institutions or in ordinary schools.

The 1997 Act distinguishes between vocational training provided by training institutes and that offered by special training and rehabilitation centres (financed by the National Fund for the Rehabilitation of Disabled Persons), which accommodate those for whom access to ordinary training centres is difficult or impossible (Section 39.3.1 of the Act).

Employers can be closely involved with the vocational training of disabled people under the terms of the 1997 Act. They can claim back 75% of the cost of providing vocational training to disabled people who undergo at least 24 months of training in conformity with targets set out in their contract. As far as retraining is concerned, the Committee notes that people who lose their job as a result of their state of health and who have been certified fit for vocational retraining are entitled to a training grant. The Committee asks what conditions must be fulfilled for a person to receive such a grant. It also asks what obligations an employer is under if the worker's disability is the result of an occupational disease or industrial accident.

Staff qualifications

The Committee notes that the National Fund for the Rehabilitation of Disabled Persons has set up an institute with specific responsibility for training people who work with the disabled.[1] It asks whether the institute awards diplomas authorising the holder to work as a trainer or advisor and whether any form of further training or refresher course is available to enable them to keep abreast of new developments.

The Committee also observes that the private sector plays a very important role in the vocational training of disabled people. The 1997 Act stipulates that tasks connected to the vocational, social and medical rehabilitation of disabled people may be entrusted to non-governmental organisations that have signed a contract with the National Fund for the Rehabilitation of Disabled Persons. The Committee requests that the next report indicate whether this contract contains specific provisions on the training of those who work with disabled people and/or quality control mechanisms for the training offered.

Suitability of vocational training to the needs of disabled persons

The report states that there is no data relating to the number of specialised institutions, places available and applications received. The Committee would therefore like to know how many disabled people attend ordinary training centres and how many undergo specialised training.

Furthermore, with regard to the financing of vocational training for disabled people, the Committee notes from the report that the National Fund for the Rehabilitation of Disabled Persons organises the funding of various types of training. For example, disabled people (except those receiving an invalidity pension) who are registered unemployed are entitled to free vocational training. However, the Committee is unable to

---

[1] *Vocational rehabilitation and employment of disabled people*, International Labour Conference, 86th session, 1998.

determine whether those undergoing training also receive a grant. It requests that this be clarified in the next report.

The Committee notes that the Fund's spending on vocational training increased significantly between 1992 and 1999 (e.g. 1,316 million PLZ in 1997 compared to 197 million PLZ in 1995). However, since the Fund's total budget is not indicated, the Committee cannot calculate what proportion it devotes to vocational training. It requests that the next report clarify this matter.

Equal treatment of nationals of other Contracting Parties

The Committee asks whether a person's nationality and/or place of residence affects their entitlement to vocational training.

Conclusion

Pending receipt of the information requested, the Committee defers its conclusion.

Paragraph 2 – Placement arrangements for the disabled

As mentioned in its conclusion on Article 15 para. 1, the 1997 Act on the vocational rehabilitation, social resettlement and employment of disabled persons stresses the importance of equal job opportunities for disabled people. This approach takes the form of a vocational integration policy which, in conformity with Article 15 para. 2, promotes measures to increase access for disabled people to the ordinary labour market and to support them in their work.

Recruitment services

The regional and voivodship employment offices are responsible for the recruitment of disabled people in Poland as well as for vocational training. Their wide range of tasks includes liaising with specialised and general administrative bodies, local authorities, non-governmental organisations and foundations involved in the employment and vocational rehabilitation of disabled people. The Committee would like to know how this co-operation works in practice.

Employment policy for disabled people: methods and results

Poland has established a quota system whereby companies with more than 25 employees (under previous legislation, it only applied to those with over 50 employees), are exempt from paying monthly contributions to the National Fund for the Rehabilitation of Disabled Persons if 6% of their employees are disabled. Companies offering sheltered employment pay reduced contributions to the Fund as long as their employees are paid a salary.

Employers' obligations concerning the employment of disabled people, as set out in the 1997 Act, therefore rely on dissuasive measures such as the aforementioned contributions, although certain incentives are also in place. For example, the Act makes provision for certain tax deductions for employers who reach the 6% quota of disabled employees.

The Committee would like to be able to determine how many employers benefit from the quota system. To this end, it requests that the next report summarise how the 1997 Act has been implemented, indicating changes in the actual working hours of disabled people and in the level of contributions made to the Fund.

The Committee observes that the employment of disabled people in the ordinary job market is subject to specific regulations governing working hours, compulsory breaks, holiday and pay. The Committee would like to know how employment in sheltered workshops is regulated (see below).

With regard to measures taken to ensure the safety of disabled workers, the 1997 Act gives employers a fixed period of time in which they must provide a workstation specially adapted to the needs of employees who become disabled as a result of an industrial accident or occupational disease. Employers who fail to respect the deadline must pay a sum equal to fifteen times the person's average wage to the National Fund for the Rehabilitation of Disabled Persons (Section 23 of the 1997 Act). The Committee asks whether specific measures are in place or are planned to protect disabled workers against unlawful dismissal.

The 1997 Act contains a series of provisions making it easier for disabled job-seekers registered with a regional employment office to work in a self-employed capacity. For example, they can apply for a loan to help them set up a company or agricultural undertaking. These loans, financed by the National Fund for the Rehabilitation of Disabled

Persons, are awarded by the employment office manager provided the applicant fulfils certain requirements set out in the contract and conditions concerning the duration of the self-employed activity (24 months). Repayment of the loan can be deferred, reduced or even cancelled if difficulties arise. Credit facilities are also available. The report states that 8,869 new jobs were created as a result of these loans between 1992 and 1998.

The sheltered employment sector is regulated by the 1997 Act, which stipulates the proportion (and category) of disabled workers necessary for a company to acquire the status of a sheltered workshop as well as health, safety and medical service requirements. The status is granted for a three-year period by the minister responsible for disabled people. Sheltered workshops enjoy tax benefits, but are obliged to pay 10% of their profits to the National Fund for the Rehabilitation of Disabled Persons.

Equal treatment of nationals of other Contracting Parties

The Committee asks whether access to the above-mentioned vocational integration services is dependent on nationality.

Conclusion

Pending receipt of the information requested, particularly concerning success in recruiting disabled workers to the ordinary labour market, the Committee defers its conclusion.

Article 17 — The right of mothers and children to social and economic protection

Article 72 of the Polish Constitution of 1997 guarantees the rights of the child.

The Office of the Commissioner for citizen's rights is also responsible for protecting the rights of the child. The Committee wishes to receive further information on the functioning of this Office.

The Committee notes that the Constitution provides for the establishment of a Commissioner for children's rights, and that according to the report a draft law on this is currently under consideration. The Committee wishes to be kept informed of all developments on this issue.

Establishment of parentage and adoption

The Family and Guardianship Code does not stipulate a separate procedure for determining maternity. If necessary maternity may be established on the basis of the provisions of the Civil Procedure Code.

According to the Family and Guardianship Code, paternity may be established either through:

- a presumption that the mother's husband is the child's father;
- acknowledgement of paternity by the child's father;
- a court determined paternity.

At the request of the mother (or where the child has reached the age of majority the child itself), the court may determine the paternity of a child. A public prosecutor may also bring an action for the determination of paternity.

The report states that the mother's consent is necessary for the child to be acknowledged. The Committee asks if this the case even where paternity is to be determined by the courts.

In accordance with Article 114 of the Family and Guardianship Code, only children under age may be adopted and only where it is in their best interest. The adoption of a child who has reached the age of 13 years can only be done with his consent. A child under 13 years of age may be heard by the court if he or she can understand the concept of adoption.

The adoption is effected through the guardianship court's order at the adopting persons' request.

The biological parents' consent is necessary for the adoption except in certain circumstances, for example where the parents have been deprived of parental authority.

The adoption creates legal bonds identical to those between children and their biological parents. Two types of adoption exist, full adoption and incomplete adoption. A full adoption consists in the adoptee acquiring rights (and in the future his descendents) and duties deriving from the relationship with regard to the relatives of the adopting person with the simultaneous cessation of rights and duties between the adoptee and his biological relatives. An incomplete adoption confines the relationship to the adoptee and the adopter.

The Committee wishes to be informed whether there exist "adoption agencies", whether these are private or state run and whether compensation may be paid to a party involved in the adoption. It also wishes to receive information on the number of children placed for adoption on an annual basis.

Child welfare

According to the report, mother and child protection is carried out through the organs of central government and local government. NGO's are also active in this field. The Committee wishes to receive more specific information on these organs and on the NGO's.

Children in public care

A child who is not under parental authority is deemed to be in "legal custody". The Family and Guardianship Code regulates the institution of "legal custody". A guardianship court institutes legal custody proceedings *ex officio* for minors:

– whose parents are unknown;

– who are orphans;

– whose parents have no parental authority (parents have been deprived of parental authority, or whose parental authority has been suspended).

The custody of the child is exercised by a guardian, appointed by the court. The court should appoint as guardian, a person indicated by the parents, or a relative, if possible. If no such person is available, the court will request that the appropriate organ of the municipal authorities or a social organisation taking care and custody of minors designate a person to whom the custody of the child may be entrusted. The custody of siblings should, if possible, be entrusted to one person.

According to the Family and Guardianship Code, whoever is appointed as a guardian by the court must accept this duty. A guardian discharges his duty under the supervision of the court.

A child deprived of their family may be placed in the care of an adoptive family, foster family or in an institution.

A foster care placement normally follows the guardianship court's custody order. A child may, however, be placed in the care of foster parents without an order from the guardianship court on the application of the child's parents, on the basis of a written "child entrustment contract" between the foster parents and the *starosta* (the successor of the school superintendent). In choosing a foster family, precedence should be given to a family related to the child if the choice of that family guarantees an improvement in the child's life situation. Siblings should be place in the same foster family if possible.

The child's opinion should be heard and taken into account when deciding whether to place a child with a foster family.

Financial assistance (and other assistance) is granted to foster carers, depending on the level of their income. Increased financial assistance is available where the child to be placed has problems. One-off cash benefits are also payable.

The *starosta* may dissolve the child entrustment contract if necessary.

The report mentions the existence of other establishments caring for children: emergency care centres, educational centres, correctional institutions for juveniles, and children's homes. The Committee wishes to receive further information on these, and on the number of children placed in these institutions as well as the number of children placed with foster families. It also wishes to receive information on the number of children subject to "custody" orders of the guardianship court.

The Committee wishes to receive information as to whether there is any body responsible for monitoring care in institutions and whether any specific procedure exists for complaining about care or treatment in institutions and on the conditions under which an institution may interfere with a child's property, mail, personal integrity and right to meet with persons close to the child. It also wishes to receive information on the procedures for reviewing placements in institutions.

Protection of children against ill-treatment and abuse

The law provides for measures to be taken against parents who do not properly discharge their duties towards children. As a last resort the court may suspend or divest parents of parental authority. In accordance with Article 109 of Family and Guardianship Code the court may also:

– impose upon the child's parents the obligation of appropriate conduct;

– determine certain activities that parents may not undertake without the court's consent;

– subject the parents to supervision;

– refer the young person to an organisation or institution for occupational training or other establishment caring for children;

– place the young person in care, or with a foster family.

The Penal code provides that those who commit crimes against, *inter alia*, children, such as abuse, ill-treatment, abduction shall be prosecuted and punished.

The Committee wishes to receive further information on the facilities available to children who are subject to ill-treatment, neglect or abuse.

It recalls from the information provided under Article 7 para. 10 that several measures were taken during the reference period to raise awareness and prevent violence within the family, with particular reference to alcohol related violence. Several programmes were specifically sought to protect children ("Physical and sexual violence towards children from communities threatened with alcoholism").

The Committee wishes to know whether legislation prohibits all forms of corporal punishment of children, in schools, in institutions, in the home and elsewhere.

Children and the law – Young Offenders

The age of majority is 18 years. Majority is also attained by a female who has reached the age of 16 if she marries. Women may marry at the age of 16 with the consent of their family and guardianship court, otherwise the age is 18 years. Men may marry at the age of 21 years unless they have the consent of the Guardianship Court.

The Constitution provides that there shall be no discrimination between children based on the status of their birth.

Statutory inheritance rights are the same for all children irrespective of whether their parents were married. A child from parents who were not married inherits, again irrespective of the manner in which paternity was established, in exactly the same way as a child of married parents, both from his mother and the mother's relatives and from his father and the father's relatives.

The Committee wishes to know at what age a child can be heard directly in court and under what circumstances.

As regards children and the criminal law, the Committee notes that the basic rule is that a young offender who has committed a criminal offence is not liable under the Penal Code unless he has reached the age of 17 years. For young offenders between the age of 17 and 18 years instead of penal measures, educational measures may be imposed if the circumstances of the case and the characteristics of the defendant warrant it.

A life sentence may not be imposed on a person under the age of 18 years.

Under certain circumstances, a young offender who has reached the age of 15 years will be liable under the Penal Code; if he has committed an offence laid down in the code, if the circumstances of the case, the degree of the defendant's mental development, his characteristics and personal situation warrant such liability and if previously applied educational or corrective measures have proved ineffective. In these cases the penalty may not exceed two thirds of the statutory maximum penalty.

The Committee wishes to receive information on the number of 15 year olds sentenced to a term of imprisonment under the Penal Code as well as the number of 17 year olds. It also wishes to know how may young persons are in custody awaiting trial. Further it wishes to receive information on the maximum periods young persons may be imprisoned or held in custody pending trial. It wishes to receive confirmation that young offenders are not held in prisons with adult offenders. As regards young offenders (and those who demonstrate "demoralisation") between the ages of 13 and 17 years (except where the Penal Code applies to those above 15 years) custodial, educational or correctional proceedings may be instituted in accordance with specific legislation on the proceedings in cases relating to juveniles. The family courts have jurisdiction over such cases. The legislation provides that educational measures such as admonition, good behaviour order, placing a juvenile under a curator's supervision, placing a juvenile with an individual that will supervise and vouch for him, prohibition on driving vehicles, an order for the forfeiture of personal items may be imposed. Further, placement in an institution or organisation for occupational training, in a foster home, or in an educational establishment, may be ordered or if the young person has committed a criminal offence placement in a correctional institution.

It appears to the Committee from the report that the family court may start proceedings and impose a wide range of "educational" measures on young persons who demonstrate symptoms of "demoralisation" but have not necessarily committed a criminal offence. The Committee wishes to receive further information on this concept and on the number of persons subject to proceedings on this ground.

Conclusion

Pending the receipt of the information requested, the Committee defers its conclusion.

Article 18 — The right to engage in a gainful occupation in the territory of other Contracting Parties

Paragraph 4 – The right of nationals to leave the country

Polish law guarantees nationals the right to leave the country to engage in a gainful occupation abroad (under the Passports Act of 29 November 1990). The only restrictions permitted concern cases where judicial proceedings have been brought against the person concerned (section 6 of the Act). These are based on grounds of public interest and national security and are therefore compatible with Article 31 of the Charter. The Committee notes that a person who has been refused a passport may appeal against the decision.

The Committee concludes that the situation in Poland is in conformity with Article 18 para. 4 of the Charter.

Chapter 12 – Conclusions concerning Articles 7, 8, 11, 14, 17 and 18 of the Charter in respect of Portugal

Article 7 — The right of children and young persons to protection

Paragraph 1 – Minimum age of admission to employment

The Committee takes note of the information provided in the Portuguese report.

In addition, it takes note of the detailed information provided in the Portuguese Government's report on the measures taken to apply the Committee of Ministers Recommendation No. Rec ChS (98) 5 and Resolution No. Res ChS (99) 4, adopted following Complaint No. 1/1998 – International Commission of Jurists v. Portugal.

During the reference period, the Portuguese Constitution was amended by Constitutional Act No. 1/97 of 30 September 1997 so as to include the prohibition of employing school children in Article 69. Portugal ratified ILO Convention No. 138 in 1998.

Further developments, outside the reference period, are described in the reports. Act No. 58/99 of 30 June 1999 amended the Legal System of the Regulation of the Employment Contract. Section 122 subsection 1 of the latter now provides that the minimum age for admission to employment is, as noted in the previous conclusion, 16 years. Subsection 2 now defines light work. Section 5 of this Act 58/99 extends the minimum age rule to self-employment.

A series of statutes was enacted in August 1999 to reinforce labour sanctions (Acts Nos. 113, 114, 116 and 118/99). The illegal employment of children is a very serious infringement. The level of fines varies with the size of the enterprise. Criminal sanctions may also be applied.

The report describes initiatives taken by labour inspectors against the employment of children, with increased inspection visits at the start of the academic year 1999/2000 in the regions and sectors where the problem is most acute. The Committee takes note of the information provided on the continuing activities undertaken within the context of the Plan for the Elimination of the Exploitation of Child Labour (PEETI), which concentrates on awareness-raising, prevention and alternative solutions. Government Resolution 1/2000 extended the mandate of PEETI to the end of 2003. The reports also describe the Integrated

Programme for Education and Training (PIEF), which aims to provide an individualised solution to children at risk of abandoning their education. The Committee asks for information on the progress and results of these measures to be included in the next report. Noting that further data will be made available on the basis of a second survey conducted in October 1999 investigating the effect of child work on education, the Committee asks to receive the results in the next report under this provision.

The Committee recalls that it previously found the situation not to be in conformity with the Charter on account of the "significant lack of respect" in practice for national legal provisions on the minimum age of admission to employment. Taking account of the data obtained from the family survey conducted in October 1998, and considered in Complaint No. 1/1998 – International Commission of Jurists against Portugal, the Committee reiterates that, during the reference period, the situation was not in conformity with the Charter.

The Committee concludes that because of the extent of child labour in Portugal during the reference period, the situation is not in conformity with Article 7 para. 1 of the Charter.

Paragraph 2 – Higher minimum age in certain occupations

As in its previous conclusion, the Committee notes that the minimum age for admission to employment is 16 years in Portugal. Having already considered the provisions of Order No. 715 of 3 August 1993, which prohibits or restricts the employment of young persons in activities involving contact with scheduled hazards (see Conclusions XIII-5, pp. 85-186), the Committee concludes that the situation is in conformity with the Charter. It asks that the next report include information on the number of occupational accidents and diseases among young workers.

The Committee concludes that the situation in Portugal is in conformity with Article 7 para. 2 of the Charter.

Paragraph 3 – Safeguarding the full benefit of compulsory education

The Portuguese report confirms that children under 16 years old who have not yet completed their compulsory schooling may not be employed, not even in light work.

In its previous conclusion, the Committee considered that the situation was not in conformity with the Charter since children aged 16 years old who have not completed their compulsory education may combine work with training for up to 40 hours per week. The report stresses that the work concerned is necessarily part-time work, since such children remain subject to compulsory education and must attend classes for part of the week. The Committee considers that this information permits it to revise its previous assessment.

The Committee takes note of the scheme set up under Joint Ordinance No. 123/97 of the Ministries of Education and Labour to provide education and training modules to children who either reach the end of compulsory schooling without a qualification, or who obtain the corresponding diploma but do not wish to continue their education. Under the Joint Ordinance, classes are provided to allow the former group obtain an educational qualification, and both groups to obtain a recognised vocational qualification.

As noted under Article 7 para. 1, a second survey of school children was carried out in October 1999, following up on the findings of the family survey conducted in September 1998 in co-operation with the International Labour Organisation (ILO). The Committee requests the results of the more recent survey, as well as the Government's comments.

The Committee concludes that the situation in Portugal is in conformity with Article 7 para. 3 of the Charter.

Paragraph 4 – Working hours for young workers and apprentices

The Committee recalls that since 1 January 1997, the minimum age of admission to employment in Portugal is 16 years old and that, as a consequence, young people aged between 15 and 16 are only allowed to perform light work. It further recalls that the personal scope of Article 7 para. 4 covers young persons under the age of 16.

Under these circumstances, the Committee concludes that the situation in Portugal is in conformity with Article 7 para. 4 of the Charter.

Paragraph 5 – Fair remuneration for young workers and apprentices

The Committee notes that there exists no general legislation in Portugal fixing remuneration levels on the basis of age. Act No. 45/98 prohibits wage discrimination of young workers and amends Legislative Decree No. 69-A/87 which henceforth provides that the statutory minimum wage can only be reduced where the capacity of the worker is reduced or where the work has the character of practical training for a skilled or highly skilled occupation. In the latter case the reduction may not exceed 20% for a maximum duration of one year (six months where certain types of training are concerned).

The report states that the legislative framework for apprenticeship training has been reformed by Legislative Decree No. 205/96 which repeals Legislative Decrees Nos. 102/84, 436/88 and 383/91. The new legislation provides for various forms of financial support for young persons undergoing training such as regular grants to cover expenses for food, accommodation, transport, etc., training grants for young unemployed persons in training, grants relating to work carried out by young persons as part of their training (i.e. remuneration for work performed) and development grants in special cases, for instance in priority sectors where there is a particular training need.

Grants relating to work carried out in the context of training are calculated as a percentage of the statutory minimum wage for the previous year and as a function of the number of hours. The percentage is 30% the first year, 40% the second year and 50% the third year. The Committee considers the resulting remuneration to be low, especially in the second and third year. It recalls its case-law according to which apprentice wages on an indicative basis must not be lower than about a third of the starting wage of an adult wage at the beginning of the apprenticeship and about two-thirds at the end. It asks whether the remuneration paid to apprentices by employers in practice is higher than the minimum percentages mentioned above.

The Committee takes note of the information on average monthly wages of young workers (between 15 and 19 years of age) and adult workers in the 20-24 age group with different levels of qualification in 1997. It notes that the difference between the two age groups is generally rather modest: a skilled young worker earns on average 67,759 escudos (PTE) per month compared to 77,842 PTE for a worker in the 20-24 age group. An unskilled young worker earns on average 64,150 PTE per month compared to 69,219 PTE in the 20-24 age group. It is recalled that the statutory minimum wage in 1997 was 56,700 PTE (51,450 PTE for domestic workers).

However, the Committee underlines that in order to assess the situation it must have information on the minimum or lowest wages of young workers and apprentices calculated net, i.e. after deduction of taxes and social security contributions. In addition, it needs information on starting wages or minimum wages of adult workers, also calculated net. Net calculations should be made for the case of a single person. The Committee recalls that in Conclusions XIV-2 (pp. 644-645) it deferred its conclusion under Article 4 para. 1 pending receipt of similar information (minimum and average net wages of adult workers).

Pending receipt of the information requested, notably in respect of apprentice wages, the Committee defers its conclusion.

Paragraph 6 – Treatment of the time spent in vocational training as forming part of the working day

The Committee notes from the Portuguese report that Act No. 26/81 has been repealed by Act No. 116/97 which lays down the legal framework for "student-workers" attending official state education courses or equivalent courses . Under the new legislation the weekly time to be set aside for participation in training without any reduction in wages is determined as follows as a function of weekly working hours:

– working hours between 20 and 29 hours per week give entitlement to 3 hours training weekly;

– between 30 and 33 hours per week to 4 hours;

– between 34 and 37 hours per week to 5 hours;

– more than 38 hours per week to 6 hours.

Moreover, the act provides for a leave of two days without pay reductions in connection with the sitting of exams (the day of the exam plus the day prior to the exam).

The report states that these rules apply in the absence of an agreement on the matter between the "student-workers", the workers' representation structures and the employer. It further emphasises that more favourable rules are often laid down in collective agreements. In certain sectors, for instance agriculture, dock work, the automotive industry, the ceramic industry and the paper and glass industry, collective agreements provides for between one and a half and two hours training daily without loss of remuneration. According to the report these provisions apply to young workers as well as to adult workers.

In the light of the information provided, the Committee concludes that the situation in Portugal is in conformity with Article 7 para. 6 of the Charter.

Paragraph 7 – Annual holiday of young persons under eighteen

The Committee notes that there have been no changes to the situation which it has previously found to be satisfactory.

It therefore concludes that the situation in Portugal is in conformity with Article 7 para. 7 of the Charter.

Paragraph 8 – Prohibition of night work for young persons under eighteen

The Committee notes that the sole change relevant to this provision of the Charter which has occurred during the reference period is the introduction of special legislation on employment relationships on board fishing vessels. Act No. 15/97 provides that young persons between 16 and 18 years old may perform night work between 11 p.m. and 7 a.m. on board fishing vessels subject to certain restrictions (including a requirement for annual medical control). For minors night work is prohibited in the period between midnight and 4 a.m. except in special circumstances. According to the report, the new act takes into account the night work provisions of Community Directive 94/33.

The Committee takes note of the information on the number of young workers engaged in night work. A total of 4,000 men and 2,800 women between 16 and 18 years of age performed night work during 1998, the majority in the service sector. The Committee wishes to continue to receive information on the number of young persons engaged in night work.

The report states that outside the reference period Legislative Decree No. 409/71 was amended by Act No. 58/99 which transposes Community Directive 94/33. Henceforth Section 33 of the Decree lays down a general prohibition of night work for young persons under the age of 16 between 8 p.m. and 7 a.m. and between 11 p.m. and 7 a.m. for young persons over the age of 16. For the latter group a number of exceptions apply. The Committee will assess the new legislation in its next conclusions.

However, as there was no general prohibition of night work for young workers aged 16 to 18 in non-industrial establishment during the reference period, the Committee concludes that the situation in Portugal is not in conformity with Article 7 para. 8 of the Charter.

Paragraph 9 – Provision of regular medical control for young workers under eighteen

The Committee notes from the Portuguese report that Act No. 15/97 on employment relationships on board fishing vessels in its Section 35 para. 3 provides for pre-employment medical examinations as well as subsequent annual examinations of young workers under 18 who will be engaged in night work (see also Article 7 para. 8).

The Committee further notes that Act No. 58/99 which was adopted outside the reference period and which transposes Community Directive 94/33 introduced amendments to existing legislation of relevance to this provision of the Charter. The Committee will examine these amendments in its next conclusions.

In reply to the Committee's question, the report states that Legislative Decree No. 26/94 applies to all workers and self-employed without exception and in all economic sectors, except in those where special legislation apply (the merchant navy, the fishing industry and retail). The Committee takes this as a confirmation that minors working in family businesses are also covered.

The Committee concludes that the situation in Portugal is in conformity with Article 7 para. 9 of the Charter.

Paragraph 10 – Special protection for children and young people from physical and moral dangers to which they are exposed

The Committee notes the information contained in the Portuguese report.

It refers to its conclusion under Article 11 in respect of measures to prevent drug addiction and alcoholism.

The Committee wishes to be informed as to whether legislation prohibits the use of children in the sex industry, and to receive information on any supervisory system and sanctions that may accompany this prohibition.

The Committee concludes that the situation in Portugal is in conformity with Article 7 para. 10 of the Charter.

Article 8 — The right of employed women to protection

Paragraph 1 – Maternity leave

1. Right to maternity leave

The Committee recalls its previous conclusion (Conclusions XIII-5, p. 194) that, in the absence of a compulsory six-week postnatal leave period, the situation in Portugal did not conform to the Charter.

The report indicates that during the period under review (1997-1998) the situation remained unchanged, the maternity leave stipulated for all working women being of 98 days' duration, of which only 14 were compulsory; 60 days were to be taken following childbirth and the remaining 30 either before or after (Act No. 17/95).

The report nevertheless explains that Act No. 142/99, whose entry into force postdates the reference period, prescribes a compulsory leave period of 6 weeks following childbirth. Furthermore, there have been extensions of the total leave period, to 110 days (applicable from 1 January to 31 December 1999) and to 120 days with effect from 1 January 2000 (Act No. 18/98). The Committee welcomes this improvement, from which it infers that whereas under Section 10 sub-section 3 of the Act No. 17/95 of 9 June 1995 a mother could relinquish her leave to the father, this will now only be possible after the six weeks of compulsory leave.

The employer's non-compliance with these provisions is defined as a very serious offence, fineable at rates of 300,000 escudos (PTE) to 9 million PTE maximum (Section 9 of Act No. 118/99 of 11 August 1999). The Committee asks that the next report provide information on the application of the legislation in practice, particularly by stating if possible the number of breaches recorded by the labour inspectors.

The Committee recalls that Article 8 para. 1 requires the right to maternity leave to be secured by law to all gainfully employed women, with a minimum duration of 12 weeks including 6 weeks of compulsory postnatal leave.

The Committee concludes that the situation in Portugal is not in conformity with Article 8 para. 1 of the Charter on this point because, during the reference period in question (1997-1998), the postnatal leave of six weeks was not obligatory. In 1999, a statutory amendment which occurred outside the reference period nevertheless redressed the situation.

2. Right to adequate benefit

As the Committee noted in its previous conclusion (Conclusions XIII-5, p. 195) concerning Portugal, employed women irrespective of nationality who come under the general social security scheme qualify for maternity benefit. Its award is subject to completion of a six-month contributory period or the equivalent thereof (i.e. incapacity for work which entitles a claimant to sickness benefit; temporary incapacity due to an industrial accident or occupational disease entitling the claimant to compensation; periods of unemployment for which unemployment benefit is payable).

The benefit amounts to 100% of the insured person's earnings during the six months preceding the second month before the one qualifying her for benefit. The reports states that no ceiling applies to this reference remuneration.

The current report indicates that where the reference remuneration is below 50% of the minimum wage, because of part-time working for instance, the maternity benefit paid is equivalent to 50% of the minimum wage.

Pending the requested information, the Committee concludes that the situation in Portugal is in conformity with Article 8 para. 1 of the Charter in this respect.

Paragraph 2 – Illegality of dismissal during maternity leave

The Committee notes from the report submitted by Portugal that there have been no changes to the situation which it has previously considered to be in conformity with the Charter.

As the report contains no new information, the Committee concludes that the situation in Portugal is in conformity with Article 8 para. 2 of the Charter.

It requests that the next report continues to provide information on the situation in practice.

Paragraph 3 – Time off for nursing mothers

The Portuguese report states that Law No. 142/99, which came into force outside the reference period, has amended Section 12 of Law No. 4/84.

The amendments are as follows:

– women are entitled to work breaks for breastfeeding (two separate periods of up to one hour) for as long as breastfeeding continues (entitlement was previously limited to one year);

– in the case of non-breastfed babies, the mother and father can decide that one or the other will take work breaks for feeding until the child is one year old;

– entitlement to work breaks for feeding has been extended to part-time workers in proportion to the hours they work.

In the light of this information, and the fact that the entitlement entails no loss of earnings, the Committee concludes that the situation in Portugal is in conformity with Article 8 para. 3 of the Charter.

Paragraph 4 – Regulation of night work and prohibition of dangerous, unhealthy or arduous types of work for women workers

1. Regulation of night work for women in industrial employment (Article 8 para. 4*a*)

The report of Portugal states that Act No. 73/98 of 10 November 1998 incorporated Community Directive 93/104 of 23 November 1993, concerning certain aspects of the organisation of working time, into the country's domestic law.

Night work is defined as work done for a minimum period of seven hours or a maximum of eleven hours including the midnight to 5 a.m. time slot. Collective agreements fix night-time working hours in conformity with these rules. Where no such collective agreements exist, night work is considered to cover the period between 8 p.m. and 7 a.m.

The average weekly duration of night work should not exceed the equivalent of eight hours per day, and workers doing jobs that involve special risks or substantial physical or mental effort should not do more than eight hours' night work in any 24-hour period.

The employer is under obligation to make sure that employees on night work undergo regular medical check-ups to monitor their state of health. The employer must also, where possible, ensure that workers who have health problems as a result of night work are transferred to daytime work (Article 8 paras. 1 and 2 of Act No. 73/98).

"The conditions and guarantees governing the employment on night work of workers whose health or safety may be put at risk as a result shall be fixed by government order" (Section 9 of Act No. 73/98).

The previous report stated that, pursuant to Act No. 17/95 of 9 June 1995 on the protection of motherhood, pregnant women and women who have recently given birth or are breastfeeding are dispensed from night work for 112 days before and after birth. At least half of that period must be taken prior to the presumed birth date, and during the remainder of the pregnancy upon presentation of a medical certificate proving that dispensation is necessary to the worker's health or that of the unborn child.

The Committee points out that Article 8 para. 4*a* of the Charter does not require states to prohibit the employment of women on night work, but to regulate it. The regulations may be general and concern workers of both sexes, but they must strictly regulate the possibilities of night work, which must be authorised only because of particular production constraints and taking into account the specific workplace and work organisation conditions. They must also determine the conditions under which women may work at night, such as obtaining the authorisation of the Labour Inspectorate, fixing working hours, breaks and days off following periods of night work, entitlement to be transferred to a daytime job in the event of health problems linked to night work, etc. The Committee also recalls that the regulations must make allowance for pregnant women and women who have recently given birth or are breastfeeding.

In the case of Portugal, the Committee observes that the regulations make satisfactory allowance for pregnant women and women who have recently given birth or are breastfeeding. It also notes that night work by men and women is regulated insofar as working hours are fixed and provision is made for regular medical check-ups and for transfer to day work where night work gives rise to health problems. However, the information supplied does not say in what circumstances night work is authorised, whether Labour Inspectorate authorisation is required, for example, or whether provision is made for days off following periods of night work.

Pending receipt of the information it has requested, the Committee defers its conclusion. It also requests whether the draft Bill following the ratification in 1994 by Portugal of the International Labour Office Convention No. 171 of the regarding night work has been adopted.

2. Prohibition of the employment of women in dangerous, unhealthy or arduous types of work (Article 8 para. 4*b*)

The Committee points out that Article 8 para. 4*b* contains a dual restriction:

– it prohibits the employment of women workers in underground mining, a restriction strictly limited to actual extraction work and

– it prohibits the employment of women, "as appropriate, on all other work which is unsuitable for them by reason of its dangerous, unhealthy or arduous nature", the expression "as appropriate" being understood to allow for the restriction to be limited solely to those cases where it is necessary, in particular to protect pregnant women and women who have recently given birth or are breastfeeding.

Concerning the former restriction, the Committee recalls that, in keeping with this provision of the Charter, Portuguese law prohibits the employment of women in any work in underground mines (Act No. 27891 of 27 July 1937 and Order No. 186 of 13 March 1973). The report states in this respect that Act No. 118/99 of 11 August 1999 provides for non-compliance to be punished by a fine, the size of which has increased and now ranges from 80,000 escudos (PTE) to 1,450,000 PTE. The report adds that during the reference period concerned (1997-1998) the Labour Inspectorate reported no violations of this rule.

Concerning the other restriction, the report supplements the information supplied in previous reports, stating that Order No. 229/96 of 26 June 1996, implementing Community Directive 92/85, also covers Appendices I and II of the Directive, which contain the non-exhaustive list of substances and working procedures and conditions prohibited to pregnant women and women who have recently given birth or are breastfeeding. They include such hazards as ionising radiation, mercury and lead and their derivatives which are likely to be absorbed by the human body.

The Committee requests that the next report state whether the Labour Inspectorate has identified any violations in this area. It points out that the penalties incurred are the same as for violations of the law prohibiting work in underground mining to women.

Pending this information, the Committee concludes that the situation in Portugal is in conformity with Article 8 para. 4*b*.

Article 11 — Right to protection of health

Paragraph 1 – Removal of the causes of ill-health

The Committee takes note of the information in the Portuguese report on the Charter, the 1997 report to the World Health Organisation[1] and the Ministry of Health Internet site.[2]

State of health of the population – general indicators

Life expectancy and main causes of mortality

The Committee observes from the OECD statistics[3] that life expectancy at birth for women has risen from 78 years in 1992 to 78.8 in 1997 and for men from 70.7 in 1992 to 71.6 in 1997. However, Eurostat statistics[4] show that women's life expectancy remains below the average for the countries of the European Union and the European Economic Area (the European average was 80.6 in 1996) and that men's life expectancy is by far the lowest of these countries.

According to the report, the main causes of death are circulatory diseases (40% of deaths in 1998, 20% attributable to cerebro-vascular conditions), followed by cancers (21%).

The Committee observes from the 1995 Eurostat data that deaths from cerebro-vascular diseases were the highest among the European Union countries and 2.5 times higher than the average (167 deaths per 100,000 women, compared with an average of 67.9, and 212.8 per 100,000 men, compared with 84).

The same applies to the number of deaths from sugar diabetes (*mellitus*), which have more than doubled since 1975 and are nearly twice the European average. The report states that reducing diabetis mellitus is now a public health priority and that significant steps have been taken to improve the care of diabetics and improve the training of those looking after them.

---

[1] *Highlights on Health in Portugal* (Internet site of the WHO European regional Office: www.who.dk).

[2] www.min-saude.pt

[3] OECD, *Health Data* 1999.

[4] Eurostat Yearbook , *A statistical eye on Europe,* 1988-1998 data.

The Committee finds that, in contrast to the general trend in Europe, the number of diagnosed AIDS cases and the number of deaths from AIDS continued to rise during the reference period, before finally falling. The report notes that under an order of 1996, antiretroviral treatments are provided free of charge and without restrictions. The Committee hopes that these measures will have significant effects in the coming years and defers reaching a conclusion to the next examination of Article 11.

Infant and maternal mortality

According to the Eurostat statistics, the infant mortality rate in Portugal fell steeply during the reference period, from 9.3 per 1,000 live births in 1992 to 6.0 in 1998. The rate varies widely from region to region, with the highest rates recorded in the Alentejo region. Nevertheless, the Committee notes that the rate remains higher than the average for the countries of the European Union and the European Economic Area (5.3 in 1997). Infant mortality is an avoidable risk, which countries must bring under control to comply with Article 11 of the Charter. It advises the Portuguese authorities that trends in the infant mortality rate will be critical for assessing the situation and strongly encourages them to pursue their efforts to secure an outcome as close as possible to zero.

The Committee notes that the rate of maternal mortality continues to decline (6.3 per 100,000 live births over the 1995-97 period, compared with an average rate of 8.3 for 1992-94), and that Portugal is now at the European average.

Health care system

Access to health care

Since 1979, there has been a national network of hospitals and health centres, the SNS, financed from taxes. In principle, it offers universal coverage. Civil servants and their dependents (about 13% of the population) are covered by their own health scheme, which is based on reimbursement and financed by the government, together with an employees' contribution (2.5% of salary). The banking and insurance sectors and a few public enterprises are also covered by specific contributory schemes. The SNS forms part of the Ministry of Health and for organisational, operational and management purposes is divided into regional and sub-regional authorities, which reflect the country's administrative divisions.

According to the aforementioned OECD statistics, total health spending represented 7.9% of GDP in 1997, compared with 7.2% in 1992. The proportion of total health spending attributable to the public sector, 60% in 1997, is by far the lowest of the OECD's European member countries.

Patients can choose their doctor from among the salaried health centre general practitioners in their local area. They must be registered on a particular doctor's list, which must include 1,500 patients. The Committee would like to know whether this list system guarantees universal access to a general practitioner.

The first report said that medical care was in theory free, but that this freedom from payment was relative since flat-rate charges were levied when patients used supplementary out-patient diagnostic and treatment facilities or medical care in hospital emergency units or health centres. Various groups of the population, such as children under 12, pregnant women and pensioners whose income is below the national minimum wage, are exempted from these payments.

There is no charge for persons admitted to the shared rooms (or individual rooms, if the doctor so recommends) of public hospitals, and other Ministry of Health approved establishments if there is a waiting list. However, patients who opt for an individual room or for a private hospital or clinic must bear the full cost.[1]

Depending on the type of illness, the SNS meets 100, 70 or 40% of the cost of medicines on the official health service list. The lower percentages are increased by 15% for pensioners whose income is below the national minimum wage.[2] According to the OECD statistics, the average rate of reimbursement of pharmaceutical products was 65% in 1997.

With reference to Recommendation No. R (99) 21 of the Committee of Ministers of the Council of Europe on criteria for the management of waiting lists and waiting times in health care, the Committee would like information on the reasons for waiting lists for admission to public hospitals in Portugal and on how these lists are managed (admission criteria and follow-up).

---

[1]European Commission, *Social Protection in the Member States of the European Union, Situation on 1 July 1999 and evolution,* Missoc.

[2]*Ibidem.*

Having noted in the aforementioned WHO report that private insurance systems are playing an increasingly important role, the Committee would welcome the Portuguese government's comments on the reasons for this trend and, if relevant, measures taken to ensure access to supplementary insurance.

Health professionals and equipment

The Committee observes from the OECD statistics that the total number of hospital beds continues to decline (40,700 in 1997) and that at 4.1, the bed ratio per 1,000 inhabitants is one of the lowest among the OECD's European countries. Acute hospital beds represent 82% of the total, and those allocated to hospital psychiatric care 17.5%. The private hospital sector has increased, representing around 22% of all hospital beds.

In 1997, the density of general practitioners and specialists per 1,000 inhabitants were 0.6 and 2.1 respectively. The density of dentists (0.3 per 1,000 inhabitants) is one of the two lowest among the OECD's European countries. The density of pharmacists (0.7 per 1,000 inhabitants) is in line with the European average.

In its previous conclusions, the Committee referred to significant regional variations in the provision of doctors and hospital beds. According to the OECD,[1] these variations are matched by regional variations in the state of health. During the XIII-5 supervision cycle, the government indicated that resolving these problems was a priority, that it had been decided to increase substantially state spending on health and that negotiations were under way with the various participants in the health sector to determine how the system's capacity to respond to needs could be increased. However, the Committee has not found anything in the report to suggest that a better geographical allocation of health facilities is one of the Portuguese government's priorities or that a general strategy to rectify the situation has been drawn up. It also notes that the public sector's share of total health spending has fallen since the last reference period (see above). The Committee stresses that this situation could cast doubts on the country's compliance with Article 11 para. 1 of the Charter and asks the government for its comments on this matter.

---

[1] *OECD Economic Surveys*, Portugal, 1998.

Conclusion

The Committee finds that certain indicators reveal negative developments in the health care system. However, it decides to defer its conclusion pending the information requested.

Paragraph 2 – Advisory and educational facilities

The Committee takes note of the information in the Portuguese report.

Developing a sense of individual responsibility

Health education in schools

The Committee has noted in previous reports that health education in schools may be included in the normal curriculum or form part of special health education projects, particularly ones aimed at drawing young persons' attention to the problems of drugs, alcohol and tobacco. School health teams (see below) take part in these activities and training programmes are organised for teachers. Since 1994, there has been a joint project with the Ministry of Education called the School Health Promotion Network.

According to the current report, during the reference period Resolution 15/98 of the Portuguese Assembly recommended that the government make sex education compulsory, that road safety education be incorporated into the curriculum and that an oral health promotion campaign be conducted among children and young persons.

The Committee considers that this information is too limited for it to assess the situation. It would therefore like the next report to include information on how, in practical terms, health education is taught in schools, whether it forms part of the curriculum throughout school life and how much is spent on it.

Public information and awareness-raising

The reports so far submitted show that campaigns to inform and educate either the public in general or specific target groups are conducted on the major problems of public health. In particular, the Committee takes note of the efforts to prevent drug abuse and smoking and to promote healthy life styles. It also notes that a sustained effort to prevent AIDS has continued with the inauguration in 1998 of a programme organised by the national anti-AIDS commission to increase people's knowledge of the disease and their sense of personal responsibility for preventing it.

According to the report, there were also campaigns during the reference period to educate the public about how to prevent *diabetis mellitus*, particularly through the publication of a diabetics' guide, and to improve road safety, with a significant contribution from the entire media, on the theme "priority for life". The Portuguese government has also decided to revive the campaign on the threat to health posed by alcohol, which has been somewhat superseded in recent years by the fight against drugs. A charter on citizens' rights and duties concerning health has also been published to make individuals more aware of their responsibilities in this area.

Counselling and screening

Children and adolescents

Medical treatment for children under 12 years of age is free.

Child and adolescent health clinics are held in health centres: nine sessions during the first year of life, three in the second, two between the ages of 2 and 6, two between 7 and 13, one around 14 or 15 and one around 17 or 18. The Committee wishes to know whether these clinics are also held in health centre outposts.

The health centres are responsible for carrying out school health activities. These take place throughout school life, at nursery level, during the three stages of basic education (6-14) and at upper secondary level (15-18). Medical examinations are carried out by school health teams, each made up of a doctor, a nurse, a psychologist and a medical auxiliary. As a minimum, the medical examinations include eyesight, hearing, dental hygiene, posture and psychomotor development tests. The report sets out the proportion of pupils examined in the 1996-97 school year: 38% in pre-school education, 53% at first stage (6-10) and 23% at second stage (10-12), that is 29% of the school population. The Committee considers that this proportion is low and notes that the proportion of children examined since the early 1990s has substantially declined. It would like an explanation for this trend and information on the total staffing of school health teams.

Rest of the population

The Committee notes the following changes during the reference period: establishment of an anonymous AIDS screening centre, and the extension to the whole country of the 1989 campaign conducted by the

Portuguese League against Cancer (LPCC), which used buses equipped with screening equipment to identify breast cancer. The Committee would like to know what other forms of screening have been carried out.

Conclusion

Subject to the information requested, the Committee concludes that the situation in Portugal is in conformity with Article 11 para. 2 of the Charter.

Paragraph 3 – Prevention of diseases

The Committee takes note of the changes in Portugal concerning the prevention of health risks in general and of specific diseases.

Policies on the prevention of avoidable risks

General

The Committee would like the next reports to indicate, as far as possible, the proportion of public authorities' budgets devoted to the main prevention policies listed below.

Reduction of environmental risks

Air pollution – In connection with local pollution, the Committee noted in the first report that legislative-Decree No. 352/90 established arrangements for protecting and monitoring the quality of the air, that air quality management is the responsibility of the quality of the environment directorate general, and that Ministerial Order No. 286/93 establishes threshold and guideline values and measurement methods for several of the main pollutants that harm air quality (sulphur dioxide, nitrogen dioxide, suspended fine particles and lead). The Committee would like to know what steps have been taken concerning ozone, carbon monoxide and benzene, and also what air quality surveillance and reporting machinery has been set up.

Turning to global pollution, the Committee notes that Portugal signed the United Nations Framework Convention on Climate Change (Rio de Janeiro, 1992) in 1993. Portugal has undertaken, *inter alia,* not to increase emissions of the main greenhouse gases by more than 27% for the period 2008-2012, in order to achieve the objectives set for the European Union at the 1997 Kyoto conference. It has also set itself the objective of a 40% reduction in carbonic gas emissions by 2010, taking 1990 as the baseline.

The Committee observes from OECD data[1] and from the second report on the application of the Rio Convention[2] that between 1990 and 1996, the result of Portugal's efforts to control man-made emissions of traditional pollutants, and greenhouse gases in particular, was either an increase or, at best, a very limited reduction in such emissions. The aforementioned report also considers that considerable progress is needed in terms of measuring and cataloguing emissions and defining objectives, but that the creation of a national climate commission could improve the situation, at least as far as greenhouse gases are concerned. The Committee will therefore keep a close watch on how the situation develops.

Asbestos – With reference to the general question concerning the measures taken to protect the health of persons exposed to asbestos (Conclusions XIII-4 p. 116), the current report states that legislative-decree no 228/94 limits the commercialisation and use of asbestos and products containing it and that industries have special responsibilities concerning the disposal in the air or water of waste and residues containing asbestos. The Committee does not consider this information sufficient to assess compliance with Article 11.3 (outside the work setting). It needs to know the scope of the restrictions on the commercialisation and use of asbestos, and stresses that compliance with Article 11 entails prohibition of or adequate restrictions on the use, production and sale of asbestos and products containing it. Measures must also be taken to monitor the presence of asbestos in buildings, particularly those used as dwellings. The Committee asks for this information to be included in the next report.

Ionising radiation – according to the first report, Portugal does not have any nuclear power stations and since 1981 cross-border radioactive pollution has been kept under surveillance as part of the Portuguese-Spanish agreement on the safety of frontier nuclear plants. The other radiation exposure risks are covered by the following regulations: legislative-Decree No. 348/89, as applied by legislative-decree no 9/90, takes account of Euratom directives 836/80, 466/84 and 467/84; regulatory-Decree No. 3/92 increases protection against radiation used

---

[1] *OECD Environmental Data,* 1999 Compendium.

[2] FCCC/IDR.2/POR 20 October 1999, consulted on the United Nations site on the Convention (www.unfccc.de)

for the purposes of medical diagnosis, treatment or research, in toys and in foodstuffs. Legislative-Decree No. 36/95 of 14 February 1995 establishes the public's right to be informed about health protection measures in the event of radioactive risk. A national radiation protection commission has been established. The Committee would like to know whether Portuguese regulations have been amended to take account of the recommendations of the International Commission on Radiological Protection (ICRP) and the standards set in Community Directive 96/29/Euratom laying down basic safety standards for the health protection of the general public and workers against the dangers of ionising radiation.

Noise – the first report stated that statutory standards in the field of noise prevention and abatement were set out in legislative-Decree No. 252/87, as amended in 1989. This laid down sound-proofing standards for new buildings, compulsory certification of equipment used in industrial plant and commercial premises, maximum sound levels for places of entertainment and standards for noise caused by road and rail traffic. The Committee would like this information to be updated if necessary and asks whether monitoring and sound measuring equipment is currently available.

Housing hygiene

According to the first report, in conjunction with the World Health Organisation (WHO) and the United Nations Development Programme (UNDP), the Ministry of Health had set up a project on housing hygiene aimed at identifying the most serious problems in this field and drawing up further regulations. The Committee would like to be informed of the outcome of this initiative, and in particular of the methods used to inspect and monitor housing hygiene.

Food safety

In view of the threat to health represented by diseases related to food and the recent outbreaks of such diseases in particular the new variation of the Creutzfeldt-Jakob disease, as well as the emergence of new food products derived from biotechnology, the Committee has decided to look at food safety measures in all states parties to the Charter. It recalls that under Article 11 states have a responsibility to ensure a high degree of safety in this area for their populations. Referring in particular to the resolution adopted by the 53rd World

Health Assembly in May 2000 on food safety[1] and while recognising the relevance of international strategies, the Committee considers that in order to comply with the Charter in this field, states must set legal norms at the national level regarding food hygiene taking into account scientific data, and establish and maintain mechanisms for monitoring compliance with these norms throughout the food chain, develop, implement and up-date systematic prevention measures, notably by way of labelling, as well as monitor the occurrence of food-borne diseases.

The Committee has taken note in the first report of the bodies responsible for inspecting food products (the inspectorate general of economic activities and the institute for the protection of food production, in conjunction with the food quality laboratory, and the health authorities, in conjunction with the national institute of health). It would like the next report to include information on the other aspects referred to above so that it can assess the situation when it next examines Article 11.

Measures to combat smoking and alcoholism

Smoking – The Committee stresses the importance of measures against smoking in meeting the requirements of Article 11 of the Charter. It recalls that smoking, a major cause of avoidable death in developed countries (in Europe 30% of deaths from cancer are attributable to smoking), is associated with a wide range of diseases (cardiac and circulatory diseases, cancers, pulmonary diseases etc.). Smoking kills one adult in ten throughout the world. The World Health Organisation (WHO) forecasts an increase of up to one in every six deaths by 2030,[2] which is more than the figure for any other cause of death. The Committee also notes that WHO is drawing up a convention on measures to combat smoking and points out that WHO, as part of the Health for All campaign, has set a target for European countries of raising the proportion of non-smokers in the population to at least 80% and protecting non-smokers against involuntary exposure to tobacco smoke.[3]

The relevant Portuguese legislation bans smoking in certain public places (Act No. 28/88), controls smoking on public transport, estab-

---

[1]WHO Internet site : www.who.int

[2] World Health Report 1999.

[3] WHO, Health Objectives for All – Health Policies in Europe, September 1991.

lishes maximum nicotine and tar levels in cigarettes and makes all tobacco products carry a notice on the risk of smoking to health, and prohibits tobacco advertising on national commercial television channels and ones with their headquarters in Portugal, other than in motor and motorcycle events in European and world championships. The government also increases duties on tobacco products every year. The Committee notes that the government's 1998-2002 action plan to prevent smoking has the objective of increasing the number of 10 to 24 year old non-smokers by 10%. It considers this to be a very positive initiative but asks whether it can be achieved in the absence of a ban on young people smoking and on the sale of tobacco products to young persons. It would like to be informed of the government's intentions in this regard. The next report should also indicate how it is intended to ensure compliance with the legislation.

The Committee finds that the results of the anti-smoking campaign are not totally convincing since the number of cigarettes consumed per person per year has increased since 1988 and is higher than the average for the European Union and European Economic Area countries (1,681, compared with a European average of 1,646 in 1997)[1].

Alcohol – According to the previous report, legislation was intended to reduce the incidence of drink-driving, the sale of alcoholic drinks to young persons aged under 16 and alcohol advertising. The Committee considers that this information is not sufficiently detailed. It would therefore like further clarification in the next report.

It emerges from the Eurostat statistics that consumption of pure alcohol in Portugal has risen continuously since 1988, particularly among the young and women, and is one of the highest in the European Union and European Economic Area countries (11.2 litres per person aged over 15 per year, compared with a European average of 9.4 in 1997). The Committee would welcome the government's comments on this subject.

The policy of controlling the supply of alcohol is clearly insufficient to reduce the level of alcohol consumption and thus the scale of the problems linked to alcohol, in accordance with Article 11 of the Charter. The Committee therefore urges the Portuguese authorities to strengthen the policy, and if necessary the legislation, and will reach a conclusion at its next examination of Article 11.

---

[1] *Eurostat yearbook - A statistical eye on Europe*, 1988-1998 data.

Drugs – The Committee notes that significant efforts continued to be made during the reference period and that outside the reference period a national anti-drugs policy has been drawn up and a Portuguese drugs and addiction institute established. More information will be supplied in the next report.

Prophylactic measures

Epidemiological surveillance

The reports so far received show that Portugal has a monitoring and surveillance system for numerous communicable diseases and that where there is a risk of epidemic special measures and surveys may be introduced.

The Committee notes in the current report that co-ordination machinery was established in 1999, with the establishment of a national commission for co-ordinating epidemiological surveillance and approving epidemiological surveillance priorities. Portugal also takes part in the European Network for Epidemiological Surveillance and control of communicable diseases and has its own "appropriate early warning and response system".

Immunisation

Vaccinations under the national vaccination programme are compulsory and free. These cover diphtheria, tetanus, whooping cough, poliomyelitis, tuberculosis, mumps, measles and rubella. The Committee notes the vaccine take-up rates for 1997 as shown in the report: 97.4% for diphtheria, tetanus and poliomyelitis, 96% for mumps, measles and rubella and 86% for tuberculosis. It also emerges from the WHO "Portugal Immunisation Profile"[1] that there is 95% vaccine cover against Hib meningitis and 64% against hepatitis B.

Conclusion

Pending receipt of the information requested, particularly regarding anti-smoking and alcohol misuse policies, the Committee concludes that the situation in Portugal is in conformity with Article 11 para. 3 of the Charter.

---

[1]www.who.int/vaccines-surveillance/

Article 14 — The right to benefit from social welfare services

Paragraph 1 – Provision or promotion of social welfare services

The Committee takes note of the information contained in the Portuguese report.

Categories of services

The report states that Order No. 407/98 issued jointly by the Ministry of Health and the Ministry of Labour and Solidarity sets out new guidelines for integrated and targeted social services and health care for persons in a state of dependency. The aim of the guidelines is to implement a comprehensive model of provision of health care and social services which will involve all the different actors in the field and utilise more fully the existing resources while respecting the institutional competencies at regional and local level. The target group consists of persons in a state of physical, mental or social dependency and the services provided fall in three categories : social support (*appui social*), continuing health care (*soins de santè continus*) and integrated services (*réponses intégrées*).

The Committee notes the statistical information on the number of social services institutions (creches, kindergartens, daycare centres, residential homes, home help facilities, etc.), beneficiaries and staff. It observes that overall the figures increased slightly in the period covered (from 1996 to 1997).

The Committee further notes that Legislative Decree No. 133-A/97 establishes a new legal framework for the provision of private non-profit social services. It asks that the next report contain more information on the types of social services provided by private institutions and on their importance in quantitative terms.

Access to services

As regards geographical distribution of social services, the Committee notes the figures on social services institutions broken down by region, but it nevertheless asks whether in the Government's view these figures demonstrate that all social services are uniformly accessible throughout the territory of Portugal.

The Committee also asks whether there exists any length of residence requirement for nationals of other Contracting Parties asking for social services.

Supervision and quality of services

In reply to the Committee's question on supervision of the quality of social services, the report states that pursuant to Legislative Decree No. 115/98 it is incumbent on the General Inspectorate of the Ministry of Labour and Solidarity (IGMTS) to ensure inspection and auditing of institutions providing social services, both public and private. In fulfilling this task IGTMS focuses *inter alia* on operational aspects of the facilities (capacity, installations, hygiene), on the service delivery, including the participation of the users, on the personnel (quantity and quality of human resources) and on problems and malfunctions indicated by users and/or personnel. Where necessary, IGTMS will propose measures to improve the situation. In 1997 and 1998 IGTMS carried out 148 and 140 inspections respectively which were followed up by 123 and 118 audits, respectively. The majority of the inspections carried out in 1997 related to old age homes. In 1998 a nation-wide audit of children's homes was carried out totalling 251 inspection visits.

The Committee asks that the next report provide details of measures taken in pursuance of IGTMS' supervisory activities, such as recommendations, fines, and closing of facilities, if applicable.

Funding of services

According to the report expenditure by Social Security on social services increased steadily during the reference period, approximately from 96 million escudos (PTE) in 1996 to 120 million PTE in 1998, an increase of about 24%. It asks to continue receiving information on total expenditure as well as a break down according to categories of services. It notes in this respect the figures on the financial contributions of Social Security per beneficiary and per month for the different types of services.

Conclusion

Pending receipt of the information requested, the Committee concludes that the situation in Portugal is in conformity with Article 14 para. 1 of the Charter.

Paragraph 2 – Public participation in the establishment and maintenance of social welfare services

The Committee notes from the Portuguese report that a new legal framework for voluntary work was established during the reference period in the form of Act No. 71/98. Outside the reference period Legislative Decree No. 389/99 containing implementing measures in application of the act was adopted. According to the report the act is based on the general principle that the state recognises the social importance of voluntary work as an expression of the free exercise of an active and socially concerned citizenship.

The Committee takes note of the definitions of voluntary work and voluntary organisations contained in Act No. 71/98 and of the governing principles for voluntary work: solidarity, participation, co-operation, complementarity, gratuity, responsibility and convergence. It wishes to be informed of the results of the implementation of the new legislation.

The report states that the number of private non-profit organisations providing social services increased during the reference period, from 2,562 in 1996 to 2,874 in 1998.

The Committee asks that the next report contain examples with details of the social services provided by private or voluntary organisations. It also requests information on how individuals, including the beneficiaries of social services, may participate in the establishment and maintenance of social services. Finally, it asks to receive information on total expenditure allocated on an annual basis to private and voluntary social services in Portugal.

Pending receipt of the information requested, the Committee concludes that the situation in Portugal is in conformity with Article 14 para. 2 of the Charter.

Article 17 — The right of mothers and children to social and economic protection

The Committee notes the information contained in the Portuguese report.

Establishment of parentage and adoption

New legislation on adoption took effect during the reference period. The legislation, *inter alia,* sought to make the adoption process easier.

Children in public care

Children may only be separated from their parents where their parents fail to perform their fundamental duties towards them and then only by judicial decision. Even where children have been separated from their parents, the parents can still retain some parental authority.

Children deprived of their family (due to ill-treatment, etc.) may be placed firstly, in emergency units, which care for children in a crisis situation for up to 48 hours. There are 11 such units with 59 places in Portugal.

Temporary reception centres also exist for children who are unable to remain within their family. Children may only remain in these centres for six months and then must either return to their families, be placed with a foster family (or be placed for adoption) or be placed in an institution. These centres may only accommodate a maximum of 12 children at a time. There are 42 temporary reception centres with 592 places in Portugal. In 1998 these centres cared for 839 children.

Children who cannot be returned to their family are placed wherever possible with a foster family. In 1997 there were 3,399 foster families fostering 4,887 children. If no foster family can be found, a child will be placed in an institution as a last resort.

According to the report there were approximately 13,500 children living in institutions in 1998. A study on this group of children, was carried out and showed, *inter alia* that this group of children were not receiving an adequate level of vocational training. Measures have subsequently been taken to remedy this. The Committee wishes to be informed of any other conclusions of the study on children in institutions, as well as information on the types of institutions that exist.

The Committee wishes to be informed as to whether the number of children in institutions mentioned above includes the children in institutions such as Casa Pia and the children in institutions in Lisbon.

The Committee wishes to be informed on how many children are removed from their families, how many placed with a foster family and how many placed in an institution for every year of the reference period. It also wishes to know the total number of children living in institutions (orphans, homeless children etc.).

It further wishes to be informed as to whether there is any body charged with monitoring care in institutions and whether there is any specific procedure for complaining about the care and treatment in them and about the conditions under which an institution may interfere with a child's property, mail, personal integrity and the right to meet with persons close to him or her.

Protection from ill-treatment and abuse

During the reference period a programme on the protection of children at risk was established. The Committee wishes to be informed of all developments arising from this programme.

The Committee recalls that an emergency help line exists for children ("SOS for abused children") subject to ill-treatment or sexual abuse. This help line is operational throughout Portugal.

The Committee notes the statistics supplied on the ill-treatment and sexual abuse of children. It notes that the number of cases of sexual abuse reported by hospitals increased again during the reference period as did the number of cases leading to interventions recorded by the emergency help line for children.

The Committee wishes to receive information on the different bodies, public and private responsible for protecting children from ill-treatment and sexual abuse, and how these services are coordinated.

The Committee wishes to know whether legislation prohibits all forms of corporal punishment of children, in schools, in institutions, in the home and elsewhere.

Children and the law – Young Offenders

Children under 16 years of age are not considered to be criminally liable for any crimes they may commit. Article 19 of the Penal Code provides that children under 16 years of age may not be imprisoned. If a child under 16 years of age commits an offence the child is subject to the provisions of the Act on the Organisation of Care for Minors (OTM). This provides for the application of supervisory measures of protection, assistance and education not only to children who have committed a criminal offence, but also to children who are begging, involved in prostitution, drug or alcohol abuse, etc. Children in this age group who commit a criminal offence, may be questioned by a judge, if over 12 years of age, they may be brought before the youth courts (or in rural areas before the district courts), if under 12 years they usually go before protection boards, to decide what measures should be taken. Measures which may be imposed on minors under 16 years of age include non-custodial supervision ("educational placement"), placement in an apprentice or work scheme, placement in an appropriate family or in a public or private educational institution, admonishment, entrustment to parents or as a measure of last resort placement in a youth care centre.

The Committee wishes to receive information on the number of children under 16 years placed in a youth centre, as well as on the total number of children subject to the OTM as a result of committing a criminal offence.

Young people over the age of 16 years are tried by the courts of general jurisdiction, and the provisions of the Code of Penal Procedure apply to them. There are no special provisions governing the conditions under which they can be arrested by the police or placed in pre-trial detention. The Committee wishes to know how many persons aged between 16 and 18 years of age are placed in pre-trial detention, and what is the maximum period.

Offenders under 21 years of age may have their sentence reduced on account of their age. The Committee wishes to know how many persons between 16 and 18 years are sentenced to a term of imprisonment and what is the maximum length of such sentences. It also wishes to receive information on alternative punishments which may be available for this group. Finally the Committee wishes to receive confirmation that young offenders are not held in prisons with adult prisoners.

Conclusion

The Committee concludes that the situation in Portugal is in conformity with Article 17 of the Charter.

Article 18 — The right to engage in a gainful occupation in the territory of other Contracting Parties

Paragraph 1 – Applying existing regulations in a spirit of liberality

Foreign population and migratory movements

The Committee notes that 175,288 foreigners were lawfully resident in Portugal in 1997 (88,000 of them being members of the workforce), comprising some 1.8% of the total population of 10 million. European Union nationals represent one third of the foreign population[1].

Portugal is traditionally a country of emigration, but the Committee observes that migratory movements have been reversed, and that Portugal has been a country of immigration since 1993 with a regularly increasing number of entries.

Work permits

There are several documents that authorise their holders to engage in a paid occupation in Portugal:

– if a foreign national wishes to engage in a temporary paid occupation, he or she has to obtain a "work visa" (according to the Portuguese terminology), of which there are various kinds. Work visa I covers sport, visa II relates to the performing arts, visa III is for the provision of services and visa IV for paid employment. They are all initially valid for two years, and are renewable for further two-year periods. Holders also need residence visas;

– if a foreign national wishes to engage in a permanent paid occupation, he or she must obtain a residence permit, either temporary (valid for two years, and renewable) or permanent (of unlimited validity, requiring renewal every five years).

Relevant statistics

The report includes information about the number of applications for registration of employment contracts (see conclusion under Article 18

[1]OECD, *Trends in International Migration*, Sopemi, 1999 edition.

para. 2) during the reference period, it being understood that nationals of the European Union or of the European Economic Area do not need to go through this formality.

The Committee notes that there are very small numbers of applications from nationals of the Contracting Parties subject to these formalities (namely those of Poland, Turkey and Slovakia; no applications were recorded from nationals of Malta or Cyprus). The 1998 total was seven employment contracts registered. It nonetheless regrets that the report does not state how many applications were made by nationals of the countries concerned.

The Committee notes the total number (no distinction being made on the basis of nationality) of contracts in respect of which applications were made for registration and refused on grounds either of failure to comply with the formalities (see conclusion under Article 18 para. 2) or of an unfavourable opinion from the Institute for the development and inspection of working conditions (IDICT) (see conclusion under Article 18 para. 3). It observes that the rate of refusal of applications for work visas (from all nationalities without distinction) rose during the reference period, from the 1996 figure of 24% to 31% in 1998. The Committee is aware, however, that these figures predate the abolition of the quota of 10% of foreigners for enterprises which have more than five employees.

Conclusion

The Committee concludes that the situation in Portugal is in conformity with Article 18 para. 1 of the Charter.

Paragraph 2 – Simplifying existing formalities and reducing dues and taxes

Administrative formalities

Issue of work permits

The Committee refers to its previous conclusion (Conclusions XIII-5, p. 243) as regards the administrative formalities required in order to obtain the various work documents.

It also points out that, in its last report on this provision, the Portuguese Government stated that the formalities required to obtain authorisation to engage in a self-employed occupation were the same as for nationals: foreign nationals were required to appear in the trade register, make a declaration of occupation and prove that they held the necessary qualifications for the exercise of the occupation concerned.

The Committee notes that, during the reference period, a certain amount of liberalisation occurred. Under Act No. 20/98 on Employment of Foreign Workers, for instance, employers are no longer required to register employment contracts (registration was subject to payment of a fee), but may simply deposit contracts, at no charge, with the Institute for the development and inspection of working conditions (IDICT). The Committee also notes that, where nationals of Contracting Parties to the Charter are concerned, straightforward notification to the IDICT in writing of the signing of an employment contract is sufficient, according to the report.

Conditions for renewal

The report states that applications for renewal of a temporary residence permit have to be submitted to the Foreign and Frontiers Service by a deadline 30 days before expiry of its validity. During the renewal procedure, the aforementioned service checks whether the conditions for issue are still being complied with (these are that the applicant must have means of subsistence, have proper accommodation arrangements and comply with Portuguese law). The Committee deduces that renewal of such a document is not a matter of simplified formalities in comparison with the first application for a temporary residence permit. It also notes that the renewal of residence permits (temporary or permanent in comparison with the first application) is subject to payment of a fee of 1,000 escudos (PTE).

Work and residence permits

The Committee wishes the next report to specify whether work and residence visa applications come under one and the same procedure.

Time necessary for obtaining work permits

The Committee wishes the next report to indicate the average time taken between submission of an application for a work permit and the issuing of that permit. It also wishes to obtain the same information about permits issued for self-employment.

Chancery dues and other charges

The information given in the report on this subject is not very clear. The Committee asks the Portuguese Government to explain in which cases the sum of 1,000 PTE payable for the issue of a work and residence visa is applied, as the report states elsewhere that work and residence visas are issued subject to separate fees of, respectively, 13,000 PTE and 16,000 PTE in 1998 (as compared to the 1994-95 figures of 10,000 and 12,000 to 15,000 PTE respectively). The Committee notes that the sum to be paid for a permanent residence permit is high (40,000 PTE). The Committee wishes to know how payment of such a sum is justified.

Conclusion

Pending receipt of the information requested, especially concerning chancery dues, the Committee defers its conclusion.

Paragraph 3 – Liberalising regulations

Access to the national labour market

The Committee notes the repeal of the legislation (Legislative Decree No. 97/77, of 17 March 1977) which laid down that the number of foreign nationals employed in enterprises with five or more staff could not exceed 10% of the workforce: since May 1998, under the new Employment of Foreign Workers Act (Act No. 20/98), foreigners lawfully resident in Portugal have been able to work in Portugal without being made subject to an employment quota.

A work visa for engaging in a paid occupation is issued only if a favourable opinion is given by the Institute for the development and inspection of working conditions (IDICT). The Committee notes in this context that this opinion is always negative if the application for a work visa relates to an employment sector affected by unemployment. The employment situation being a decisive criterion for obtaining a work visa, the Committee wishes to know how such a situation is taken into account and whether a foreign national given this as a reason for refusal has the right to appeal against the refusal of a work visa.

The Committee noted in Conclusions XIII-3, p. 395, that certain government service occupations were prohibited to foreign nationals in cases "where the exercise of authority predominates" (Opinion No. 22/30 of the Principal State Prosecutor). The Committee wishes the next report to specify the occupations concerned as well as the reasons which justify this prohibition.

Exercise of the right to employment

The Committee noted in its previous conclusion that work visas were issued for the exercise of the intended paid occupation. It also noted then that anyone holding a residence permit could engage in waged or self-employed work, anywhere on national territory without any geographical restriction, and could change occupation or place of work. The Committee notes in this context that a residence permit may now be obtained after ten consecutive years of lawful residence in Portugal (compared to the previous requirement of twenty years). The Committee agrees that this is a positive development. It nonetheless takes the view that the requirement for ten years of continuous residence is still an excessively strict one and could be reduced.

Consequence of job loss

The Committee notes from another source[1] that a person finding him or herself out of work is not necessarily denied renewal of his or her residence permit for that reason alone, provided that he or she does not constitute a financial burden on the community. Renewal is in practice dependent on fulfilment of the criteria relating to means of subsistence and accommodation arrangements. It seems to the Committee that these conditions would be difficult to meet in the absence of regular earnings paid under an employment contract. In order to enable it to assess the situation accurately, the next report confirms that foreign nationals have a right to unemployment benefits on the same footing as nationals. It asks if the exhaustion of this right may lead to the non-renewal of the residence permit.

Conclusion

Pending receipt of the requested information concerning the consequences of job loss on residence permits, the Committee concludes that the situation is in conformity with Article 18 para. 3 of the Charter.

---

[1] *Migrant workers*, International Labour Conference, 87th session, 1999.

Paragraph 4 – The right of nationals to leave the country

As the situation remains unchanged, the Committee concludes that the situation in Portugal is in conformity with Article 18 para. 4.

Chapter 13 – Conclusions concerning Articles 7, 8, 11, 14, 17 and 18 of the Charter in respect of Spain

Article 7 — The right of children and young persons to protection

Paragraph 1 – Minimum age of admission to employment

The Committee notes from the Spanish Report that there was no change during the reference period in the legal situation which it previously considered not to be in conformity with Article 7 para. 1 of the Charter. The Spanish report maintains that the exclusion of work in family enterprises from the scope of the Workers' Statute (Article 1.3c)) is based on the particular nature of such work. As the Committee has recently had the opportunity to recall, Article 7 para. 1 of the Charter applies to "all economic sectors and all types of enterprises, including family businesses, as well as all forms of work, whether paid or not."[1] Accordingly, the situation in Spain remains in violation of this provision of the Charter.

With respect to the issue of self-employment among minors, the report maintains that even in the absence of a clear statutory prohibition on the exercise of such activity by minors, it may be deduced from the rules concerning majority in the Civil Code and the terms of the General Law on Social Security that no person under 18 years may be self-employed. The Committee considers that the legislation cited, especially the latter, is not intended to limit access to employment or work. Rather, its objective is to ensure that self-employed workers are covered by social security schemes. It therefore considers that the situation remains in violation of the Charter on this point too.

Information is provided in the report on the activities of the Labour Inspectorate in supervising the application of the law on minors' work. It appears to the Committee from these data that the number of inspections is modest. It asks the Spanish Government to comment on the level of inspection. Furthermore, the Committee requests information or estimates on the number of children who work illegally in Spain.

---

[1]Para. 27, Decision on the Merits, Complaint No. 1/1998, International Commission of Jurists against Portugal.

The Committee concludes that the situation in Spain is not in conformity with Article 7 para. 1 of the Charter since no minimum age of admission to employment applies to work within family enterprises, or to access to self-employment.

Paragraph 2 – Higher minimum age in certain occupations

According to the Spanish report, there were no changes in the legal situation during the reference period. The Committee takes note of the data provided on labour inspection, and the number of cases detected of minors performing work prohibited by law during the reference period. It wishes to receive updated information in the next report, as well as information on the rate of occupational accidents and diseases among young workers.

The Committee concludes that the situation in Spain is in conformity with Article 7 para. 2 of the Charter.

Paragraph 3 – Safeguarding the full benefit of compulsory education

The Committee notes from the Spanish report that there have been no changes in the legal situation which it previously found not to be in conformity with the Charter. Referring to its conclusion under Article 7 para. 1, the Committee concludes that the situation is not in conformity with Article 7 para. 3 of the Charter, since Spanish law does not ensure that children who work within a family enterprise are not deprived of the full benefit of their education. Furthermore, since no minimum age is laid down for access to self-employment, the Committee concludes that on this ground too the situation in Spain is not in conformity with Article 7 para. 3 of the Charter.

Paragraph 4 – Working hours for young workers and apprentices

The Spanish report recalls that the minimum age of admission to employment provided for by the Workers' Statute is 16 years and that compulsory education extends until the age of 16. Moreover, according to information previously made available by the Spanish Government, the only exceptions to this prohibition of the employment of children under 16 concern participation in performances or other sporting or cultural events. In such cases authorisation must be granted by the child's parents and the Labour Inspectorate.

However, the report confirms that the Workers' Statute does not apply to work in family businesses which is not based on an employment relationship as defined in the Statute. Therefore, as no legislation exists which limits the number of working hours of young workers under the age of 16 who are members of the family of their employers and who are not registered as employees, the Committee can only conclude again that the situation is not in conformity with the Charter.

No new information is provided as regards the self-employment of children under 18 years of age, which is not prohibited and for which there is no limitation on working hours, which is not in conformity with the Charter

The Committee concludes that the situation in Spain is not in conformity with Article 7 para. 4 of the Charter.

Paragraph 5 – Fair remuneration for young workers and apprentices

The Spanish report states that Royal Decree 2199/95 established the minimum wage for 1996 for young workers under 18 at 77% of the adult minimum wage compared to 66% in 1995. The remuneration of young workers was further improved by Royal Decree 2015/97 which fixes a minimum wage for all workers regardless of age. The gross minimum wage for 1998 was thus set at 68,040 Spanish Pesetas (PTA) per month. Given 14 payments of this amount per year, the monthly average was 79,380 PTA. The Committee notes that the adult minimum wage rose between 2.1% and 3.5% annually during the years 1996-1998.

The report also states that the situation of apprentices has improved following the entry into force of Royal Decree-Law 8/97. Under the new regulation, apprentice wages will be fixed by collective agreement, but the wage agreed upon cannot be lower than the minimum wage, in proportion to time worked (Spanish law makes no provision for remuneration of time spent on vocational training, see the conclusion under Article 7 para. 6).

Notwithstanding the improvements for young workers which occurred during the reference period, the Committee recalls that it found the minimum wage for adults to be manifestly unfair and therefore not in conformity with Article 4 para. 1 of the Charter (Conclusions XIV-2 pp. 681-682). As noted above, the adult minimum wage only increased marginally during the period 1996-1998. The wage of young workers and apprentices is not in compliance with this provision of the Charter, if the reference wage, in this case the statutory minimum wage which applies to all workers, is not in conformity with Article 4 para. 1.

The Committee underlines that it requires information on the minimum or lowest wages of young workers and apprentices calculated net, i.e. after deduction of taxes and social security contributions. In addition, it needs information on starting wages or minimum wages of adult workers, also calculated net. Net calculations should be made for the case of a single person.

The Committee concludes that the situation in Spain is not in conformity with Article 7 para. 5 of the Charter.

Paragraph 6 – Treatment of the time spent in vocational training as forming part of the working day

The Committee again notes from the Spanish report that the right of workers to vocational training is recognised by Section 4.2b of the Workers' Statute, which implies *inter alia* that workers have the right to leave for the purpose of sitting exams. It also notes that pursuant to Section 34.3 of the Workers' Statute, workers who are minors may not perform more than eight hours work per day, including any time spent on training.

However, the report confirms that no specific provision is made, whether in the form of legislation or regulations, to ensure that the time spent in vocational training during normal working hours with the employer's consent is remunerated as such. The report states that the existing legal regulations are minimum norms, the scope of which may be improved through collective agreements or in individual employment contracts. The Committee observes that the report does not contain the requested information on the extent to which collective agreements, individual contracts, etc., provide for the remuneration of time spent on vocational training. It recalls that Article 33 applies, i.e. the benefits of Article 7 para. 6 must be enjoyed by the great majority (at least 80%) of the young workers concerned.

In the absence of information showing that Spain respects Article 7 para. 6, the Committee concludes that the situation is not in conformity with this provision of the Charter.

Paragraph 7 – Annual holiday of young persons under eighteen

The Committee notes from the report submitted by Spain that there have been no changes in the situation which it has previously considered to be satisfactory. It therefore concludes that the situation in Spain is in conformity with Article 7 para. 7 of the Charter.

Nevertheless, the Committee requests clarification as to whether the requirements of Article 7 para. 7 are met with respect to workers in family businesses, whose employment does not come within the scope of the Workers' Statute.

It also asks whether annual holidays of workers are suspended in the event of illness or accident during the holidays, so that the worker has the right to take time off at another time.

Paragraph 8 – Prohibition of night work for young persons under eighteen

The Spanish report does not contain the requested information demonstrating that the great majority of persons under 18 years are prohibited from doing night work. The Committee insists that the next report furnish the necessary information.

It also repeats its question on whether any derogations are possible to the prohibition of night work in the Workers' Statute and how many young workers are subject to such derogations.

In the absence of information demonstrating that Spain respects Article 7 para. 8, the Committee concludes that the situation is not in conformity with this provision of the Charter.

Paragraph 9 – Provision of regular medical control for young workers under eighteen

According to the Spanish report, it follows from the prohibition of minors performing unhealthy, hard, harmful or dangerous work (Section 7.2 of the Workers' Statute) that the employer is obliged to assess the work to be performed by young workers under 18. This principle is regulated by Law No. 31/95 on Prevention of Labour Risks. Under Section 22.1 of this law employers have the obligation to grant workers periodical medical check-ups "in relation to the inherent work risks". The Committee asks whether objective criteria exist as to when medical control should be carried out, or whether it is left solely to the discretion of the employer. It also asks to be informed of the intervals at which medical examinations are carried out. Finally, the Committee also wishes clarification as to the sectoral scope of Law 31/95, notably whether industrial family enterprises are covered.

The Committee has previously noted that, according to Section 178 para. 3 of the 1944 Act on Employment Contracts, pre-employment examinations are required for young workers aged under 18. It asks again how the implementation of this provision is ensured in practice.

However, as no legal provision guarantees the protection required under this provision of the Charter for young workers employed in family business who do not have the status of paid employees and young self-employed workers not covered by labour law, the Committee concludes that the situation in Spain is not in conformity with Article 7 para. 9 of the Charter.

Paragraph 10 – Special protection for children and young people from physical and moral dangers to which they are exposed

The Committee notes the information in the Spanish report on the measures taken to protect workers, those in a teaching relationship, etc., from sexual harassment.

The Committee wishes to be informed as to whether legislation prohibits the use of children in the sex industry, and to receive information on the supervisory system and sanctions that may accompany this prohibition.

The Committee concludes that the situation in Spain is in conformity with Article 7 para 10 of the Charter.

Article 8 — The right of employed women to protection

Paragraph 1 – Maternity leave

1. Right to maternity leave

The report from Spain states that Act 39/1999, which came into force outside the reference period, prescribes 16 weeks of maternity leave which the mother may elect to take before or after delivery. Six weeks are nevertheless to be taken obligatorily after delivery, during which time the mother is not allowed to work. This legislation is applicable to all categories of employees and to civil servants.

The report states that it is permissible under this new legislation, where both parents are employed, for all or some of the mother's postnatal leave to be relinquished to the father at the commencement of her maternity leave, unless her return to work would endanger her health. In such cases, the obligation to take six weeks of postnatal leave no longer applies.

The Committee reiterates that the purpose of Article 8 para. 1 is to afford women special protection in case of maternity, and to meet a more general interest of public health by protecting both mother and child. The twelve-week rest period, to be split into two parts preceding and following childbirth, should therefore be regarded as a minimum according to the letter of the Charter. The period of compulsory postnatal leave fixed at six weeks by the Committee (Conclusions VIII, p. 123) is also to be regarded as a minimum which cannot be waived.

The possibility for the mother to let the father take all or some of her six-week postnatal leave is therefore contrary to the Charter.

The Committee furthermore requests that the next report furnish information on the enforcement of the legislation in practice, indicating in particular the penalties prescribed for non-compliance and stating, if possible, the number of breaches recorded by the labour inspectors.

The Committee concludes that the situation in Spain was in conformity with this aspect of Article 8 para. 1 of the Charter during the reference period (1997-1998).

2. Right to adequate benefit

In Spain, the maternity allowance is payable throughout maternity leave to all women who are affiliated to social security when pregnant and have worked and paid contributions for 180 days during the five years preceding the time of delivery. The level of the allowance is 100% of the daily wage payable in the month preceding delivery. The Committee infers that no ceiling applies to the allowance.

In reply to a question from the Committee, the report indicates that women not fulfilling the aforementioned conditions and not entitled to maternity benefit nonetheless receive medical assistance during pregnancy and after delivery.

Article 8 para. 1 allows the right to payment of benefit to be subject to conditions such as a stipulated minimum period of contribution and/or employment. The Committee nevertheless reserves the right to verify the reasonableness of these conditions. In the present case it finds that a period of 180 days' contributions and employment during the five years previous to delivery is long and difficult to complete. This requirement may in effect deprive many women of the benefit of maternity allowances. The Committee therefore asks whether, apart from the medical assistance mentioned above, the workers concerned receive any other form of adequate benefit, and the applicable conditions. The Committee also asks if periods of unemployment are calculated as working time for the granting of maternity allowance.

Pending receipt of the information requested, the Committee defers its conclusion on this point.

Paragraph 2 – Illegality of dismissal during maternity leave

Prohibition of dismissal

The Spanish report indicates that according to the Spanish Constitution and consistent Constitutional Court case-law, dismissal on pregnancy-related grounds is discriminatory and therefore shall be deemed void.

It adds that Act 39/1999, which entered into force outside the reference period and which amends the Workers Statute, introduces new provisions according to which individual dismissal of female workers during their pregnancy and until the end of their maternity leave is prohibited (Title I, Article 7 para. 2 of the 1999 Act). The Committee requests that the next report clarifies what are the exceptions to this rule.

On the other hand, the report states that the provisions in question only prohibit individual dismissals. According to Article 51 of the Workers Statute, dismissals of pregnant women or of women in maternity leave, in the context of collective redundancy, are still not prohibited. Nevertheless such dismissals are only admitted following a previous administrative authorization.

The Committee takes note of the positive development concerning the prohibition of individual dismissal of women. However it notes that, contrary to the provisions of the Charter, pregnant women might be dismissed in the context of redundancy, no matter whether the undertaking has ceased to operate. In order to have a clear view of the situation, the Committee asks whether the company redundancy plan covers workers individually.

Furthermore, the report stresses that despite the absence of specific provisions in the Workers' Statute, the employer's right to terminate domestic workers' employment contracts, through "withdrawal" (*desistimiento*), before the normal expiry date and without alleging any motive, is subject to the same constitutional safeguards prohibiting dismissals based on sex discrimination. The Committee considers that this situation is contrary to Article 8 para. 2 of the Charter and that domestic workers must be given the same protection as all other workers.

Consequences of unlawful dismissal

Pursuant to Article 7 para. 2 of the 1999 Act, an unlawful dismissal is deemed void. This situation complies with Article 8 para. 2.

The Committee requests that the next report indicate the amount of compensation owed to unlawfully dismissed female employees who do not go back to their post, either because they do not wish to do so or because the undertaking has ceased to operate. It recalls that payment of such compensation, which is admitted as an exception, must be sufficient to deter the employer and compensate the employee.

As the Spanish report does not contain information with regard to this point, the Committee asks that the next report address the matter.

Conclusion

The Committee concludes that the situation in Spain is not in conformity with Article 8 para. 2 since domestic workers are not given the same protection as all other workers.

Paragraph 3 – Time off for nursing mothers

The Committee notes that women workers in Spain - including domestic employees, home-based workers and public employees - who breastfeed their babies are entitled, until the child is nine months old, to an hour-long work-break, which may be split into two periods (Section 37.4 of the Workers' Statute). The hour is regarded as working time and paid as such.

The technical amendments to this provision of the Workers' Statute under Law No. 39/1999 of 23 March 1995 do not affect this situation, which the Committee already considered to be in conformity with the Charter.

With regard to domestic workers, the report indicates that the relevant legislation is Royal Decree 1424/1985. In the absence of specific rules on breastfeeding in this decree, ordinary law (i.e. the Workers' Statute) applies "whenever this is compatible with the peculiarities stemming from the relationship's special kind". According to the report, this means that the entitlement to feeding breaks under the Workers' Statute extends to domestic workers.

The Committee repeats its request made in the last conclusion inviting the Government to indicate expressly within each report whether such incompatibilities had been noticed by the tribunals.

Pending receipt of the information requested, the Committee concludes that the situation in Spain is in conformity with Article 8 para. 3 of the Charter.

Paragraph 4 – Regulation of night work and prohibition of dangerous, unhealthy or arduous types of work for women

1. Regulation of night work for women in industrial jobs (Article 8 para. 4*a*)

The Committee takes note of the information provided in the Spanish report.

It concluded in its previous conclusion that the legislation governing night work in industrial employment complied with Article 8 para. 4*a* of the Charter (Conclusions XIII-4, p.114).

It notes from the present report that Act 31/1995 on the Prevention of Labour Risks introduced special rules on maternity protection. Risk assessment must include determining the nature, degree and duration of the exposure of pregnant women or women who have just given birth to agents, procedures and working conditions that may adversely affect the woman's or the foetus' health. If the assessment reveals a risk to the woman's health or safety, the employer must take the necessary steps to put an end to exposure to risk. These measures must include an end to night work and transfer to another work station. If this is not possible, sick leave must be granted.

The report supplies statistics on night work by women in industrial jobs: in 1998, for example, 145,500 women were regularly working at night (for at least 15 days a month).

The Committee considered in its previous conclusion that the regulations governing night work complied with this provision of the Charter. It notes that the regulations take satisfactory account of the situation of pregnant women, women who have recently given birth and nursing mothers. In order to have a full view of the situation, however, it asks that the next report indicate the cases in which night work is permitted, whether the authorisation of the Labour Inspectorate is required, or if, before introducing night work, the employer must consult with worker representatives.

The Committee asks that the next report provide information on practice and specify the penalties prescribed for breaches of the legislation.

Pending receipt of the information requested, the Committee defers its conclusion.

Article 11 — Right to protection of health

Paragraph 1 – Removal of the causes of ill-health

The Committee takes note of the information in the Spanish report on the Charter and in the 1998 report to the World Health Organisation (WHO).[1]

State of health of the population – General indicators

Life expectancy and principal causes of death

The Committee notes from OECD statistics[2] that life expectancy at birth has increased slightly, reaching 81.7 years for women and 74.4 years for men in 1996. These levels are slightly above average for European Union and European Economic Area countries.

Cardiovascular diseases are the main cause of death, followed by cancer. The Committee notes that the death rates for these diseases are below the European average, but that the male death rate for lung cancer is above average and the death rate for cardiovascular diseases is particularly high among young people.[3] The Committee would like the government to comment on the reasons for this state of affairs.

The Committee observes that the number of Aids cases diagnosed annually (morbidity rate) declined during the reference period from 7,197 in 1994 (a record total) to 3,713 in 1997. It notes, however, that the number of new Aids cases per million inhabitants is by far the highest among the European OECD countries (160 in 1997) and that in 1995, the mortality rate for Aids was nearly three times higher than the average for European Union and European Economic Area countries. The Committee will therefore pay close attention to developments in the situation and requests information on conditions of the access to antiretroviral treatment.

---

[1] *Highlights on Health in Spain* (WHO European regional office website: www.who.dk).

[2] OECD, *Health Data* 1999.

[3] Eurostat Yearbook: *A statistical eye on Europe,* 1988-1998 data.

Infant and maternal mortality

According to Eurostat data, the infant mortality rate fell during the reference period, from 7.1 deaths per 1,000 live births in 1992 to 5.6 in 1997. The Committee notes, however, that the improvement in the situation over the past decade has been much less marked than in other European Union and European Economic Area countries and that the rate is now above the average (5.3 in 1997). The Committee emphasises that infant mortality is an avoidable risk, which countries must bring under control to comply with Article 11 of the Charter. It advises the Spanish authorities that trends in the infant mortality rate will be central to assessing whether the situation complies with the Charter, and strongly encourages them to pursue their efforts to achieve a result as close as possible to zero.

The Committee notes that the maternal mortality rate is still low (slightly over 3 deaths per 100,000 live births during the 1992-1995 period).

Health care system

Access to health care

The General Health Act 14/86 set up a national health service, which is run either by the Autonomous Communities or by the National Institute of Health (INSALUD) in those communities which have not yet been given responsibility for health matters. 99.5% of the population is covered by the health system. The system is mainly funded by taxes (80%).

According to the above-mentioned OECD statistics, total health expenditure represented 7.4% of GDP in 1997. The proportion of total health expenditure attributable to the public sector has declined and stood at 76% in 1997 (as against 78.9% in 1992).

Medical care provided under the national health service by registered general practitioners, medical centres and approved hospitals is free of charge to all persons resident in Spain who are covered by the general scheme or a special scheme.

Prescription medicine is refundable to a value of 60%. However, medicines on a special list are subject to a refund of only 10%, to a maximum value of 439 pesetas (PTA). The following categories are exempt from contributions: pensioners, hospital patients, residents over 65 years of age with insufficient resources and conscientious objectors performing social work.[1] According to OECD statistics, the average rate of reimbursement of pharmaceutical products was 75% in 1997.

The Committee wishes to know whether waiting lists have been introduced for hospital care, and, if so, would like information on how they are managed.

The Committee wishes to know whether evaluations of the functioning in practice of the national health service have been carried out and if so it asks to know the results.

Health professionals and equipment

The Committee notes from the aforementioned OECD data that the total number of hospital beds has continued to decline (154,644 in 1997) and that the bed ratio per 1,000 inhabitants (3.9) is one of the three lowest among the European OECD countries. Private hospitals account for approximately 30% of all beds.

The Committee notes from Eurostat statistics that in 1996, the number of doctors per 100,000 inhabitants was 421, one of the highest ratios among European Union and European Economic Area countries. The same applies to the number of pharmacists (one per 1,000 inhabitants), however, the ratio of dentists (37.9 per 100,000 inhabitants) is one of the lowest.

Conclusion

The Committee observes that the situation in Spain with respect to Article 11 para. 1 of the Charter presents several weak points both as far as the state of health of the population is concerned (mortality due to AIDS and infantile mortality) and as regards the health care system (low density of hospital beds). Nevertheless, it decides to wait until the next examination of Article 11 before assessing the situation and it meanwhile defers its conclusion.

Paragraph 2 – Advisory and educational facilities

The Committee takes note of the information in the Spanish report.

---

[1]European Commission, *Social protection in the member states of the European Union: situation on 1 July 1999 and evolution,* Missoc.

Encouragement of individual responsibility

Health education in schools

Under the Act governing the general education system, health education is compulsory in school curricula. Training sessions are arranged for teachers. The Committee notes that special attention is devoted to preventing drug addiction. It also wishes to know whether health education in schools deals systematically with the dangers of alcohol and smoking, sex education, including the prevention of sexually transmitted diseases, and the promotion of healthy eating.

The report states that a programme entitled "Building Health" was launched in schools in ten Autonomous Communities in 1996 and includes activities for parents, the aim being to encourage constructive use of free time through activities such as improving the environment.

Public information and awareness-raising

General information campaigns and more specific health-promotion activities are organised regularly, targeting all sectors of society and involving a range of media (e.g. booklets, television and radio advertisements and conferences). The Committee takes particular note of the efforts to prevent drug addiction among young people, for example by encouraging dialogue within families.

Counselling and screening

Children and adolescents

The previous report stated that preventive medical check-ups are provided for children and adolescents: one check-up during the first month, three more in the first 3 months, one check-up every 6 months until the age of 2, two check-ups between the ages of 2 and 5 and three check-ups between the ages of 6 and 14. A dental check-up is also carried out every two years between the ages of 6 and 14. The Committee wishes to know what body is responsible for carrying out these check-ups.

According to previous reports, school medical care is the responsibility of the Autonomous Communities and systematic examinations are carried out. The Committee requests that the next report contain more precise information, indicating the frequency of medical check-ups during schooling, what the check-ups entail, the proportion of pupils covered, the staffing resources and their qualifications.

Rest of the population

Cervical cancer screening is carried out every five years among women aged between 35 and 64 and breast cancer screening every two years among women aged between 50 and 75. Smokers and alcoholics are given a preventive examination for cardiovascular diseases every two years and men aged between 35 and 65 are screened for hypercholesterolaemia every two years.

Conclusion

Pending receipt of the information requested, the Committee concludes that the situation in Spain is in conformity with Article 11 para. 2 of the Charter.

Paragraph 3 – Prevention of diseases

The Committee takes note of the changes in Spain concerning the prevention of health risks in general, and preventive measures in particular.

Policies on the prevention of avoidable risks

General

The Committee would like the next reports to indicate, as far as possible, what proportion of public authorities' budgets is devoted to the main prevention policies listed below.

Reduction of environmental risks

Air pollution – with regard to local pollution management, the Committee has noted from previous reports that air quality standards and maximum concentration levels for the main pollutants responsible for lowering air quality have been established and that air quality surveillance machinery is in place throughout the country. The Committee would like to know whether there are specific arrangements for monitoring air quality and reducing air pollution in cities.

With regard to controlling emissions of these pollutants, the Committee notes from OECD data[1] that in 1995, Spain had failed to reach any of the objectives set for controlling emissions of sulphur oxides and nitrogen oxides.

Concerning global pollution, the Committee notes that in 1993, Spain ratified the United Nations Framework Convention on Climate Change (Rio de Janeiro, 1992). Amongst other things, Spain has undertaken not to increase emissions of the main greenhouse gases by more than 15% above the 1990 level by the 2008-2012 period, in order to achieve the objectives set for the European Union following the 1997 Kyoto conference. The Committee observes from OECD data and from the second report on the implementation of the Rio Convention[2] that the results achieved by Spain in controlling anthropogenic emissions of the three main greenhouse gases (carbon dioxide, methane and nitrous oxide) are consistent with its undertakings.

Asbestos – The report does not answer the general question concerning measures taken to protect the health of persons exposed to asbestos (Conclusions XIII-4, p. 116). The Committee requests that the next report contain detailed information on the subject and indicate whether measures have been taken to prohibit the mining, import, export, sale and production of asbestos and products containing it, and to monitor the presence of asbestos in residential buildings in particular.

Ionising radiation – The Committee notes that approximately one third of Spain's electricity is produced by nuclear power stations. In reply to the general question in Conclusions XIII-4 concerning the safety of those living near nuclear power stations, the report refers to Royal Decree No. 53/1992, which lays down standards for protecting the public and workers against ionising radiation. The Committee notes however that the Spanish regulations have not been adjusted to take account of the recommendations of the International Commission on Radiological Protection (ICRP) or Directive 96/29/Euratom laying down basic safety standards for the protection of the health of workers and the general public against the dangers arising from ionising radiation. Bearing in mind Spain's energy options, the Committee considers that

---

[1]OEC;D *Environmental Data*, 1999 Compendium.

[2]FCCC/IDR.2/ESP (31 May 2000), consulted on the United Nations Climate Convention website (www.unfccc.de).

this situation is potentially problematic as regards compliance with Article 11 para. 3. It encourages the Spanish authorities to remedy the situation and it will pronounce itself following the next examination of Article 3 para. 1 (supervision cycle XVI-2).

The report also states that a radiological surveillance network, under the authority of the Nuclear Security Council, operates throughout the country, monitoring environmental radioactivity.

Noise – The report mentions two changes: a bill is being drafted to update the general regulations governing noise (the existing general framework dates from 1972), and several local authorities have started taking steps to counter noise pollution more effectively, for example in Madrid where meters have been installed to measure traffic noise.

Food safety

In view of the threat to health represented by diseases related to food and the recent outbreaks of such diseases in particular the new variation of the Creutzfeldt-Jakob disease, as well as the emergence of new food products derived from biotechnology, the Committee has decided to look at food safety measures in all states parties to the Charter. It recalls that under Article 11 states have a responsibility to ensure a high degree of safety in this area for their populations.

Referring in particular to the resolution adopted by the 53rd World Health Assembly in May 2000 on food safety[1] and while recognising the relevance of international strategies, the Committee considers that in order to comply with the Charter in this field, states must set legal norms at the national level regarding food hygiene, taking into account scientific data, and establish and maintain mechanisms for monitoring compliance with these norms throughout the food chain, develop, implement and up-date systematic prevention measures, notably by way of labelling, as well as monitor the occurrence of food-borne diseases.

The Committee requests that the next report provide up-to-date information on these three aspects (standards, monitoring and prevention) so that it can assess the situation when it next examines Article 11.

[1]WHO Internet site : www.who.int

Measures to combat smoking and alcoholism

Smoking – The Committee stresses the importance of measures against smoking in meeting the requirements of Article 11 of the Charter. It recalls that smoking, a major cause of avoidable death in developed countries (in Europe 30% of deaths from cancer are attributable to smoking), is associated with a wide range of diseases (cardiac and circulatory diseases, cancers, pulmonary diseases etc.). Smoking kills one adult in ten throughout the world. The World Health Organisation (WHO) forecasts an increase to up to one in every six deaths by 2030,[1] which is more than the figure for any other cause of death. The Committee also notes that WHO is drawing up a convention on measures to combat smoking and points out that WHO, as part of the Health for All campaign, has set a target for European countries of raising the proportion of non-smokers in the population to at least 80% and protecting non-smokers against involuntary exposure to tobacco smoke.[2]

Anti-smoking legislation in Spain bans the sale of tobacco to persons under 16 years of age, ensures that cigarette packets contain medical warnings and information on the health risks of smoking, establishes maximum nicotine and tar levels in cigarettes and prohibits smoking in certain public places.

The Committee notes from Eurostat data that the number of cigarettes consumed per person is falling but is still higher than the average for European Union and European Economic Area countries (1,929, as against a European average of 1,646 in 1997)[3] and that the percentage of female smokers aged between 25 and 34 and that of male smokers aged between 35 and 44 are by far the highest among these countries.

The Committee would like to know how the government intends to remedy this state of affairs, and in particular what measures it intends to take to strengthen legislation. In this connection, having noted from a previous report that a draft Royal Decree envisaged a ban on the advertising of tobacco products, as well as the extension of the ban on smoking to other public places, the Committee would like to receive information on developments in legislation. It also wishes to know what means are used to ensure practical compliance with these regulations.

---

[1]World Health Report 1999.

[2]WHO, *Health Objectives for All – Health Policies in Europe,* September 1991.

[3]Eurostat Yearbook: *A statistical eye on Europe,* 1988-1998 data.

Alcohol – The Committee notes from Eurostat data that consumption of pure alcohol is in line with the average for European Union and European Economic Area countries (9.3 litres, compared with a European average of 9.4 in 1996) and has declined over the past decade. It requests that the next report contain up-to-date information on legislation aimed at reducing the supply of alcohol.

Drugs – The Committee refers to its conclusion in respect of Article 11 para. 2.

Prophylactic measures

Epidemiological monitoring

The report states that a national epidemiological surveillance network was set up under Royal Decree No. 2210/1995, involving in particular the development of a warning system for epidemiological surveillance, a data transmission system linking the Autonomous Communities and central government, and consolidation of the list of notifiable diseases.

Immunisation

According to a previous report, vaccinations are generally not compulsory; some, however, are recommended and are carried out systematically in schools in accordance with a national vaccine schedule.

The Committee takes note of the vaccine coverage rates given in the report: 94% for diphtheria and poliomyelitis, 92% for mumps, measles and rubella and 82% for hepatitis B in 1997. It would also like information on vaccine coverage rates for tetanus, tuberculosis and Hib meningitis.

Conclusion

The Committee reserves its position as regards the level of protection of the population living near nuclear power stations and the efficiency of the measures to combat smoking and while awaiting developments in the situation, defers its conclusion.

Article 14 — The right to benefit from social welfare services

Paragraph 1 – Provision or promotion of social welfare services

The Spanish report states that the implementation of the Arranged Plan on Social Services Basic Allowances in Local Corporations continues and that two new services have been introduced: economic allowances and enhancement of solidarity – social cooperation.

The Committee notes that total expenditure on the Arranged Plan increased from 58.5 billion Spanish Pesetas (PTA) in 1995 to 69.9 billion PTA in 1998.[1] It further notes that 6,506 local corporations were engaged in the Arranged Plan in 1998 and that a total of 20,514 were employed within the framework of the plan.

However, the Committee observes that the report does not contain replies to the questions asked since supervision cycle XII-2 as to whether all the autonomous communities have adopted laws organising the social services and whether the whole population is covered by such legislation. It insists that the information be included in the next report. Moreover, it asks that the next report provide a detailed overview of social services provision in Spain in the meaning of Article 14, including up-dated and complete replies to the questions of the Form for Reports.

In the absence of the above-mentioned information, the Committee is unable to assess properly the situation and it therefore defers its conclusion.

Paragraph 2 – Public participation in the establishment and maintenance of social welfare services

The Committee regrets that the Spanish report does not reply to the request for complete and updated information on all the measures taken to encourage the participation of individuals and voluntary organisations in the setting-up and running of social services, the areas of action of individuals or voluntary organisations within the social services and on the amounts devoted by the state to this area. The Committee requests that this information be contained in the next report.

Meanwhile, it defers its conclusion.

[1]According to the report the figure for 1998 is provisional.

Article 17 — The right of mothers and children to social and economic protection

The Committee notes the information contained in the Spanish report.

Establishment of parentage and adoption

The situation as regards the establishment of parentage is satisfactory.

The Committee notes that new legislation on adoption entered into force in 1996 and 1997 in order to tighten the regulations as to who may adopt and to amend the procedure.

Children in Public care

The protection and care of children separated from their families is the responsibility of the Autonomous Communities.

The Committee wishes to receive information in the next report on the procedure for separating a child from his family.

The report mentions that children removed from their families due to ill-treatment, neglect, etc. may be placed with a foster family, adopted or placed in residential care. The Committee wishes to be informed for the next reference period, how many children were removed from their families and placed with a foster family, placed in residential care or placed for adoption.

The Committee wishes to receive information on the types of institutions caring for children that exist.

It also wishes to receive information as to whether there is any body charged with monitoring care in institutions and whether there is any specific procedure for complaining about the care and treatment in institutions and about the conditions under which an institution may interfere with a child's property, mail, personal integrity and right to meet with persons close to him.

Protection from ill-treatment

Organic Law No. 1/1996 imposes an obligation on every person to notify the competent authorities of suspected child abuse.

The protection of children who are ill treated, abused, etc. is the responsibility of the Autonomous Communities, which generally have procedures for the reporting of child abuse (in some communities the minor concerned may file his/her own report), including confidential telephone lines, procedures for intervention by the appropriate bodies (health, educational personnel, police, public prosecutors, protection services) and rehabilitation services.

The criminal law has been amended during the reference period in order to provide better protection of children from abuse and domestic violence.

The Committee notes from the Concluding Observations of the Committee on the Rights of the Child in respect of Spain's first report[1] under the Convention on the Rights of the Child, that Article 154 of the Spanish Civil Code provides that parents "may administer punishment to their children reasonably and in moderation". The Committee notes that this would permit the corporal punishment of children, which is in breach of Article 17 of the Charter and it refers to its general observations on Article 17 in the General introduction. The Committee wishes to know whether this provision of the Civil Code has been amended, and further whether legislation prohibits the corporal punishment of children in schools, institutions and elsewhere. Meanwhile, it defers its conclusion.

Children and the law – Young Offenders

The Committee wishes to receive information on the minimum age for marriage.

The Committee notes that new legislation on young offenders, which sets the age of criminal responsibility at 14 years, was adopted in December 1999, but that it has not yet been published officially.

Organic Law 4/1992 currently regulates the situation of young offenders, those aged between 12 and 16 years.

The Committee requests that the next report supply further information on the situation of young offenders. It recalls that it has previously asked for this information. It wishes to receive information on the procedure for minors charged with a criminal offence, the sanctions available, the number of young offenders sentenced to a term of imprisonment, the maximum duration of any such prison sentence, whether young offenders may be remanded in custody, the length of any such remand, where young offenders are detained etc.

---

[1]CRC/C/15/Add.28.

Conclusion

Pending the receipt of information on the corporal punishment of children, the Committee defers its conclusion.

Article 18 — The right to engage in a gainful occupation in the territory of other Contracting Parties

Paragraph 1 – Applying existing regulations in a spirit of liberality

The Committee firstly notes that a regularisation programme was conducted in 1996. Under this operation, illegal immigrants were granted either a residence and work permit or a residence permit only. The Committee notes from sources[1] other than the report, that many of the estimated 20,000 foreigners who benefited from these measures had already been granted work permits in the past, but were in an illegal situation because their work permits had not been renewed.

Foreign population and migratory movements

The Committee notes that the foreign population residing lawfully in Spain is in excess of 600,000, representing 1.5% of the total population. 40% of these foreigners are from European Union countries. It also notes that following the aforementioned regularisation programme, the percentage of nationals of central and east European countries (particularly Poland, Romania, Russia, Bulgaria and Bosnia) and African States has now increased.[2]

Work and residence permits

Spain has two major categories of work/residence permit: categories A, B and C short-term permits, and category D permits, which entitle the holder to permanent residence.

The Committee notes that foreign nationals who have been granted an initial category A work permit as employees or self-employed persons are authorised to exercise specified activities or to work in a specified sector and geographical area for one year. Renewal of this initial permit entitles the holder to a category B (employee) or D (self-employed) permit. Both these permits, which are valid for two years, authorise the exercise of a series of activities, although restrictions may be imposed.

---

[1]OECD, *Trends in International Migration*, Sopemi, 1999 edition.

[2]*Ibidem.*

Lastly, on expiry of the category B and D permits, permanent and unrestricted permits (employee or self-employed) are issued.

Relevant statistics

The Committee recalls that Spain issues work permits either in accordance with either a quota system or other general regulations (see also conclusion under Article 18 para. 3).

It takes note of the statistics on quotas established per annum (on the understanding that this quota does not apply to nationals of countries in the European Union or the European Economic Area) and on numbers of permits actually issued. It also takes note of the number of permits granted under the general regulations. These data do not, however, differentiate between nationals of Contracting Parties to the Charter that are not members of the European Union or parties to the European Economic Area Agreement and nationals of other countries. The Committee consequently requests that the next report should provide information drawing a distinction between these two categories of nationals. It also asks whether any special measures are provided for in the quota system for nationals of Contracting Parties to the Charter that are members neither of the European Union or party to the European Economic Area Agreement.

Conclusion

Pending receipt of the information requested, particularly on the application of the quota system to nationals of Contracting Parties to the Charter that are not members of the European Union or party to of the European Economic Area Agreement, the Committee defers its conclusion.

Paragraph 2 – Simplifying existing formalities and reducing dues and taxes

The Committee notes from the report the entry into force of Organic Law 4/2000 of 11 January 2000 on rights and freedoms of foreigners in Spain and their social integration, repealing Organic Law 7/85 of 1 July 1985. The Committee observes that this new law does not concern the present reference period (1995-1998).

Administrative formalities

Issue of work permits

The Committee takes note of the various documents required to obtain a work permit: copy of passport, certificate stating applicant's police record, medical certificate and identity photographs.

It observes that Law 7/1985 on foreigners, approved by Royal Decree 155/1996 introduced measures to simplify the procedure, including a new prior consultation procedure to prevent subsequent refusal of work and residence permits, and exemption from production of the required documents where they have already been forwarded to the administration.

Where self-employed activities are concerned, the report states that in pursuance of Section 34 of Organic Law 4/2000 persons wishing to exercise a self-employed activity in Spain must obtain the same administrative authorisations and fulfil the same formalities as nationals.

Conditions for renewal

Under the terms of Organic Law 7/1985 applications for renewal of work permits must be submitted before, or within three months after, the date of expiry. The Committee notes that Law 4/2000 provides for automatic renewal of the residence/work permit if the person concerned is in receipt of unemployment benefit or social assistance (see also conclusion under Article 18 para. 3).

Work and residence permit

In light of the information noted above on the procedure for prior consultation introduced by Law 7/1985 on foreigners, it appears to the Committee that the procedures for obtaining a work permit and residence permit are different. The Committee wishes to receive clarification of this point in the next report.

Time necessary for obtaining work permits

The Committee would like the next report to provide information on the average period of time between the submission of an application for a work permit and the issue of this document, differentiating between the various types of permit. It also requested information on authorisations for exercising self-employed activities.

Chancery dues and other charges

The report does not answer the question put in the previous conclusion (Conclusions XIII-4, p. 316) on adapting charges to the foreign worker's level of remuneration. On the other hand, the Committee notes that the new Organic Law 4/2000 abolishes the charges payable by workers for an employee's work permit.

Conclusion

Pending receipt of the information requested the Committee concludes that the situation in Spain is in conformity with Article 18 para. 2 of the Charter.

Paragraph 3 – Liberalising regulations

The Committee recalls that during the reference period (1993-1998) Spanish policy on employment of foreign nationals was based on Organic Law 7/85 of 1 July 1985. As noted in its conclusion under Article 18 para. 2, a new law has subsequently come into force (Organic Law 4/2000 of 11 January 2000).

Access to the national labour market

The Committee observes that in Spain work permits can be issued either under the quota system in force since 1993 in respect of nationals of states not members of the European Union or party to the European Economic Area Agreement (apart from 1996, when no employment quota was set) or with reference to general regulations. The Committee would like the next report to explain the quota system (rate established, the criteria applied, possible exceptions) and indicate any links between the two procedures.

Broadly speaking, the Committee notes that the decision to grant the initial work permit takes account of the following factors: lack of available workers from Spain, the European Union or the European Economic Area, the economic activity and geographic area where it is performed. It recalls that the work permit initially issued is only valid for one job and one geographical area. However, it notes from the report that such restrictions can be lifted at the request of the foreign worker under a duly reasoned decision. The Committee asks in which cases the issuing authorities can derogate from the restrictions on initial work permits.

Exercise of the right to employment

Foreign workers are entitled to a permanent, and therefore unrestricted, work permit after six years' occupational activity in Spain. The Committee notes with interest that Law 7/1985 provides that such workers can appeal against decisions not to issue residence and work permits.

Moreover, the Committee notes from the report that under the terms of Article 13 para. 2 of the Constitution only Spaniards "have the right to access to public office" as laid down in Article 23 of the Constitution. The Committee would like the next report to specify the types of employment subject to a nationality criterion and to set out the reasons for excluding non-nationals from each of these posts.

Consequence of job loss

The Committee notes that if foreign workers who have been made redundant can produce evidence that the competent authorities have granted them entitlement to unemployment benefit (contributory benefit), they are entitled to automatic renewal of their residence permit.

Section 59 of the regulations enforcing Organic Law 7/1985 provides that residence permits are renewed if the conditions for its issue have not changed or if fresh circumstances entitling the person to the permit have transpired. These fresh circumstances include the receipt of an unemployment benefit. The Committee also notes from a different source that in order to qualify for unemployment benefit, the person in question must have paid at least a year's contributions. It deduces from this that foreign workers whose contracts have been terminated through no fault of their own before they can fulfil the contribution conditions are not eligible for unemployment benefit and therefore cannot apply for renewal of their residence permit. It would like to know whether, in such circumstances, an extension of the residence permit is provided for in order to allow the person in question sufficient time to find a new job. It also asks whether an extension of the residence permit is provided for pending a judicial decision on an appeal submitted by the foreign worker against dismissal.

Conclusion

Pending receipt of the requested information concerning the quota system and the, cases in which the authorities can derogate from the restrictions on initial work permits, the Committee defers its conclusion.

Paragraph 4 – The right of nationals to leave the country

In the absence of any change, the Committee concludes that the situation in Spain is in conformity with Article 18 para. 4 of the Charter.

However it wishes the next report to explain the application in practice of the rule that a passport may be refused on the grounds that the person concerned must perform his military service.

Chapter 14 – Conclusions concerning Articles 7, 8, 11, 14, 17 and 18 of the Charter and Articles 1 and 4 of the 1988 Additional Protocol in respect of Sweden

Article 7 — The right of children and young persons to protection

Paragraph 1 – Minimum age of admission to employment

The Committee takes note from the Swedish report of the amendments to the Work Environment Act (AML) that took effect as of 1 January 1996. Whereas previously the act did not extend to minors employed in the employer's household, this group is now subject to its provisions (Chapter 1, Section 4(2)). As the Committee had considered the exclusion of this group from the general statutory framework not to be in conformity with the Charter, it welcomes this development.

The Committee notes that the time for which children under the age of 15 years may work during school holidays has been reduced to a maximum of 7 hours per day and 35 hours per week. In addition, the leave period which must be granted to such children has been increased from three to four weeks. It refers in this respect to its observations in its conclusion under Article 7 para. 3 of the Charter.

In reply to the Committee's general question on children employed in family businesses, the report indicates that they enjoy the same level of statutory protection and that such workplaces are subject to labour inspection.

Finally, the Committee takes note of the information provided in response to its question on the employment of children under the age of 13 years in performances. Section 10 of Ordinance 1996:1 Minors at Work, permits such work on the basis of individual permits granted by the Labour Inspectorate, where it is satisfied as to the suitability of the work for the child concerned. The work must be "harmless" and entail "only a slight degree of physical or mental strain". Any permits issued in this way are for a fixed duration.

The Committee concludes that the situation in Sweden is in conformity with Article 7 para. 1 of the Charter.

Paragraph 2 – Higher minimum age in certain occupations

The Committee takes note of the provisions of Ordinance 1996:1 Minors at Work, issued by the Swedish National Board of Occupational Safety and Health, which took effect during the reference period. In particular, it takes note of the duty of employers to exercise "great care" in the assignment of work to minors, so as to provide adequate safeguards against accidents, injuries and risks to their health (Section 2). Minors must be provided with the appropriate training and information to ensure their safety at work.

The employment of minors in a series of scheduled hazardous occupations, contained in the first Appendix to the Ordinance, is prohibited unless it takes place within the context of formal instruction under appropriate supervision. Certain tasks, listed in the second Appendix, are completely prohibited to minors.

The Committee notes from another source[1] that reported occupational injuries among minors fell from 1,818 in 1989 to 92 in 1996. It asks to receive updated information in the next report under this provision.

The Committee concludes that the situation in Sweden is in conformity with Article 7 para. 2 of the Charter.

Paragraph 3 – Safeguarding the full benefit of compulsory education

The Swedish report under this provision describes the contents of Ordinance 1996:1 Minors at Work issued by the National Board of Occupational Safety and Health, which came into force on 1 November 1996. The Committee takes note of the special provisions contained in Section 9 that apply when a minor is engaged for work as an employee before the calendar year in which they reach the age of 16 or before compulsory schooling has been completed:

– Section 9.2 permits the employment of children under the age of 15 years during school holidays for a maximum of 7 hours per day and 35 hours per week. A child who has reached the age of 15 may work

[1] *Priorities and Strategies in Occupational Safety and Health Policy in the Member States of the European Union, Country Report, Sweden*. European Agency for Safety and Health at Work.

for up to 8 hours per day and 40 hours per week. The Committee considers these hours to be long, but as they only apply during part of the school holidays, they do not constitute a violation of Article 7 para. 3 of the Charter;

– Section 9.3 provides that children may not be employed between 8 p.m. and 6 a.m. The Committee recalls that it has previously held that children should not be allowed to perform any work before going to school in the morning, since such activity is likely to deprive them of the full benefit of their education (Conclusions VIII, p. 108). However, it notes that Section 9.7 provides that permission is required from school management for work that takes place before or after school if this involves more than five school days per term. It requests information on the application of this procedure in practice and on the nature and extent of such work. Pending receipt of this information, the Committee reserves its position on this matter;

– Section 9.6 provides that minors shall have at least four weeks' continuous leave from work per calendar year, at a time which is free from timetabled instruction. The Committee considers that the main purpose of school holidays is to let children rest in order to benefit from school after the holiday. It refers to its case-law that the rest period must cover at least half of the holiday period for children still subject to compulsory education. This not being the case in Sweden, the Committee finds that the situation is not in conformity with Article 7 para. 3 of the Charter.

The Committee asks that the next report under this provision include information on the activities of the Labour Inspectorate in ensuring compliance with the above regulations.

The Committee concludes that the situation in Sweden is not in conformity with Article 7 para. 3 of the Charter as the mandatory rest period during school holidays for children still subject to compulsory education is not sufficient to ensure that they benefit from such education.

Paragraph 4 – Working hours for young workers and apprentices

The Committee notes that there have been no changes to the situation which it has previously considered satisfactory.

It therefore concludes that the situation in Sweden is in conformity with Article 7 para. 4 of the Charter.

Paragraph 7 – Annual holiday of young persons under eighteen

The Committee notes from the Swedish report that young workers under the age of 18 are entitled to statutory holiday under the Holidays Act in keeping with the requirements of this provision of the Charter. Under Section 9 of the Ordinance 1996:1 Minors at Work, a minor who is employed before the calendar year where he/she attains the age of 16 shall have at least 4 weeks of continuous leave from work every calendar year.

The Committee concludes that the situation in Sweden is in conformity with Article 7 para. 7 of the Charter.

Paragraph 8 – Prohibition of night work for young persons under eighteen

From the information contained in the Swedish report, the Committee notes that pursuant to Section 8 of Ordinance 1996:1 Minors at Work, night work between 10 p.m. and 6 a.m. or between 11 p.m. and 7 a.m. is prohibited for young workers under the age of 18. Minors employed before the calendar year where they attain the age of 16 may not perform work between 8 p.m. and 6 a.m.

In the light of this information the Committee concludes that the situation in Sweden is in conformity with Article 7 para. 8 of the Charter.

Paragraph 9 – Provision of regular medical control for young workers under eighteen

The Committee notes from the Swedish report that protection of young workers relevant to this provision of the Charter has been improved somewhat under the Ordinance 1996:1 Minors at Work, through the introduction of a new Section 3 which stipulates that, where necessary, a young worker's health should be examined, in a recurrent manner if required, in order to a assess whether the work entails a special risk to the health or safety of the young worker. Moreover, Section 2 has been reworded to accentuate the employer's duty, in that tasks for young workers shall be chosen with great care and that adequate security must exist against accidents and harmful effects.

However, as regards certain prescribed occupations of a hazardous nature listed in Schedule 1 of the Ordinance for which young workers may be employed on condition that they have completed vocational training for that particular work (or if the work is performed as part of vocational training), the Committee notes that the approval of a medical doctor for the admission to employment of a young worker is only required for a limited number of these occupations. In addition, there is no express provision for regular (periodical) medical control, except for the general provision of the above-mentioned Section 3 which would seem to leave it to the discretion of the employer whether pre-employment examination and regular examination is necessary. The Committee recalls in this respect that Article 7 para. 9 of the Charter requires compulsory regular medical control of the young workers in the occupations concerned.

In consequence, as regular medical control of young workers in the occupations concerned is not guaranteed in legislation and as it has not been demonstrated that a guarantee exists in practice, the Committee concludes that the situation in Sweden is not in conformity with Article 7 para. 9 of the Charter.

Paragraph 10 – Special protection for children and young people from physical and moral dangers to which they are exposed

The Committee notes the information provided in the Swedish report on the protection of working children. It refers in this respect to its conclusion under Article 7 para. 2.

The Committee notes that it is a criminal offence in Sweden to procure or attempt to procure casual sexual intercourse with a person under 18 by promising or giving consideration. The Committee notes that the sexual offences legislation is under review, and wishes to be kept informed of all relevant developments. The Committee asks whether legislation prohibits the use of children in the sex industry as a whole, and to receive information on any supervisory system and sanctions that may accompany this prohibition.

The Committee concludes that the situation in Sweden is in conformity with Article 7 para. 10 of the Charter.

Article 8 — The right of employed women to protection

Paragraph 1 – Maternity leave

The Committee takes note of the information given in the Swedish report.

1. Entitlement to maternity leave

Women in Sweden are entitled to seven weeks' leave prior to confinement and seven weeks thereafter (Parental Leave Act No. 584 of 1995). This leave is not compulsory and remains at the mother's discretion.

The report says that, while the leave is not compulsory, virtually all women take it in practice. They are also entitled to parental leave. Various forms of leave for mothers and fathers are in fact provided for in the Parental Leave Act. The report nevertheless states that the Parental Leave Act has been amended in order to bring the situation into line with Community Directive 92/85, of 19 October 1992, on the introduction of measures to encourage improvements in the safety and health at work of pregnant workers and workers who have recently given birth or are breastfeeding. Thus, with effect from 1 July 2000, women will, in accordance with the directive, be obliged to take two weeks' leave, either before or after confinement.

The Committee recalls that the aim of Article 8 para. 1 is to ensure women have special protection in cases of maternity and to meet the general public health interest through the protection of mother and child. The period of 12 weeks of rest apportioned before and after confinement, is to be considered a minimum, as the text of the Charter itself states. The period of compulsory post-natal leave set at 6 weeks by the Committee (Conclusion VIII, p. 125) is also to be seen as a minimum period permitting no derogation. The Committee adds that even if in practice the majority of women enjoy post-natal maternity leave longer than the compulsory 2 weeks, this does not mean that all women enjoy post-natal maternity leave of 6 weeks. It considers it necessary that the relevant texts expressly provide for 6 weeks of compulsory leave after confinement.

The absence of 6 weeks' compulsory post-natal leave leads the Committee to conclude that the situation in Sweden is not in conformity with Article 8 para. 1 of the Charter on this point.

2. Right to adequate benefits

As Swedish legislation provides for virtually complete equality between mothers and fathers, there are no provisions specific to mothers.

In reply to the Committee's general question raised in Conclusions XIII-1, p. 172, the report indicates the parental benefit entitlement conditions. The benefit is paid for 450 days. Mothers may claim it for the 60 days prior to the presumed date of confinement, and one of the parents may claim up to the child's 8th birthday. Where both parents are looking after the child, they may divide between them the days in respect of which the benefit is paid, with the exception of the 30 days allotted solely to father or mother. In order to be entitled to this benefit, the mother or father must have been affiliated to the social security scheme for a continuous period of 180 days (around 6 months) prior to submission of the application. Mothers (or fathers) affiliated for 240 days receive the benefit at a higher rate. Periods of unemployment are taken into account for the calculation of entitlement.

The Committee asks that the next report give the conditions which apply to women working part-time.

Everyone who lives in Sweden is affiliated to the social security scheme. Parental benefit is thus paid to mothers or fathers, whether or not they are in work. The minimum rate of the benefit, paid to those not in work or in occasional work, is 60 Swedish Kroner (SEK) per day. Mothers or fathers in work whose income is greater than 8,800 SEK per year and have been affiliated to the social security scheme for a continuous period of 240 days receive a higher rate equivalent to sickness benefit, which is 80% of pay.

The Committee recalls that the closer benefits are to the previous salary, the more they maybe considered as satisfactory, and vice versa. It considers in the present case that the level of parental benefit is adequate.

Finally, in reply to a question from the Committee about the maximum rate of benefit, or ceiling, the report states, without specifying the rate, that 3.2% of all recipients of parental allowance in 1997 were women receiving the maximum rate, while 14.4% of all recipients were men being paid the maximum rate. It also states that there is no compensation for loss of earnings exceeding the ceiling. In order to be able to assess the situation, the Committee asks that the next report indicate the maximum rate of benefit.

In the meantime, the Committee defers its conclusion on this point.

Paragraph 3 – Time off for nursing mothers

Sweden's report again mentions the broad scope for extended leave and part-time work available to women following childbirth.

The Committee takes the view that this cannot be regarded as the equivalent of time off for nursing within the meaning of Article 8 para. 3, for the concept of "time off" implies that this is taken during work time.

It also points out that this time off, which counts as working hours, must be remunerated as such. Thus the absence of a guarantee of remuneration for time off for nursing is not in conformity with the requirements of the Charter.

The Committee notes from the Governmental Committee, 13th report (IV), p. 82, para 323, that a possibility exists for obtaining partial parental leave, for instance, two hours per day, the distribution of the leave being subject to agreement between the employer and the employee.

The Committee requests that the next report contain more detailed information on this possibility.

Meanwhile, it concludes that the situation in Sweden is not in conformity with Article 8 para. 3 of the Charter.

Article 11 — Right to protection of health

Paragraph 1 – Removal of the causes of ill-health

The Committee takes note of the information contained in the Swedish report and its appendices.

Population's state of health - general indicators

Life expectancy and principal causes of death

The Committee takes note of the general indicators of the state of health of the Swedish population. It notes that life expectancy at birth increased significantly from 80.8 years in 1992 to 81.8 years in 1997 for women and from 75.4 years in 1991 to 76.7 years in 1996 for men. Life expectancy for men is higher in Sweden than in any other European OECD country.[1]

According to Eurostat,[2] the main causes of death in 1995 were cardio-vascular diseases, followed by cancer and diseases of the respiratory system. The Committee observes that skin cancer rates among men and women are double the European average and the highest in any European Union country. It requests that the next report contain the latest data.

The Committee notes that the number of new AIDS diagnoses per year fell sharply during the reference period, from 192 in 1995 to 56 in 1998.

Infant and maternal mortality

The infant mortality rate in Sweden was lower than in the previous reference period, falling from 5.3 deaths per 1,000 live births in 1992 to 4 in 1996. The average maternal mortality rate, decreased from 5.3 deaths per 100,000 live births between 1998 and 1991 to 3.8 between 1993 and 1996.

---

[1]OECD, *Health Data*, 1999.

[2]Eurostat Yearbook: *A statistical eye on Europe* 1988-1998 data.

Health care system

Access to health care

Health care in Sweden is available to the whole population. The health care system is funded through taxes, with each of the 25 general councils entirely financing its own medical services.

The health care system is split into primary, county and regional care. Primary care is the most important, comprising basic services such as child and mother health care centres, district health centres and care homes. Primary care is available in 288 municipalities. Hospital care is provided at county and regional levels.

In 1997, 8.6% of GDP was devoted to health expenditure. The proportion of health care funded by the state is constantly falling, but was still around 83.3% in 1997.

Patients pay part of the cost of out-patient medical and hospital care. Their contribution varies from 100 SEK to 140 SEK for a consultation, from 120 SEK to 250 SEK for specialist treatment and from 120 SEK to 300 SEK for emergency treatment. They pay a maximum of 80 SEK per day for hospital care. Dental care is free up to the age of 20, after which patients pay 1,300 SEK for a course of treatment.

Patients pay the full cost of medicines up to a maximum of 400 SEK per year, 50% of the cost between 400 SEK and 1,200 SEK, 25% between 1,200 SEK and 2,800 SEK, i.e. 400 SEK at the most, and 10% of the cost between 2,800 SEK and 3,800 SEK. In 1997 patients' contributions to the cost of medicines were limited to 1,300 SEK per year. Medicines are free for the chronically ill.

According to OECD data, the average reimbursement rate for hospital care[1] fell from 99.5% in 1992 to 98% in 1997, whereas the average rate for pharmaceutical products rose from 70.6% in 1992 to 71% in 1997. The Committee observes that these rates are among the highest in European OECD countries. Meanwhile, the reimbursement rate for out-patient medical care fell sharply from 77.4% to 72%, which is about average for European OECD countries.

The Committee notes in the report under Article 4 of the Additional Protocol that there is a system of waiting lists for hospital care and primary care. A "care guarantee" was introduced in 1992 with the aim of reducing waiting lists and waiting times for access to hospital care. It

[1]The proportion of total expenditure usually paid by the state.

applies to twelve different types of treatment which must be offered to a patient within three months. As from 1996, the care guarantee has been extended so as to include also access to primary care in order to guarantee that patients are able to contact primary care staff on the same day, to see a doctor within eight days and to see a specialist within four weeks after referral. The report states that waiting lists and waiting times were reduced, but the effect was of short duration and the county councils have difficulty in meeting the deadlines. Moreover, the care guarantee was criticised and several studies showed its insufficiency as far as patients with severe acute or chronic illnesses or terminal patients were concerned. An act came into force in 1997 laying down the guidelines for prioritisation in health care: human dignity, need and solidarity and cost-efficiency, in that order. It entails high priority for patients with serious or long-term illnesses and with reduced ability to make independent decisions and for terminal patients. A report evaluating the impact of this policy was drawn up by the National Board of Health and Welfare in 1999. The Committee would like to receive this report as well as any other relevant information on the management and the follow-up in respect of waiting lists for access to hospital care and primary care.

Health professionals and equipment

The number of hospital beds continued to fall, reaching 46,177 in 1997, only one-third of the number in 1975. Expressed in proportion to the population (5.2 beds per 1,000 inhabitants in 1997), this is one of the lowest among European OECD countries. The report states that this drop is the result of cost-cutting measures designed to promote outpatient care rather than overnight stays in hospital.

Psychiatric institutions accounted for 13.5% of all beds in 1997. The private sector continues to grow, with 23.6% of all beds compared to 6.5% at the beginning of the 1980s.

In 1995 there were 0.5 general practitioners per 1,000 inhabitants, a below-average figure for European OECD countries. The density of specialists, on the other hand, which was 2.2 per 1,000 inhabitants in 1996, is one of the highest, as is the density of dentists, which remained virtually unchanged from the previous reference period (0.9 per 1,000 inhabitants).

Conclusion

The Committee concludes that the situation in Sweden is in conformity with Article 11 para.1 of the Charter.

Paragraph 2 – Advisory and educational facilities

The Committee takes note of the information contained in the Swedish report.

Encouragement of individual responsibility

The Committee noted in its previous conclusion that the main purpose of the National Institute of Public Health, a public body set up in 1992, is to provide health education for the whole population, targeting groups such as young people and teenagers. The Institute, which has ninety members of staff, supports local authority and independent public health initiatives, including in the education sector. Its tasks include monitoring developments in public health and drawing up prevention strategies, which might include promoting co-operation between the partners concerned. According to the previous report, the Institute's campaigns tackle the following areas: accident prevention, smoking, alcohol and drug abuse, sex education, especially AIDS prevention, promotion of healthy lifestyles and allergy prevention.

Previous reports indicate that health education is provided in all schools by class teachers and the school health services. The Committee would like more detailed, up-to-date information on the way in which health education is taught in schools and particularly whether there is a national health education syllabus, whether health education is taught at every level of school education and what financial resources are devoted to it.

The Committee would also like regular information on campaigns designed to inform the public about major public health issues in Sweden, on the partners involved, the means of action used and the budget devoted to this kind of prevention.

Counselling and screening

Children and adolescents

The Committee notes that, in conformity with Article 11 para. 2, children in Sweden receive preventive health care from services operating in accordance with child health screening and monitoring standards laid down in 1991 by the National Board of Health and Welfare. As well as offering vaccinations, they carry out numerous screening tests covering all aspects of children's physical and mental health.

The Education Act stipulates that medical checks and basic health care should be provided for preventive purposes. Previous reports indicate that all schoolchildren undergo regular medical examinations carried out by municipal school health services and that health care is available in all schools. The report states that a study is under way with a view to improving the quality and efficiency of school health services. The Committee requests information on the measures taken in this respect, the frequency of school medical examinations and the resources devoted to these services (staff and funding).

Rest of the population

Sweden has never provided information on screening for diseases that cause high rates of premature death. The Committee therefore insists that the next report contain detailed information, especially concerning screening for types of cancer that are particularly common in Sweden.

Conclusion

Pending receipt of the information requested, the Committee concludes that the situation in Sweden is in conformity with Article 11 para. 2 of the Charter.

Paragraph 3 – Prevention of diseases

The Committee takes note of developments in Sweden concerning the prevention of health risks in general and diseases in particular.

Policies on the prevention of avoidable risks

General

The Committee requests that future reports indicate, as far as possible, how much public funding is devoted to the main prevention policies listed below.

Reduction of environmental risks

Air pollution – As far as local pollution is concerned, previous reports state that air quality targets and limit values for the concentration of the main pollutants responsible for air quality deterioration have been laid down and that an air quality monitoring mechanism is in place.

The Committee observes from OECD data[1] that Sweden's efforts to control anthropic emissions of traditional pollutants (sulphur oxides, nitrogen oxides, particles, carbon monoxide, volatile organic compounds) have, on the whole, been very successful.

As far as global pollution is concerned, the Committee notes that Sweden ratified the United Nations Framework Convention on Climate Change (Rio de Janeiro, 1992) in 1993 and has been pursuing a highly active policy of reducing the main types of greenhouse gas emission since 1988. It observes from OECD data that the emissions control policy is producing excellent results despite a slight increase in carbon dioxide emissions since 1990.

Asbestos – The Committee observes that Swedish regulations and legislation cover all aspects related to Article 11 para. 3. These include:

– a total ban on crocidolite and a ban on the use, conversion or processing of other types of asbestos fibre or asbestos material;

– obligations on property owners to establish the presence of asbestos and to take any necessary action, and on public authorities to establish the presence of asbestos in all public places;

– specific obligations on companies concerning the disposal of asbestos waste.

Ionising radiation – In 1998 Parliament adopted a new Act on the closure of nuclear power stations and authorised the government to shut down the reactors at the Barsebäck power station (which generates around 30% of the country's electricity). The government intends to promote renewable energy sources and new technologies that use fewer resources.

Given the current situation in Sweden, the safety of the population from nuclear hazards (see general question in Conclusions XIII-4) remains an important factor in the Committee's assessment of Sweden's conformity with Article 11 para. 3. In this connection, the Committee notes from the aforementioned appendix that, on the initiative of the Swedish Radiation Protection Institute (*SSI*), in co-operation with the Swedish Nuclear Energy Inspectorate (*SKI*) in particular, radiation protection is now strictly regulated, radioactivity in the vicinity of nuclear

[1]OECD, *Environmental Data*, 1999 Compendium.

power stations is closely monitored and studies of possible strategies to be implemented in the event of an accident are carried out. With regard to dose limits, the Committee observes that, despite its request in Conclusions XIV-2 (p. 797), Sweden has not reported any progress towards adapting its regulations in order to implement the maximum values recommended in 1990 by the International Commission on Radiological Protection (ICRP). However, the Committee expects rapid progress to be made when Community Directive 96/29/Euratom on the protection of the health of workers and the general public against the dangers arising from ionising radiation is transposed into Swedish law. It would like to be informed of any developments in the next report on Article 3.

Noise – The previous report stated that an anti-noise action plan was carried out in order to assess and limit damage caused by noise in general, including inside residential buildings. Anti-noise provisions were brought in to protect the population from land and rail transport noise. The Committee requests that the next report update the situation, particularly with regard to legislation and steps taken to enforce it, together with performance indicators if possible.

Food safety

In view of the threat to health represented by diseases related to food and the recent outbreaks of such diseases in particular the new variation of the Creutzfeldt-Jakob disease, as well as the emergence of new food products derived from biotechnology, the Committee has decided to look at food safety measures in all states parties to the Charter. It recalls that under Article 11 states have a responsibility to ensure a high degree of safety in this area for their populations.

Referring in particular to the resolution adopted by the 53rd World Health Assembly in May 2000 on food safety[1] and while recognising the relevance of international strategies, the Committee considers that in order to comply with the Charter in this field, states must set legal norms at the national level regarding food hygiene taking into account scientific data, and establish and maintain mechanisms for monitoring compliance with these norms throughout the food chain, develop, implement and up-date systematic prevention measures, notably by way of labelling, as well as monitor the occurrence of food-borne diseases.

---

[1]WHO Internet site: www.who.int

Previous reports state that food hygiene regulations cover every stage of the food chain, that strict safety standards are in place and that checks are carried out. The Committee requests that the next report provide more specific information on the aspects set out above so that it can assess the situation on the next occasion that Article 11 is examined.

Measures to combat smoking and alcoholism

Sweden has been actively fighting smoking and alcohol abuse for many years, with extremely tight restrictions on the sale of alcohol and tobacco. The Committee observes that this policy has been successful since tobacco and alcohol consumption are constantly falling and are the lowest in the European Union[1].

Prophylactic measures

Epidemiological monitoring

The Committee notes from previous reports that a system for the collection of data and monitoring of numerous transmittable diseases is in operation in Sweden. It also observes that specific measures can be taken and *ad hoc* investigations launched if an epidemic seems likely to break out.

Immunisation

The Committee reported in its previous conclusion that all recommended child vaccinations are optional and free.

The Committee takes note of the vaccination rates recorded in the Swedish profile drawn up by the World Health Organisation (WHO)[2]: in 1995, 99% of children were vaccinated against diphtheria and polio and 96% against measles.

The Committee requests that the next report contain up-to-date information on vaccination rates and on policy concerning tuberculosis and hepatitis vaccinations.

---

[1]Eurostat Yearbook: *A statistical eye on Europe,* 1988-1998 data.

[2] www.who.int/vaccines-surveillance/

Conclusion

Pending receipt of the information requested, the Committee concludes that the situation in Sweden is in conformity with Article 11 para. 3 of the Charter.

Article 14 — The right to benefit from social welfare services

Paragraph 1 – Provision or promotion of social welfare services

The Committee takes note of the information contained in the Swedish report, notably the replies to the questions raised in the previous conclusion.

The report recalls that provision of social services is the responsibility of the municipalities and covers the following three categories of services :

i. Services for individuals and families

– Social assistance to adults including social allowance, preventive and non-institutional measures;

– Children and young persons aged 0-20 in need of support and protection, including care in special supervisory homes, other types of institutions and homes and non-institutional supportive measures;

– Rehabilitation of drug and alcohol abusers in different types of institutions and by non-institutional measures;

– Family law services and municipal family counselling.

ii. Childcare for children 0-12 years

– 0-6 years, childcare before school age;

– 7-12 years, childcare after school.

iii. Services to the elderly and the disabled

In reply to the Committee's question, the report gives figures on the number of people using social services. Childcare accounted for 721,000 beneficiaries in 1998, there were 367,300 social allowance recipients, services were provided to 244,800 elderly and an estimated 70,000-80,000 disabled. The figures reveal no uniform trend in the number of beneficiaries during the reference period, for some services the number has increased (e.g. childcare) while for others it has decreased (e.g. services to the elderly).

The report also gives figures on municipal staffing levels in social services which indicate that the majority of staff are employed to provide services to the elderly and disabled (171,100 employees in November 1998) and to provide childcare (113,900 employees). 22,100 persons were employed in services for individuals and families in November 1998. Having noted that staffing levels decreased slightly from 1997 to 1998 the Committee asks what is the explanation for this development.

The report states that no figures are available in respect of privately produced services, but the Committee nevertheless asks that the next report provide an estimate of the staffing levels and the number of beneficiaries of the private services concerned.

Finally, the Committee wishes to receive up-dated information on how the quality of services is supervised, not only within and between the municipalities but also in relation to the private providers hired by the municipalities.

Pending receipt of the information requested, the Committee concludes that the situation in Sweden is in conformity with Article 14 para. 1 of the Charter.

Paragraph 2 – Public participation in the establishment and maintenance of social welfare services

In reply to the Committee's question in the previous conclusion, the Swedish report provides information on the participation of disabled persons in the organisation of the assistance they receive. Under the Assistance Benefit Act persons with certain functional impairments have the right to an assistance benefit through the social insurance system to cover the cost of personal assistance. The most important means of facilitating the participation of disabled persons themselves is their possibility of deciding for themselves how the assistance is to be arranged. They can turn to the municipality or a personnel co-operative for a personal assistant, or they can be the employer themselves.

The municipalities are responsible for personal assistance amounting to less than 20 hours per week and for complementary service to the assistance benefit. This is governed by the Functional Impairments (Support for Certain Categories) Act, which also provides that the measure can be given either as personal assistance or as financial support to cover reasonable expenditure on such help.

As regards measures taken to encourage the participation of individuals and voluntary organisations in the setting up and running of social services in general the report states that voluntary organisations may receive state grants, both for organisational work and for projects to support individuals. According to the report, the organisations of the disabled are among the most important actors in this field. In 2000 these organisations will receive 129,248,000 Swedish kronor (SEK) for organisation work and 78,394,000 SEK for certain specified activities. The Committee asks that the next report provide a more complete picture of the role of voluntary organisations, their funding and notably the nature of the services they provide or participate in providing.

Meanwhile, the Committee concludes that the situation in Sweden is in conformity with Article 14 para. 2 of the Charter.

Article 17 — The right of mothers and children to social and economic protection

The Committee notes the information contained in the Swedish report.

Establishment of parentage and adoption

The situation as regards adoption is satisfactory. Adoption orders must be made by the courts, the parent's consent must be obtained and no payment must be made or promised.

The Committee recalls that the guiding principle is that every child whether born of married, cohabitating or separated parents or parents who have never lived together, has the right to know his parents. In this respect it notes that a child born with the help of medically assisted reproduction techniques (donor insemination) is entitled, if it has achieved sufficient maturity, to be appraised of the particulars concerning the donor.

Children in public care and Protection of children against ill-treatment and abuse

The municipal social welfare committee is responsible for ensuring that children are not neglected or abused within the family. It may offer families in difficulty support and various types of assistance. It may also offer placement of the children away from the home. Parental agreement will be sought if possible. However, if agreement cannot be reached, the social welfare authorities can still intervene under certain conditions, with a care order. Care orders are made by the court and can be appealed.

The municipal social welfare committee may place a child in a foster family or in a children's home. Most children are placed in a foster family. The Committee wishes to receive information on the number of children taken into care and placed with a foster family or in an institution and on the types of institutions that exist. It also wishes to receive information on the number of children receiving support and assistance in the home.

The municipal social welfare committee and county administrative boards supervise foster families.

Institutions (residential homes) are supervised by the National Board of Institutional Care. The Committee wishes to receive information on the procedures available to children in institutions who wish to complain about the care or treatment in the institution. Further it wishes to receive details on the conditions under which an institution may interfere with a child's property, mail, personal integrity, and right to meet with persons close to him.

According to the second Swedish report submitted under the United Nations Convention on the Rights of the Child,[1] if a child has been placed in care, normally legal custody remains with the parents although *de facto* custody devolves on the municipal social welfare committee. Legal custody may be transferred by court order if this is in the best interests of the child. According to the report, very few custody transfers of this kind actually occur.

If a parent fails to care for his/her child so that its health and development is at risk, the court may deprive the parent of custody.

The Code of Parenthood and Guardianship expressly provides that children may not be subjected to corporal punishment or other degrading treatment.

The Committee notes that the sexual offences legislation is currently under review. Changes to the law are being considered regarding the protection of young persons between the ages of 15 to 18 from being used for the production of pornographic images, and the recruitment of young persons for sex clubs. The Committee wishes to be kept informed of all development in this area.

Children and the law – Young Offenders

Children who commit crimes when they are less than 15 years of age may not be punished under the Penal Code, nor be remanded in custody. They may however in certain circumstances be arrested and subject to a preliminary investigation. In certain very exceptional cases (cases where the young person is suspected of having committed a very serious crime) a court may adjudicate whether the young person has committed the crime. Young offenders under 15 years of age are treated within the social services.

A young person under 18 years may only exceptionally be remanded in custody. Under the Penal Code a sentence of imprisonment may be passed for a crime committed before the age of 18 only if there are exceptional reasons for doing so. The basic principle is that a young

[1] CRC/C/65/Add. 3.

offender under 18 should if possible be dealt with by the social services; the court will make this order and often also impose a fine or an order for community service. Only if this is not appropriate will the court impose probation or a prison sentence.

If a prison sentence is necessary, the court will sentence the young offender to institutional youth care unless there are special reasons to the contrary.

A new form of custodial sanction was introduced in 1998; closed juvenile care, to replace the imprisonment of young offenders in prisons.

Institutional youth care and closed juvenile care are of a fixed duration; not less that 14 days and not more than four years. The National Board of Institutional Care supervises both types of custody. The Committee wishes to receive information on the number of young offenders sentenced to institutional youth care and closed juvenile care as well as the average length of sentence.

The Committee also wishes to know if young offenders are still exceptionally remanded in custody or sentenced to a term of imprisonment, if so how many and the maximum periods of any such detention.

Conclusion

The Committee concludes that the situation in Sweden is in conformity with Article 17 of the Charter.

Article 18 — The right to engage in a gainful occupation in the territory of other Contracting Parties

Paragraph 1 – Applying existing regulations in a spirit of liberality

Foreign population and migratory movement

On 1 January 1998 there were an estimated 522,000 foreigners living in Sweden (i.e. 6% of the total population). The Committee notes that the main groups of nationals of Contracting Parties to the Charter were from Finland (the largest group, forming 20% of the foreign population), Denmark, Norway and Turkey (4% each).[1]

Work permits

There are three types of work permits in Sweden. Seasonal work permits are valid for up to three months. Temporary work permits, valid for up to 18 months for work with a single employer (see also conclusion under Article 18 para. 2) can be used to remedy a shortage of workers in a particular sector or occupation. Temporary permit holders do not require a residence permit. Finally, permanent work permits are only granted for specific posts (see also conclusion under Article 18 para. 2).

Relevant statistics

The Committee asked the Swedish Government to explain the fall in the number of temporary residence and work permits granted between 1992 and 1993. The reasons given in the report refer to the overall employment situation, but these are not backed up by statistics showing the grounds on which permits were refused.

Following Sweden's accession to the European Economic Area Agreement in 1994, nationals of parties to the agreement no longer need a work permit which, in the light of the migratory flows described above, explains why relatively few have since been issued. The Committee also notes from a source other than the report that most

---

[1]OECD, *Trends in International Migration*, Sopemi, 1999 edition.

permits were granted to highly qualified industrial workers and self-employed individuals.[1]

Generally speaking, the Committee notes that statistics on the number of work permit applications received and appeals against refusal to grant such permits are not available. It is therefore unable to assess whether regulations governing the employment of foreign workers are being enforced. However, it observes that a new system introduced in 1999 will make it possible to produce such data. The Committee would therefore like to receive this information during the next supervision cycle that deals with this provision and points out that it should cover all nationals of Contracting Parties to the Charter which are not members of the European Union or party to the European Economic Area Agreement.

Conclusion

Owing to the lack of relevant statistics on the application of regulations concerning nationals of Contracting Parties to the Charter which are not members of the European Union or party to the European Economic Area Agreement, the Committee defers its conclusion.

Paragraph 2 – Simplifying existing formalities and reducing dues and taxes

Administrative formalities

Work permits

Regulations on the issue of work permits stipulate that applications should be made to the Swedish diplomatic authorities in the applicant's country of origin. Foreigners are thus unable to work in Sweden until they have obtained such authorisation. The Committee asks whether exceptions are made for foreigners already staying in Sweden and requests clarification of the situation of nationals of Contracting Parties to the Charter in this regard.

Applications must be accompanied by the offer of employment, a passport and a photograph. They are submitted to the Immigration

---

[1] *Ibidem.*

Board, which decides whether the work permit should be granted after consulting the appropriate County Labour Board.

The Committee requests that the next report explain the formalities that must be completed in order for a foreigner to work in a self-employed capacity.

Work and residence permits

Foreigners issued with a permanent residence permit are entitled to work for any employer in any occupational sector. However, holders of a temporary work permit are granted a residence permit valid only for the period covered by their work permit.

The Committee notes that foreigners are entitled to a permanent permit if they have worked for more than four years under a temporary permit. However, this only applies to people with "exceptional qualifications".

Renewal conditions

The Committee observes that conditions for the renewal of temporary work permits are stricter than before. The report indicates that, in order to prevent people who initially came to work in Sweden on a temporary basis from settling permanently in the country, the validity of temporary work permits was cut from 48 to 18 months. The Committee notes that this makes it more difficult to obtain permanent resident status and therefore restricts access for foreigners to the Swedish labour market under the same conditions as nationals.

The Committee asks whether the administrative formalities for the renewal of temporary permits are the same as for the initial permit, or whether they are simpler.

Waiting period

The Committee requests that the next report indicate the average length of time that elapses between an application being submitted and the work permit being granted, distinguishing between the various permits available and including those issued to self-employed workers.

Chancery dues and other charges

The Committee notes that there are no charges for work and residence permits. Only nationals who require a visa, including Turkish nationals, must pay chancery dues.

Conclusion

Pending receipt of the information requested concerning exceptions to the obligation to obtain a work permit before entering Swedish territory, the Committee concludes that the situation in Sweden is in conformity with Article 18 para. 2 of the Charter.

Paragraph 3 – Liberalising regulations

Access to the national labour market

As mentioned in the conclusion concerning Article 18 para. 2, work permit applications are submitted to the Immigration Board, which decides whether the work permit should be granted after consulting the appropriate County Labour Board. It is recalled that work permits are only granted in specific circumstances (i.e. for a specific job with a specific employer), subject to highly restrictive conditions being met (e.g. shortage of workers). Permanent work permits are only issued to workers who possess exceptional qualifications. Foreign workers cannot appeal against a refusal to grant a work permit. The Committee finds that these rules governing access for foreign workers to the Swedish labour market are too restrictive to be compatible with the aim of liberalising regulations set out in Article 18 para. 3.

The Committee also notes that, under the terms of Section 5 of the Aliens Act (SFS, 1989:526), the government can decide in some cases that a work permit is not required. The Committee would like to know under what circumstances a work permit is not required and whether such exceptions are granted in practice.

The report states briefly that foreigners holding a permanent residence permit may apply for any job except certain posts which may only be held by Swedish citizens "for reasons of national security and suchlike interests". The Committee requests that the next report clarify the situation for nationals of Contracting Parties to the Charter concerning access to certain posts. It asks in particular for an indication of the posts (civil service and others) to which foreigners are denied access and for an explanation of the legal grounds for such restrictions.

Exercise of the right to employment

Since temporary work permits are only granted for work with a specific employer, foreigners may not change employer during the permit period. They must therefore apply for a new work permit.

Consequences of job loss

The report states that if a person holding a work permit for work with a particular employer loses their job, they are not allowed to change employer. They may, however, remain in Sweden until their residence permit expires. The Committee requests that the next report explain the situation of a foreign worker whose residence permit expires shortly after their dismissal. It would like to know in particular whether the residence permit can be extended in order to give the holder sufficient time to find another job. Similarly, the Committee asks whether the residence permit of foreign workers who appeal against their dismissal may be extended pending a court decision.

Conclusion

The Committee concludes that the situation in Sweden is not in conformity with Article 18 para. 3 because of the restrictive nature of the regulations concerning the granting of work permits.

Paragraph 4 – The right of nationals to leave the country

Since the situation in Sweden has not changed, the Committee concludes that it is in conformity with Article 18 para. 4 of the Charter.

Article 1 of the 1988 Additional Protocol — The right to equal opportunities and equal treatment in matters of employment and occupation without discrimination on the grounds of sex

The Committee takes note of the information provided by the Swedish report.

The situation in law and in practice

The Committee refers to its general observation on Article 1 of the Additional Protocol (Conclusions XIII-5, pp. 255-257) and its conclusion for Sweden in that cycle of supervision.

With respect to vocational guidance and training, the Committee notes that according to Section 7 of the Equal Opportunities Act No. 433/1991, an employer shall, through training, skills development and other suitable measures, promote an equal distribution between men and women in various types of work and within different categories of employees. If the employer fails to comply with this, pursuant to Section 35 of the Act, the Equal Opportunities Commission may, at the petition of the Equal Opportunities Ombudsman, issue an order to the employer to fulfil the obligations, under penalty of a fine. It is not clear, however, whether the individual worker has recourse to legal action in matters of this kind. Recalling that states are obliged to ensure through legislation the right of workers to take legal action in matters covered by Article 1 of the Protocol, the Committee requests an explicit clarification on this point.

In its previous conclusion, the Committee noted that differences exist between part-time and full-time workers as regards possible entitlement to unemployment benefits and partial pensions and on those grounds raised the issue of possible indirect discrimination.

The Committee now notes that during the period 1995-1998, the proportion of women on the labour market was on average 48% and that of men 52%. During the same period, 83% of the part-time workers were women and 17% were men. From an appendix to the report,[1] the Committee notes that approximately twice as many women as men worked "short" part-time in 1997 with a working time of less than 19 hours per week. Recalling that the benefit entitlements in question are contingent on a working week of at least 17 hours, the Committee

---

[1]Women and men in Sweden, facts and figures 1998, Statistiska Centralbyrån, 1998.

notes that this in effect may operate to place women in a less favourable position than men. Noting that the Swedish report states that there are no statistics on the proportion of part-time workers who do not qualify for benefits, the Committee underlines the importance of this point and insists on finding this information in the next report.

In general, wage differentials between women and men have not decreased during the 1990s according to a Government circular (1999/2000:24) appended to the report. In 1997, women earned on average 83% of male wages. There were less differences in the private sector than in the public sector, with female workers in the private sector on average earning 89% of male wages. The most important wage differentials were to be found in the administration of the provinces (landsting) where female wages were only 71% of male wages. However, if the level of education, profession and age factors are taken into consideration, women on average earned 93% of male wages. The Committee takes note of the extensive measures taken by the Swedish Government to improve the situation.

As regards differences in terms of employment and working conditions between women and men, an appendix to the report shows that current research is concerned with tools from an ergonomic perspective. The National Institute for Working Life will run a research project on "Gender, Employment and Health" which is expected to continue for four or five years. The Committee asks to be kept informed of the results.

The Committee takes note of the information provided in the report on the conditions for being accepted to the police force, the fire and rescue services and the army. It also takes note of the figures supplied on the proportion of women employed in these services (17% of the police force, 0,1% of the part-time fire-fighters, 0,16% of the full-time fire-fighters, 2,4% of regular army officers and 0,7% of reserve officers). According to the report, the physical demands are very exacting in the fire and rescue services and few women can meet them. However, work is in progress with a view to possibly altering the municipal rules of admission so as to facilitate the recruitment of women.

Positive action

The Equal Opportunities Act requires every employer to conduct, within the scope of the business operation concerned, target-referenced activities for the active promotion of equal opportunities at work. In addition, every employer with 10 or more employees shall draw up an annual plan of equal opportunities promotion. The plan shall chart conditions at the workplace and shall also include concrete targets and guidelines with respect to working conditions, recruitment, training, and competence development and pay questions. The Equal Opportunities Ombudsman monitors the drafting of equal opportunities plans.

Conclusion

Pending receipt of the information requested on the proportion of female/male part-time workers who do not qualify for unemployment and pension benefits, the Committee again defers its conclusion.

Article 4 of the 1988 Additional Protocol — The right of elderly persons to social protection

The Committee takes note of the information on developments concerning the right of elderly persons to social protection and the replies to the questions posed in its previous conclusion, contained in the Swedish report and the appendices thereto.

General policy for the elderly

The report states that, in 1998, 17.4% of the population was over 65, and 4.9% over 80 years old.

To adapt policies to growth in the number of elderly people and their changing needs, parliament adopted a national plan of action in June 1998, which defines the objectives of policy for the elderly. The Committee notes that these objectives are consistent with the commitments entered into under Article 4 of the Additional Protocol: to enable elderly persons to lead an active life and have some influence in society; to assure people that they will be able to grow old in security, while retaining their independence and being treated with respect; and to guarantee access to good-quality health services. A total of 1.2 million Swedish Kronor (SEK) has been earmarked for implementation of this plan during the 1999-2001 period, in particular for launching a new gerontology research programme and training staff supervising services for the elderly.

In December 1998 the government asked a parliamentary committee to look at how policies for the elderly in all sectors of society should be designed from the year 2005 onwards.

A standard of living enabling elderly persons to remain full members of society for as long as possible (Article 4 para. 1)

The Committee noted from the previous report that, according to government estimates, elderly persons' standard of living exceeded 90% of that enjoyed by households in the active age groups.

Financial resources

The public old-age pension scheme provides for a basic national pension, which is non-contributory and is payable to anyone who has lived in Sweden for at least 3 years or paid 3 years' ATP contributions (see below) between the ages of 16 and 64, and a supplementary national pension (ATP), which depends on the level of income from employment (which must exceed a base amount), is contributory and is not subject to any minimum period of scheme membership. To receive a full basic pension, a person must have lived in Sweden for 40 years or have been credited with 30 years' ATP contributions. Otherwise, the pension is reduced on a proportional basis. The Committee wishes to know what proportion of elderly people receive the basic pension as their sole source of income. It would also like to receive information on the amount of the basic pension or the pension guaranteed under the new scheme introduced in 1998.

For a description of the conditions governing retirement, the Committee refers to its previous conclusion.

The above rules apply irrespective of nationality. For nationals of other Contracting Parties who do not meet the residence requirement, cumulating periods of insurance abroad is possible in the case of nationals of European Union and European Economic Area member states and countries with which bilateral agreements have been concluded. Since Sweden has not accepted Article 12 para. 4, it has not entered into any commitment under the Charter with regard to coordination of social security schemes.

The report states that foreigners living in Sweden who do not qualify for a pension may receive social benefits. This applied to 10,000 people in 1998 (out of the 132,000 foreign nationals over 65 years of age resident in Sweden). The Committee notes that equality of treatment in social assistance matters is guaranteed in accordance with Article 13 para. 1 of the Charter (Conclusions XV-1, p. 573).

Noting that the basic pension is non-contributory, within the meaning of the Charter, the Committee considers that the 3 year residence requirement for acquisition of entitlement is not excessive and does not breach Article 4 of the Additional Protocol.

Cost of community services

The report states that 90-95% of the cost of social services for the elderly is borne by the municipalities, the remainder being financed by charging individual users. It is the local council which determines the level of charges, subject to the requirements, laid down in the Social Services Act, that charges must be reasonable, that they must not exceed the actual cost to the municipality and that the individual must be left with enough money to provide for his or her personal needs. According to the report, a survey conducted in 1996 showed that 70% of municipalities take account of both income levels and "consumption" as criteria for determining charges for home services, and 65% apply income-related charges for special forms of accommodation. The National Board of Health and Welfare found that there were deficiencies concerning the requirement that an individual be left with enough resources to provide for his or her personal needs, and the law was therefore amended to specify the minimum amount that must be reserved for the individual and to provide that municipalities might modify the charges payable where these constituted a financial obstacle to a person's remaining in his or her own home.

The Committee would like the next report to indicate the results of the investigation into the effect of systems of charges on use of services, mentioned in this report, which were published in 1999.

Availability of care

In its previous conclusion the Committee noted that a "care guarantee" had been introduced with the aim of improving the availability of health care and reducing waiting periods. The report contains information on the results of this reform. Since the Committee examined these under Article 11 para. 1 of the Charter, it refers to its conclusion concerning that provision.

Services and facilities allowing elderly persons to lead independent lives in familiar surroundings (Article 4 para. 2)

In Sweden 90% of elderly people live in ordinary housing, and half of them own their home. The principle is that the decision to move a person to special accommodation is taken only as a last resort, when that person can no longer lead an independent life.

Assessment of needs

Under the Social Services Act, municipal authorities are responsible for assessing elderly persons' needs, in particular through home visits made with the permission of the persons concerned, and for determining the measures to be taken to satisfy those needs. The report states that there was a decrease in home visits in the early nineties because of the economic recession but that, under the above-mentioned plan of action, funds have been specifically earmarked for re-launching these activities.

Types of services and facilities

A broad range of community services and facilities exists, with the aim of enabling elderly persons to remain in their own home for as long as possible. The Committee has noted from previous reports that these include special transport services, home help and daycare (meals, leisure activities and other daytime activities). The report specifies that 8% of elderly people living in ordinary housing receive home-help services. With regard to accommodation, the report mentions the existence of a special grant from the municipality for adaptation of housing to individual requirements, including the needs of persons with reduced mobility, impaired vision or impaired hearing.

Operational responsibility

The report states that during the nineties it became increasingly common for municipalities to sub-contract operational responsibility for care of the elderly. A nationwide survey in 1999 showed that over 50% of municipalities relied on private service-providers. However, the municipal authority still has overall responsibility for service provision, as regards both keeping track of individuals' situations and supervising services provided by private firms.

Specific protection afforded to elderly persons living in institutions (Article 4 para. 3)

The report specifies that approximately 9% of people over 65 years of age currently live in special forms of accommodation. The above-mentioned plan of action includes a special appropriation for increasing intake capacity and improving the quality of life in institutions.

In its earlier conclusions the Committee noted the types of accommodation available in institutions, the arrangements for supervising standards and the running of institutions and the right of recourse of persons wishing to complain about shortcomings in the services provided.

With regard to equipment, the report states that 80% of people living in an institution now have individual toilets. It also specifies that in most special forms of accommodation there are residents' councils, which are consulted on a regular basis but have no official say in decisions. The Committee wishes to know whether measures are envisaged to guarantee elderly people living in institutions effective participation in decisions concerning living conditions, as required by Article 4 of the Additional Protocol.

Conclusion

Pending receipt of the information requested, the Committee concludes that the situation in Sweden is in conformity with Article 4 of the Additional Protocol.

Chapter 15 – Conclusions concerning Articles 7, 8, 11, 14, 17 and 18 of the Charter in respect of the United Kingdom

Article 7 — The right of children and young persons to protection

Paragraph 2 – Higher minimum age in certain occupations

The Committee takes note of the information provided in the report of the United Kingdom, and of the numerous appendices relating to various dangerous occupations in which the employment of minors is either prohibited or subject to restriction. The report indicates that, during the reference period, the Health and Safety (Young Persons) Regulations 1997 entered into force. These have since been incorporated into the Management of Health and Safety at Work Regulations 1999, which entered into force on 29 December 1999. Section 19 of the Regulations prohibits the employment of young persons in work which entails exposure to danger. Young persons who have completed compulsory schooling, i.e. are over the age of 16, may however perform such work under competent adult supervision if this is necessary for their training and any risk is reduced to the lowest level that is reasonably practicable.

In addition to binding regulations on the employment of minors in dangerous activities, the Committee also takes note of the use of Approved Codes of Practice, issued under the Health and Safety at Work Act 1974 or the Health and Safety at Work (Northern Ireland) Order 1978. These Codes contain both the relevant regulations and provide advice to employers on how best to comply with the law. Failure to observe a code is not an offence, but may constitute proof that an employer has contravened health and safety law.

The Committee concludes that the situation in the United Kingdom is in conformity with Article 7 para. 2 of the Charter.

Paragraph 3 – Safeguarding the full benefit of compulsory education

The Committee takes note from the report of the United Kingdom of the legislative amendments made during the reference period, in particular the Children (Protection at Work) Regulations 1998 and the Employment of Children Regulations (Northern Ireland) 1996.

Situation in Great Britain

According to the report, one of the effects of the 1998 Regulations has been to introduce some additional national standards on the employment of children. Previously, certain matters, such as the duration of children's work during school holidays, were regulated on the basis of local authority bye-laws. The minimum age for employment is 13 years, although children of this age may only perform light work for their parents. Children aged 14 to 15 years may perform light work for other employers, subject to a series of restrictions. As regards working time, such children may work for up to 17 hours per week during the school year, calculated as follows:

– no more than 2 hours per day on a school day. This may include one hour before school, but no earlier than 7 a.m. No work may be performed after 7 p.m.;

– no more than 5 hours' work on Saturdays;

– no more than 2 hours' work on Sundays.

Children between the age of 15 and minimum school leaving age[1] (MSLA) may work for slightly longer during the school year, as they are permitted to be employed for up to 8 hours on a Saturday.

The Committee recalls that it has previously held that children should not be permitted to do any kind of work before going to school in the morning (Conclusions VIII, p. 108) as such work may deprive them of the full benefit of their compulsory education. However, in the light of the restrictions applying (a maximum of one hour before school, not before 7 a.m., not in an industrial undertaking), the Committee wishes to know how these are supervised and it also asks to be informed of the nature and extent in practice of early morning work before school. Pending receipt of this information, the Committee reserves its position on this matter.

During school holidays, children under the age of 15 may be employed in light work for up to 5 hours per day and 25 hours per week. Children

---

[1]Children are required to attend school until the last Friday of June of the school year in which they reach the age of 16. Thus, the youngest age at which a child may finish school is 15 years and 10 months.

over 15 may be employed for up to 8 hours per day and 35 hours per week. The Committee considers that these rules are not contrary to the Charter.

A mandatory rest period of 2 weeks during the summer holidays now applies to employed children. The Committee takes note of this improvement in the situation, but considers that this period of rest is insufficient. The Committee considers that the main purpose of school holidays is to let children rest in order to benefit from school after the holiday. It refers to its case-law that the rest period must cover at least half of the holiday period for children still subject to compulsory education. This not being the case in the United Kingdom, the Committee finds that the situation is not in conformity with Article 7 para. 3 of the Charter.

As regards the situation in practice, the Committee notes from another source[1] that employment is common among children aged 11-15 years, concerning between 1.1 and 1.7 million in this group. The Committee wishes to receive information in the next report under this provision on the activities of local authorities in enforcing the above regulations, especially the issuing of employment cards. It also asks about the number of prosecutions or other forms of sanction.

Situation in Northern Ireland

The rules applicable in Northern Ireland differ from the above in the following regard:

– maximum weekly working time for children under the age of 15 is 27 hours. For children over 15 but under minimum school leaving age, maximum weekly working time is 37 hours;

– children may only be employed in work that is expressly permitted in the schedule to the 1996 Regulations.

The Committee considers that these rules are not contrary to the Charter, but it asks that the next report state what measures have been taken to ensure supervision of employers' compliance with these rules in practice.

[1] House of Commons Library Research Paper 98/18, 3 February 1998.

Conclusion

The Committee concludes that the situation in the United Kingdom is not in conformity with Article 7 para. 3 of the Charter because the mandatory rest period during the school holidays for children still subject to compulsory education is not sufficient to ensure that they may benefit from such education.

Paragraph 5 – Fair remuneration for young workers and apprentices

The Committee notes from the report of the United Kingdom that young workers aged 16 and 17, i.e. coming within the scope of this provision of the Charter, are exempted from the national minimum wage which was introduced in 1999.

According to the report the government's priority is that young people of 16 and 17 continue with their education and acquire the skills and opportunities they need to progress. It wishes to ensure against the risk that the provision of a set minimum wage rate might discourage them from staying on in education and training or discourage employers from hiring them.

The Committee further notes the information on average gross weekly pay for those aged 16-18 on full-time rates as of April 1999. For male manual workers the average per week was 138.60 British Pounds (GBP) and for female manual workers it was 144.90 GBP. From another source[1] it notes that the comparable average wage for adults was 335 GBP for male manual workers and 221.90 GBP for female manual workers. The average gross wage of young workers is thus well below half that of adult workers.

However, in order to assess compliance with Article 7 para. 5 the Committee needs information on the starting wages of adult workers, or in effect the minimum wage, and the lowest remuneration paid to young workers and apprentices, in both cases calculated net, i.e. after deduction of taxes and social security contributions. As such information is not included in the report, the Committee requests that it be contained in the next report.

[1]www.statistics.gov.uk/statbase.

The report states that a number of tax and benefit reforms to boost the wages of low paid workers were introduced outside the reference period. The Committee observes that this only accentuates the importance of supplying information on the net value of wages and it asks whether the new tax measures will also benefit young workers.

The Committee notes from a recent report by the Low Pay Commission[1] that a not insignificant number of young workers under 18 earn 2 GBP gross per hour compared to the statutory minimum wage for adults of 3.60 GBP per hour (3 GBP for the 18-21 year olds), i.e. a difference of about 44%. Other material made available by the Low Pay Commission[2] reveals that hourly pay may in certain cases be even lower, which would indicate that the situation is not in conformity with the Charter. This information is evidently not in itself sufficient to assess the situation, but as it reached a negative conclusion under Article 4 para. 1 as regards adult wages (Conclusions XIV-2, p. 771) and given the fact that the report does not demonstrate that the situation of young workers and apprentices has improved, the Committee renews its previous conclusion that the situation in the United Kingdom is not in conformity with the Charter.

The Committee wishes to underline in response to observations in the report that the Charter does not require that young workers be paid at the same rate as "experienced workers" nor indeed should employers be "obliged to pay them the full adult rate." The Committee holds on an indicative basis that a reduction of about 20% in comparison with an adult worker's starting wage (or minimum wage) is fair for a young worker. For an apprentice a satisfactory remuneration could range from at least one-third at the beginning of the apprenticeship to at least two-thirds at the end. In the opinion of the Committee, concerns for the continued education of young people and for their prospects of gaining access to employment are not incompatible with the guarantee of a fair wage in the meaning of Article 7 para. 5 of the Charter.

The Committee concludes that the situation in the United Kingdom is not in conformity with Article 7 para. 5 of the Charter as the Committee has held that the wages of adult workers are not in conformity with Article 4 para. 1 of the Charter and as the government has not shown

---

[1]The National Minimum Wage. The Story So Far. Second report by the Low Pay Commission, February 2000.

[2] www.lowpay.gov.uk

that the wages of all young workers have reached a level which can be considered fair.

Paragraph 6 – Treatment of the time spent in vocational training as forming part of the working day

The United Kingdom report recalls that terms and conditions of employment, including whether time spent on vocational training is included in normal working hours, are matters for agreement between employer and employee and are reflected in the individual's employment contract. However, the report also states that under the Work-Based Training for Young People scheme (WBTYP) providing vocational qualifications to young people aged 16-25, all employers treat vocational education and training taking place during normal working hours as part of the working day for remuneration purposes.

The Committee observes that initiatives relevant to this provision of the Charter have been taken outside the reference period. A new employment right to time off for study or training came into force on 1 September 1999. Through the Teaching and Higher Education Act 1998, the Government has amended the Employment Rights Act 1996 so that 16 and 17 year old employees who have not achieved a certain standard of education/training, are entitled to reasonable paid time off during normal working hours to pursue approved qualifications in the workplace, at college or with a training provider. In Northern Ireland legislation entitling young people to time off to undertake study or training leading to a relevant qualification has been put in place and will shortly be implemented. Under the legislation, young people will have a right to time off for study or training and to remuneration from their employer for the time taken off at the appropriate hourly rate.

In view of the absence of a statutory guarantee of the principle laid down by Article 7 para. 6, the Committee has previously requested information demonstrating that at least 80% of young employed persons undergoing training benefit from having time spent on the training treated as normal working hours. The report states that data from the Labour Force Survey (LFS) show that in 1998 20% of employees aged 16-18 did not receive wages while doing some form of off-the job training. "Employees" did not include young people on government programmes such as WBTYP mentioned above.

The Committee emphasises that information must be included in each report demonstrating that at least 80% of the persons concerned are covered by the Charter's guarantee.

Pending receipt of the information requested, the Committee concludes that the situation in the United Kingdom is in conformity with Article 7 para. 6 of the Charter.

Paragraph 9 – Provision of regular medical control for young workers under eighteen

The United Kingdom report states that the Control of Lead at Work Regulations 1998 require that employees in any occupation where their exposure to lead is significant (as defined by the Regulations), must be placed under medical surveillance. All employees must have their blood monitored regularly to detect any absorption of lead before clinical effects become evident.

The Committee asks that the next report provide up-dated information on occupations in which medical examinations are stipulated for persons under 18, indicating the conditions in which and how often these examinations are made.

Meanwhile, it concludes that the situation in the United Kingdom is in conformity with Article 7 para. 9 of the Charter.

Paragraph 10 – Special protection for children and young people from physical and moral dangers to which they are exposed

The Committee notes the information contained in the report of the United Kingdom.

As regards the protection of working children the Committee refers to its conclusions under Article 7 paras. 2 and 3.

The Committee further refers to its conclusion under Article 11 para. 2 in respect of measures taken to prevent drug addiction and alcohol abuse.

The Committee wishes to be informed as to whether legislation prohibits the use of children in the sex industry, and to receive information on any supervisory system and sanctions that may accompany this prohibition.

The Committee concludes that the situation in the United Kingdom is in conformity with Article 7 para. 10 of the Charter.

Article 8 — The right of employed women to protection

Paragraph 1 – Maternity leave

1. Entitlement to maternity leave

The report states that the regulations on maternity leave have been amended and that, since 15 December 1999, outside the reference period, the 14 week ordinary maternity leave has been extended to 18 weeks for all employees, including policewomen, regardless of length of service (*the Maternity and Parental Leave Regulations, 1999*). Of these 18 weeks, only 2 weeks have to be taken after the birth of the baby. For women factory workers this compulsory leave period lasts 4 weeks.

The report states that the 2 weeks' post-natal maternity leave are in line with the requirements of Community Directive 92/85 on the introduction of measures to encourage improvements in the safety and health at work of pregnant workers and workers who have recently given birth or are breastfeeding. It also maintains that, in practice, where a woman is entitled to the basic 18 weeks' ordinary maternity leave, she starts her maternity leave 11 weeks before the expected date of childbirth and has 7 weeks after the birth of the baby. It states, finally, that it is for women to decide how to use their maternity leave and when to return to work after the birth.

The Committee recalls that the aim of Article 8 para. 1 is to ensure women have special protection in cases of maternity and to meet the general public health interest through the protection of mother and child. The period of 12 weeks of rest, apportioned before and after confinement, is to be considered a minimum, as the text of the Charter itself states. The period of compulsory post-natal leave set at 6 weeks by the Committee (Conclusion VIII, p. 125) is also to be seen as a minimum period permitting no derogation. The Committee adds that even if in practice the majority of women enjoy post-natal maternity leave longer than the compulsory 2 weeks, this does not mean that all women enjoy post-natal maternity leave of 6 weeks. It considers it necessary that national law expressly provide for 6 weeks of compulsory leave after confinement.

Consequently, in the absence of a compulsory period of 6 weeks' post-natal leave, the Committee concludes that the situation in the United

Kingdom is not in conformity with Article 8 para. 1 of the Charter on this point.

2. Entitlement to adequate allowances

The Committee notes that the report makes no reference to any significant change in a situation which it has considered to be in breach of the Charter since the XI supervision cycle.

It recalls that, in the United Kingdom, women are entitled to statutory maternity pay (SMP). They must have worked for their employer for at least 6 months before the 15th week preceding the birth and have had average earnings in the 8 weeks preceding the 15th week before the birth such that they were paying national insurance contributions. During the first 6 weeks this maternity pay, which is not subject to any ceiling, is payable at 90% of the woman's average earnings (subsequently at a rate of 57.70 GPB per week (in 1998).

Women who do not satisfy the SMP qualifying conditions can receive maternity allowance for 18 weeks if they have worked and paid national insurance contributions for at least 26 weeks during the 66 weeks preceding the expected date of childbirth. There are two rates of maternity allowance: 57.70 GPB per week (in 1998) if the beneficiary was gainfully employed in the reference week for entitlement to the allowance; 50.10 GBP per week (in 1998) if the beneficiary was not working or was self-employed in the reference week for entitlement to the allowance.

The Committee asks if periods of unemployment are reckoned as working time for the granting of maternity allowance.

Finally, a woman who does not satisfy the conditions either for SMP or for maternity allowance is entitled to sickness benefit (amounting to 57.70 GBP per week) for six weeks before the birth and for fourteen days after.

The Committee again notes that the SMP is paid at an adequate rate (90% of the previous earnings) for only six weeks. Furthermore, a weekly allowance of 57.70 GBP (SMP or maternity allowance) paid for the following twelve weeks or for eighteen weeks cannot be considered adequate. The Committee recalls in this connection that in April 1999 the minimum wage was set at 144 GBP per week.

The Committee concludes therefore that the situation in the United Kingdom is not in conformity with Article 8 para. 1 of the Charter on this point.

Article 11 — Right to protection of health

Paragraph 1 – Removal of the causes of ill-health

The Committee takes note of the information in the United Kingdom report on the Charter, on the National Health Service (NHS) Internet site[1] and in the 1999 report of the European Observatory on Health Care Systems.[2]

State of health of the population – General indicators

Life expectancy and principal causes of mortality

The Committee observes from the OECD statistics[3] that life expectancy at birth has risen from 78.9 years in 1992 to 79.5 in 1996 for women and from 73.4 in 1992 to 74.3 in 1996 for men. Eurostat statistics[4] show that women's life expectancy in the United Kingdom is below the average for the countries of the European Union and the European Economic Area (the European average was 80.6 in 1996).

According to the report, the main causes of death in 1998 in England and Wales were cancers (25%), followed by heart disease (22%) and respiratory conditions (16%), while in Northern Ireland they were circulatory diseases (42%), cancers (24%) and respiratory diseases (18%).

The Committee notes from the Eurostat data that in 1995 death from ischaemic cardiopathy was significantly higher than the European average (380 deaths per 100,000 inhabitants compared with an average of 247). The mortality rate caused by diseases of the respiratory tract, particularly pneumonia (120 deaths per 100,000 inhabitants, compared with an average of 48), was twice as high as the average for the other European Union countries. The Committee emphasises that death from pneumonia must be considered to be an avoidable risk since this is a curable disease. It therefore considers that a significant rate of mortality from this disease indicates a problem in the provision of care and patients' medical treatment. However, with a view to pronouncing itself on the basis of more complete information, it wishes

---

[1]www.nhsdirect.nhs.uk

[2]Health Care Systems in Transition Profile (www.observatory.dk).

[3]OECD Health Data 1999.

[4]Eurostat yearbook, *A statistical eye on Europe,* 1988-1998 data.

to know the mortality rate due to diseases of the respiratory system, in particular pneumonia, broken down according to age of the deceased persons and it decides to pronounce itself in the light of the evolution of the situation during the next reference period.

The Committee notes that the number of AIDS cases diagnosed halved over the reference period, from 1,740 cases in 1995 to 81 in 1998.

Infant and maternal mortality

According to the OECD statistics, the infant mortality rate in the United Kingdom continued to decline: from 6.6 per 1,000 live births in 1992 to 5.9 in 1997. The Committee observes that the rate remains higher than the average of the countries of the European Union and the European Economic Area (5,3 in 1997). It emphasises that infant mortality is an avoidable risk which States must control in order to comply with Article 11 of the Charter. It indicates to the British authorities that the evolution in the infant mortality rate will be central to assessing the conformity of the situation and it encourages the authorities to pursue its efforts to approach as close as possible to "zero risk".

The average maternal mortality rate remained stable in relation to the previous reference period.

Health care system

Access to health care

The British health system offers universal, free and uniform health coverage. Nearly all care is provided under the NHS.

General practitioners, who are paid directly by the NHS, have a central role. In particular, it is they who direct patients towards specialist services. Under the 1991 reform, governed by the NHS and Community Care Act, health authorities and certain general practitioners, known as fund holders, were given responsibility for managing budgets for purchasing health services, to introduce competition between hospitals and clinics, which are grouped together into hospital trusts. In the 1997 white paper, *The New NHS, Modern, Dependable*, the incoming government launched a new approach based on collaboration between service purchasers and providers rather than competition. One of the main reforms to stem from this approach is the requirement for general practitioners to belong to primary health groups.

NHS financing mainly comes from taxes (84%).

According to the aforementioned OECD statistics, total health spending has remained stable since the last reference period, representing 6.9% of GDP in 1997. The proportion of health spending accounted for by the public sector also remained stable and was 84.6% in 1997.

Patients are not required to make any contribution to medical or hospital costs. For dental care under the general dental service, patients pay for 80% of the cost of treatment, up to 340 pounds sterling (GBP), but certain groups (pregnant women, young persons aged under 18 and persons in receipt of social assistance allowances) are exempt from payment. There is a charge of 5.80 GBP for prescribed medicines, again with exemptions for certain groups, in particular pregnant women, mothers with children under one year, persons aged over 60, young persons under 16 and persons in receipt of social assistance allowances, and for persons suffering from certain conditions.[1]

According to the OECD statistics, the average "reimbursement" rates for out-patient medical care, hospital costs and pharmaceutical products, respectively 88%, 99% and 90% in 1997, are among the highest in the OECD's European countries.

Waiting lists for hospital admission and appointments with specialists are a structural feature of the British health system, as a consequence of the fact that services are free. The Committee notes from another source than the report[2] that in England between 1990-1991 and 1995-1996 the average waiting time for admission to hospital increased from 35 to 45 days while the percentage of patients admitted after waiting for more than a year fell from 20% to 3%. In 1997, 74% of patients were admitted within 3 months and 87% were admitted within 6 months. In 1997 the new Government set itself the objectives of ensuring that waiting time in no case should exceed 18 months and in a second phase, 12 months, and that the total number of patients on waiting lists should be reduced. According to the above-mentioned report of the European Observatory on Health Care Systems, none of these objectives were attained during the reference period. On the contrary, the number of patients on waiting lists continued to increase. As regards waiting lists for an appointment with a general practitioner,

[1]European Commission, *Social protection in the Member States of the European Union, situation on 1 July 1999 and Overview*, Missoc

[2]Research paper 99/60, House of Commons, Hospital waiting lists and waiting times.

the proportion of persons having obtained an appointment within 13 weeks diminished from 83% to 77% from 1997 to 1999. The total number of persons having waited more than 26 weeks for an appointment with a general practitioner nearly doubled from 1997 to 1999.

The Committee is aware that the fact that waiting lists are getting longer has more than one cause and may in particular reflect growing demand and expectations of the population. However, the Committee notes that the duration of waiting times is long in absolute terms, that the situation is not improving and that simultaneously the number of hospital beds continues to decrease (see below). It considers that on the basis of these data, the organisation of health care in the United Kingdom is manifestly not adapted to ensure the right to health for everyone. Nevertheless, before pronouncing itself on compliance with Article 11 para. 1 and referring to Recommendation No. R Chs (99)21 of the Committee of Ministers of the Council of Europe on criteria for the management of waiting lists and waiting times in health care, the Committee requests information on the way in which waiting lists are managed (admission criteria and follow-up). The Committee underlines that it will pay particular attention to whether access to treatment is based on transparent criteria, agreed at the national level, taking into account the risk of deterioration, in clinical terms as well as in terms of quality of life.

Health professionals and equipment

According to the OECD statistics, the number of hospital beds continues to fall (264,500 in 1996, compared with 310 500 in 1992), and at 4.5 per 1,000 inhabitants, bed density is one of the lowest among the OECD's European member countries. Of the total number of beds, 45.4% are in acute hospitals and 20% are allocated to psychiatric care. Private hospital beds accounted for 3.7% of the total in 1993.

The total density of doctors, general practitioners and specialists per 1,000 population is one of the two lowest in the European OECD countries (1.7 in 1996). The same applies to the density of general practitioners per 1,000 inhabitants (0.6 in 1996). The Committee notes that this situation is not compensated for by a higher rate of hospital posts. The density of dentists (0.4 per 1,000 inhabitants) is around the European average and the number of pharmacists (0.6 per 1,000 inhabitants is one of the lowest.

Conclusion

Pending receipt of the information requested, the Committee defers its conclusion.

Paragraph 2 – Advisory and educational facilities

The Committee takes note of the information in the United Kingdom report and its appendices.

Developing a sense of individual responsibility

Health education in schools

The Committee has noted in previous reports that health education is part of the school curriculum and entails co-operation between teachers, school health staff and, sometimes, parents, and between local authorities and health services. The areas covered include, in particular, the prevention of smoking, alcohol misuse and drug taking, dental hygiene and healthy eating, and AIDS prevention.

Since 1993, the United Kingdom has been a member of the European Network of Health Promoting Schools, established by the World Health Organisation Regional Office for Europe, the European Commission and the Council of Europe.

In England, the government's strategy is to strengthen health education in schools through a national pilot project called the Healthy Schools Programme. This has a budget of 4 million GBP for 1999-2000. The programme, based on a partnership between education and health authorities, identifies a number of standards in this area and offers schools various means of achieving them: an Internet site (Wired for Health) to help young people develop a sense of personal responsibility for their health, the Cooking for Kids programme to make children more aware of the importance of a healthy diet for their health and support for programmes to encourage physical activity in or on the way to and from school.

Strengthening and improving health education is also one of the health policy priorities in Scotland. The Committee notes in particular the establishment of 60 "new community schools" to offer children and their families full and integrated support in such areas as health education.

Public information and awareness

Campaigns to inform and educate the public in general or specific target groups are regularly conducted in England and Wales by the Health Education Authority. Throughout the country, the information and public awareness strategy is based on a multidisciplinary approach involving local authorities, employers, schools, NGOs, the media and health services. The Committee particularly notes the sustained efforts to prevent drug abuse, smoking and alcohol misuse, encourage physical activities and prevent the spread of AIDS. It also notes that a telephone line, *NHS direct*, and a Web site, *NHS Direct On-line*, enable people to obtain general and specialised information and advice on health matters, twenty-four hours a day. Finally, the Committee notes the establishment of the Good Start programme for parents on their children's health.

Consultations and health screening

There are medical staff, either a doctor and nurse and just a nurse, in every school. School nurses monitor children's health and development from the age of five through hearing and eyesight tests and by measuring their height and weight. They are responsible for health promotion in schools, offer children and young persons health care and advice and are trained in specific aspects of juvenile health, such as sexuality, allergies and asthma. Pupils are then encouraged to initiate consultations themselves with the school doctor or nurse. Dental examinations are carried out annually on all school-age children and vaccinations are also administered in school.

The Committee asks whether childcare services offer paediatric consultation for children from birth up to school age.

Conclusion

The Committee concludes that the situation in the United Kingdom is in conformity with Article 11 para. 2 of the Charter.

Paragraph 3 – Prevention of disease

The Committee takes note of the changes in the United Kingdom concerning the prevention of health risks in general and specific diseases.

Policies on the prevention of avoidable risks

General

The Committee would like the next reports to indicate, as far as possible, the proportion of public authorities' budgets devoted to the main prevention policies listed below.

Reduction of environmental risks

Air pollution – The Committee notes, on the basis of OECD data,[1] that the United Kingdom's performance in terms of controlling man-made emissions of traditional pollutants (sulphur oxides, nitrogen oxides, carbon monoxide and volatile organic compounds) is generally positive.

Turning to global pollution, the Committee notes that the United Kingdom signed the United Nations Framework Convention on Climate Change (Rio de Janeiro, 1992) in 1993. With others, the United Kingdom has undertaken to maintain the main greenhouse gas emissions at 1990 levels by 2000 and reduce them by 12.5% by 2008-2012, in order to achieve the objectives set for the European Union at the 1997 Kyoto conference. It has also set itself the objective of a 20% reduction in carbon dioxide emissions by 2010, taking 1990 as the baseline. It appears from the second report on the application of the Rio Convention[2] that the United Kingdom is one of a few states to have achieved, and even exceeded, the objectives set under the Convention for the three main greenhouse gases: carbon dioxide, methane and nitrogen protoxide.

Turning to the management of local pollutants, and having regard to the high level of deaths caused by respiratory diseases (see conclusion under Article 11 para. 1), the Committee would like the next report to indicate whether concentration limits and information and warning thresholds have been set for the main pollutants that cause air pollution (ozone, sulphur dioxide, nitrogen dioxide, lead, suspended fine particles, carbon monoxide and benzene), and whether equipment for monitoring air quality has been installed, particularly in urban areas.

Asbestos – With reference to the general question concerning the measures taken to protect the health of persons exposed to asbestos (Conclusions XIII-4 p. 116), the Committee noted in its last conclusion

---

[1] *OECD Environmental Data*, Compendium 1999.

[2] FCCC/IDR.2/GBR of 17 December 1999, consulted on the United Nations site on the Convention (www.unfccc.de).

on Article 3 (Conclusions XIV-2, p. 764) that the Asbestos Regulations 1992 banned the import, supply and use of all amphibole asbestos fibres. The Committee also wishes to know what measures are taken to monitor the presence of asbestos in buildings, particularly those used as dwellings, and the specific obligations placed on businesses concerning the disposal of asbestos waste.

Ionising radiation – In 1995, 26.7% of the electricity produced in the United Kingdom was of nuclear origin. In reply to the general question on protecting the health of persons living in the vicinity of nuclear power plants (Conclusions XII-2, p. 168), the report states that the radiation dose limits in the regulations are now the same as those recommended by the International Commission on Radiological Protection (ICRP). This information supplements that in earlier reports on the monitoring of radiation pollution, the information and consultation activities of local community liaison councils and the information supplied regularly to people living in the vicinity of nuclear plants. The Committee therefore considers that the United Kingdom is in compliance with Article 11 para. 3 of the Charter on this point.

Noise – previous reports have shown that noise abatement has been an integral part of the United Kingdom's environmental policy for several years. Noise thresholds have been set for vehicles and various noise-abatement measures have been introduced. The Environmental Protection Act 1990, as amended in 1993, gives local authorities wide-ranging powers to prevent, abate or stop noise from vehicles, machinery and equipment in the street. Failure to comply can result in fines or imprisonment. In Scotland, the police are empowered to intervene on their own initiative in response to noise nuisance. The Committee wishes to know whether monitoring and sound measuring equipment is currently available.

Food safety

In view of the threat to health represented by diseases related to food and the recent outbreaks of such diseases in particular the new variation of the Creutzfeldt-Jakob disease, as well as the emergence of new food products derived from biotechnology, the Committee has decided to look at food safety measures in all states parties to the Charter. It considers that under Article 11 states have a responsibility to ensure a high degree of safety in this area for their populations.

Referring in particular to the resolution adopted by the 53rd World Health Assembly in May 2000 on food safety[1] and while recognising the relevance of international strategies, the Committee recalls that in order to comply with the Charter in this field, states must set legal norms at the national level regarding food hygiene taking into account scientific data, and establish and maintain mechanisms for monitoring compliance with these norms throughout the food chain, develop, implement and up-date systematic prevention measures, notably by way of labelling, as well as monitor the occurrence of food-borne diseases.

As regards in particular the food-related infection by Bovine Spongiform Encephalopathy (BSE), the Committee notes that the British population is currently the most affected by this infection and that several deaths due to the new variation of the Creutzfeldt-Jakob disease caused by BSE have occurred during the reference period. The Committee expresses its concern about the seriousness of the situation and asks that the next report contain information on the evolution of the situation and on the measures taken with a view to preventing and curbing the infection of human beings, in particular measures to supervise compliance with the regulations in practice.

Measures to combat smoking and alcoholism

Smoking – The Committee stresses the importance of measures against smoking in meeting the requirements of Article 11 of the Charter. It recalls that smoking, a major cause of avoidable death in developed countries (in Europe 30% of deaths from cancer are attributable to smoking), is associated with a wide range of diseases (cardiac and circulatory diseases, cancers, pulmonary diseases etc.). Smoking kills one adult in ten throughout the world. The World Health Organisation (WHO) forecasts an increase to up to one in every six deaths by 2030,[2] which is more than the figure for any other cause of death. The Committee also notes that WHO is drawing up a convention on measures to combat smoking and points out that WHO, as part of the Health for All campaign, has set a target for European countries of raising the proportion of non-smokers in the population to at least 80% and protecting non-smokers against involuntary exposure to tobacco smoke.[3]

---

[1]WHO Internet site : www.who.int

[2]World Health Report 1999.

[3]WHO, Health Objectives for All – Health Policies in Europe, September 1991.

It is clear from previous reports that legislation to reduce the supply of tobacco in the United Kingdom is relatively under-developed compared with other contracting parties, in contrast to the information and education policy aimed at reducing the demand for tobacco, in which significant sums are invested each year (see the conclusion under Article 11 para. 2). The sale of tobacco to children under 16 is prohibited, under the Children and Young Persons (Protection from Tobacco) Act 1991. Restrictions on tobacco advertising are based on agreements between the government and the tobacco industry. The provision of non-smoking areas is also based on an agreement, with the hospitality industry.

The number of cigarettes consumed per person has been falling since the early 1990s, and is close to the average for the countries of the European Union and the European Economic Area (1,515 compared with a European average of 1,646 in 1997).

The report states that the new government has made the anti-smoking campaign a public health priority and the White Paper entitled "Smoking Kills", which is appended, includes a number of important measures, including a ban on advertising tobacco products, in accordance with Community Directive 98/43, closer monitoring of the ban on tobacco sales to young persons and a charter on tobacco use in public places. As it will take several years to implement these measures, the Committee will reach a conclusion on the basis of information supplied when it next considers Article 11.

Alcohol – the policy to combat alcohol misuse is also mainly based on information and education campaigns, targeted according to the type of behaviour or age-group concerned (see conclusion under Article 11 para. 2). Recommendations concerning tolerance levels are regularly disseminated and objectives set. Previous reports have shown that the main methods of controlling the supply of alcohol are restricting the times when the sale of alcohol in licensed premises is authorised, setting age-limits for the consumption of alcoholic drinks (18) and admission to licensed premises (14), making it a criminal offence to be drunk in a public place and setting limits on drivers' authorised levels of alcohol in the blood. It hopes that the next report will update this information, if necessary, and state what steps have been taken to restrict advertising. Consumption of pure alcohol fell between 1990 and 1996 and is below the average for the European Union and the European Economic Area (7.7 litres compared to a European average of 9.4 in 1996).

Prophylactic measures

Epidemiological surveillance

The reports so far received show that the United Kingdom has a monitoring and surveillance system for numerous communicable diseases and that where there is a risk of epidemic special measures and surveys may be introduced, as was the case during the reference period with the resurgence of tuberculosis. The United Kingdom also takes part in the network for the epidemiological surveillance and control of communicable disease in the Community (established by a joint decision of the European Parliament and Council of 24 September 1998), the competent surveillance body being the Public Health Laboratory Service.

Immunisation

Vaccinations are not obligatory in the United Kingdom but are recommended by the NHS. Vaccines are administered free to children and young persons. The programme covers diphtheria, tetanus, poliomyelitis, whooping cough, Hib meningitis, tuberculosis, mumps, measles and rubella. Since November 1999, that is outside the reference period, the programme has also included vaccination against meningococcal Group C disease.

The Committee notes that the United Kingdom has maintained high rates of vaccination coverage: at least 90% for all the vaccines recommended by WHO except the one against mumps, measles and rubella, whose coverage has fallen steeply (87% in 1999). The report explains that media coverage of certain medical publications has shaken confidence in the vaccine, but that steps have been taken, particularly with the aid of "counter-reports", to re-establish this vaccine, restore confidence in its safety and thus avoid the risk of epidemics. The report also indicates that severe problems with the manufacture of the BCG, DTP-Hib and DT vaccines have led to the suspension of vaccinations. The Committee stresses that Article 11 para. 3 entails the maintenance of high rates of vaccination coverage, not only to reduce the incidence of the diseases in question but also to neutralise the reservoir of the virus and thus achieve the WHO objectives, and will keep the situation under close review. It would also like the next report to include information on vaccination coverage rates against hepatitis.

Conclusion

Pending receipt of the information requested, notably as regards food safety, the Committee defers its conclusion.

Article 14 — The right to benefit from social welfare services

Paragraph 1 – Provision or promotion of social welfare services

The Committee takes note of the information contained in the report of the United Kingdom and its appendices, including on the situation in Scotland and the Isle of Man.

Categories of services

The report states that social services are the responsibility of the local authorities who exercise their functions under the general guidance of the Secretary of State for Health. Arrangements for the organisation, management and administration of local authority social services are set out in the Local Authority Social Services Act 1970. The local authorities co-operate with the voluntary sector and private care organisations, as well as with other state agencies in providing the services.

Social services provide a wide range of care and support for children (fostering, accommodation in children's homes, adoption and monitoring of children at risk), the elderly (nursing homes, home care, day centres, meals-on-wheels, etc.), families (particularly where children have special needs), persons with physical or learning disabilities, people with mental problems, drug and alcohol addicts and young offenders.

The Committee asks that the next report contain information on the number of beneficiaries of the various types of social services in Great Britain.

With respect to Scotland, the report states that social welfare services are broadly similar to those in England and Wales. The Committee notes as regards elderly care that there are 1,618 residential homes in Scotland with a total of 24,848 places. Over 24,000 people attend day centres for adults and about 75,000 people receive a home care service. The total number of meals on wheels served per year is estimated at about 2.5 million.

In the Isle of Man the Social Services Division of the Department for Health and Social Security is responsible for the provision of social services in three service areas: older people and mental health, disabilities and children and families. The Committee takes note of the detailed information on the types of services provided within each of these areas.

The Committee asks that the next report contain information on the provision of social services in Northern Ireland.

Access to services

The local authorities are responsible for assessing people's social care needs and for deciding what services to provide. The report states that under the Community Care Act 1990 local authorities have a duty to give a community care assessment to anyone who, in their view, might be in need of services. The specifics of an individual's assessment are a matter for the local authority concerned and it is for them to decide how best to assess the needs of their local population. The report states in respect of health services that decisions to provide services are taken "in accordance with local policy and eligibility criteria following a multi-disciplinary assessment of the patient's needs... ".

The Committee requests up-dated information on the nature of the eligibility criteria applied by the local authorities for the different services, and information on the possibility of appeal against decisions in this respect.

Supervision and quality of services

The Committee notes that the social services are also responsible for inspection and registration of care homes and other services, to ensure adequate standards and safeguards for users. According to the report, effective systems to monitor and manage performance of social services have been put in place. The Best Value Regime requires authorities to secure continuous improvements in performance, and to deliver services that bear comparison to the best. The Performance Assessment System within the Best Value regime brings together information from a number of sources to provide a comprehensive overview of the performance of each council.

Furthermore, the Committee notes that a Care Standards Bill has been put before Parliament, which will set up a National Care Standards Commission to regulate social care services in accordance with minimum national standards. It will also set up a General Social Care Council to raise professional and training standards for the social care workforce, only about 20% of whom currently have relevant qualifications. The Committee wishes to receive further details on this legislation in the next report.

While noting the information on social services staff in Scotland and the Isle of Man, the Committee repeats its question on the number and the qualifications of staff in the social services in Great Britain.

Funding of services

According to the report local authorities' net expenditure on community care services was 6,188 million British Pounds (GBP) in 1997/1998. The Committee asks to receive figures showing expenditure broken down according to categories of services.

Net expenditure in Scotland exceeded 1,080 million GBP in the same period of which 231 million GBP were spent on children's services and 670 million GBP on community care. In the Isle of Man the social services budget increased from about 9 million GBP in 1995 to about 13 million GBP in 1998.

Conclusion

Pending receipt of the information requested, the Committee concludes that the situation in the United Kingdom is in conformity with Article 14 para. 1 of the Charter.

Paragraph 2 – Public participation in the establishment and maintenance of social welfare services

According to the report of United Kingdom, voluntary organisations make a major contribution to health and social care as providers of service. It is estimated that some 80,000 voluntary organisations work in the health and social care field, mostly at local level. Their involvement spans a wide range of activities including involvement in the planning of services, assisting with the delivery of some aspects of service (e.g. provision of residential care for vulnerable groups) and health education and promotion activities.

The Department of Health provides grant aid to voluntary organisations through 28 different schemes. The largest is the Section 64 General Scheme of Grants, which is primarily aimed at funding national voluntary organisations to run national projects within England, which are in line with Department of Health's priorities. This scheme presently funds around 400 different national organisations. Total grant aid to the voluntary sector from Department of Health for 1998/99 was approximately 54 million British Pounds (GBP). The Committee asks for clarification as to whether this figure also covers Scotland and Northern Ireland. If not, it asks that the relevant information be contained in the next report.

The Committee notes that in 1998 a joint "Compact on Relations between Government and the Voluntary and Community Sector in England" was introduced in order to promote working in effective partnership. The Committee wishes to be informed of developments.

Meanwhile, it concludes that the situation in the United Kingdom is in conformity with Article 14 para. 2 of the Charter.

Article 17 — The right of mothers and children to social and economic protection

The Committee notes the information contained in the report of the United Kingdom.

Establishment of parentage and adoption

There have been no changes to the primary legislation relating to adoption. However, changes were made to the regulations under the Children Act 1989 applying to adoption; for example, an adoption agency is required to obtain information about any criminal convictions when assessing a prospective adoptive parent, likewise a local authority is required to carry out a police check.

In 1996 and 1997 two reports looked at adoption and identified a number of problems related to it. As a result guidance, "Adoption: Achieving the Right Balance" was issued to local authorities and to voluntary adoption agencies. This guidance focuses attention on adoption as an important and beneficial option in the care of children and is intended to bring adoption back into the mainstream of children's services. Adoption services are being monitored.

According to the findings from the survey into the implementation of the above mentioned guidance, in the year ending 31 March 1999, 2,162 children in public care were adopted, which represented 4% of the total children in care at that time. However, at the same date adoption was planned for 5,183 children and on 1 July 1999 for 6,915 children. The Social Services Inspectorate was concerned by the high number of children still awaiting families. Measures have been taken to find more adoptive parents.

The Committee considers that as regards the establishment of parentage and adoption, the situation is satisfactory.

Children in public care and protection from ill-treatment

Programmes entitled "The Quality Protects Programme" and the Social Services White Paper "Modernising Social Services" (both launched in 1998) set out eight social services objectives for children. They aim to make explicit what is in the Children Act and help to strengthen some of the planning provisions under the Act. The objectives include *inter alia*, to ensure that children are protected from emotional, physical and sexual abuse and neglect (significant harm). They focus on working with the most vulnerable children, for example children in public care. Extra money has been made available by the government to local authorities in order to enable them to improve the situation of the children in their care.

The Government has issued during the reference period revised guidance on how all agencies with child protection responsibilities – social services, the National Society for the Prevention of Cruelty to Children (NSPCC), police, health, education, probation and the voluntary sector should work together (Working Together to Safeguard Children). It sets out the role and responsibilities of different agencies and practitioners; outlining the way in which joint working arrangements should be agreed, implemented and reviewed through the mechanism of Area Child Protection Committees.

Children who have been ill treated or neglected, or who are at risk of serious harm, may be the subject of certain orders laid down in the Children Act 1989 such as care and supervision orders, emergency protection orders, etc. They may if removed from their family, be placed with a foster family, in residential care, lodgings or residential employment.

The Committee notes from the information provided in the report that out of 11 million children and young people under 18 years of age in England, approximately 350,000 are estimated to be in contact with social services and approximately 50,000 are looked after by local authorities (in public care). Of the 50,000 in care approximately 65% are placed with foster families, 13.5% are placed in children's homes and 4-5% are adopted.

According to the report, between 1994 and 1998, there was an 8% increase in the number of children in the care of local authorities. However, the number of children in residential care declined, while the number of children placed with foster parents, for adoption or placed with their parents on care orders increased.

The Committee wishes to continue to receive the above type of information for each reference period. It also wishes to receive similar information on the situation of children looked after by local authorities in Northern Ireland and Scotland.

The Committee recalls that the situation of children in residential care in England and Wales has been a matter of ongoing concern. Several reports and enquiries have taken place over the years. In 1997, the Government published the Review of the Safeguards for Children Living Away from Home, which had been conducted following reports of widespread abuse of children in care. The report revealed a "woeful tale of failure at all levels to provide a secure and decent childhood for some of the most vulnerable children", elementary safeguards were not in place or not enforced and many children in residential care were harmed. The report made 20 principal recommendations, in order to, *inter alia*, improve protection for children in foster and residential care, in schools and in the penal system; provide more effective avenues of complaint and to increase access to independent advocates. In 1998, the British Government published its response, the Children's Safeguards Review. In this response, it states that it will, *inter alia*, establish new regulatory bodies to regulate children's homes, independent fostering agencies, and local authority fostering services. The Committee notes that regulations have already been introduced which restrict the opportunities for those with criminal records for offences against children to be employed or considered for fostering or work in certain settings with children.

The Committee wishes to receive information on any new regulatory bodies. It also wishes to be informed whether there is any specific procedure for children to complain about care and treatment in institutions and on the conditions under which an institution may interfere with a child's property, mail, personal integrity and right to meet with persons close to him.

The Committee wishes to receive copies of any reports on local authority services for children carried out by the Social Services Inspectorate over the next reference period.

The Committee notes that most children leave care at 16 years of age, and that this has been an issue of some concern, as it is known that "the future of these children is precarious". [1]It notes that the Government undertook to introduce new measures to ensure that young people only leave care when ready to do so and to improve their life chances. The Committee wishes to be informed of these measures.

As regards corporal punishment, the Committee notes that it was prohibited in private schools by the School Standards and Framework Act 1998, with the result that corporal punishment is now prohibited in all schools. The Committee wishes to be informed whether legislation prohibits corporal punishment in other institutions caring for children. It notes that not all forms of corporal punishment are prohibited within the family. The Committee refers to its general observations on Article 17 in

[1]Review of the Safeguards for Children Living Away from Home, 1997.

the General introduction and decides to defer its conclusion on this point pending more information from the British Government on the situation and on its intentions in this regard. It also wishes to receive information on the situation in Northern Ireland and Scotland.

Children and the law – Young offenders

The age of criminal responsibility in England and Wales is 10 years.[1] Sanctions may be imposed on children from 10 years up. The Committee finds the age of criminal responsibility to be low and wishes to receive the Government's comments on this.

A special procedure and special courts exist for children aged between 10 and 17 years suspected of or charged with a criminal offence. However, in certain circumstances, a child may be tried in the adult courts, for example when charged with a "grave" crime or murder they must be tried in an adult court.

All 12, 13 and 14 year old boys and girls as well as 15 and 16 year old girls are remanded to local authority secure accommodation. The Committee wishes to know the maximum duration of remand in such accommodation.

The Government's policy is currently to prevent the remand of 15 –16 year olds to prison service custody. The Crime and Disorder Act 1998, which entered into force in 1999 provides that where a place in local authority secure accommodation is available a vulnerable (defined by the legislation) 15-16 year old males should not be remanded to a prison (Section 98). The legislation also provides, as an alternative, where local authority secure accommodation is not available or the young person in question has not been deemed vulnerable, that a young person (15-16 year old male) may be remanded to a remand centre. The Committee wishes to be informed how many 15-16 year olds continue to be remanded to prison (Young Offender Institution). It also wishes to know how many young offenders under 18 years of age are remanded to prison and what is the maximum length of remand.

The following custodial measures are available for young offenders under 18 years of age:

[1]The rebuttable presumption of criminal law that a child aged 10 or over is incapable of committing a criminal offence was abolished by Section 34 of the Crime and Disorder Act 1998.

– Detention in a place approved by the Secretary of State; young people who commit grave crimes, punishable in the case of an adult by custody of 14 years or more or who indecently assault a woman, can be detained in a place approved by the Secretary of State up to the adult maximum for the offence. The Committee wishes to be informed how many young offenders are detained in a place approved by the Secretary of State and where they are held.

– Detention during Her Majesty's Pleasure: Young offenders who commit murder are detained during Her Majesty's Pleasure. Within this they must initially serve a period of time for punishment and retribution; the tariff. Following a judgment of the European Court of Human Rights[1] the tariff will now be set by the judiciary. After expiry of the tariff, the sentence is kept under review and release on licence is decided by the Parole Board. A person detained during Her Majesty's Pleasure who is released on licence is liable to be recalled throughout his life, subject to the decision of the Parole Board. The Committee wishes to be informed where persons detained are held.

– Detention in a young offender institution: young offenders aged between 15-17 years may be sentenced in certain circumstances (for example where only a custodial sentence would be adequate to protect the public from serious harm from the juvenile or where the offence was so serious that a non-custodial sentence could not be justified) to detention in a young offender institution up to a maximum of 24 months. The Committee wishes to know how many offenders are detained in such institutions.

– Detention in a Secure Training Centre, persistent young offenders aged 12-14 may be given a Secure Training Order. This may last from six months to two years, with half being served in a Secure Training Centre and half under the supervision of the local community. The Committee notes that there are three secure training centres and wishes to be informed how many young offenders are the subject of Secure Training Orders.

The Crime And Disorder Act 1998 introduced a new Detention and Training Order to replace Detention in a Young Offender Institution and Secure Training Order. This entered into force in April 2000. The Committee wishes to be informed how it operates and of the number of offenders sentenced to it.

[1]Case of V. v The United Kingdom, Judgement 16 December 1999.

The Committee notes the efforts made by the Government to improve the situation in young offender institutions. However it is concerned about reports on the number of young offenders in young offender institutions and on the conditions in these institutions.[1] It wishes to be kept informed of all further measures taken to improve the situation further and defers its conclusion pending this information and information that the situation has improved.

A variety of community sanctions are also available: community service orders, attendance centre orders, absolute or conditional discharge, fines and supervision orders. The Crime and Disorder Act 1998 provides for action plan orders, reparation orders and orders of referral to a youth offender panel. These were to be introduced gradually throughout 2000. The Committee requests information on the implementation of these schemes.

The Committee notes that emergency legislation in Northern Ireland permits the detention of young persons from the age of 10 for 7 days without charge. It asks whether the government intends to repeal this provision.

The Committee wishes to receive information on the youth justice system in Northern Ireland and Scotland in so far as it differs from that in England and Wales.

Conclusion

Pending the information requested on the number of young offenders in young offender institutions, and on measures taken to improve the conditions within these institutions, as well as the information requested on corporal punishment, the Committee defers its conclusion.

---

[1]For example Reports of HM Inspector of Prisons on Young Offender Institutions during the reference period; Tough Justice- Responding to children in trouble by Barry Goldstone and Eleanor Peters, published by the Children's Society 2000.

Article 18 — The right to engage in a gainful occupation in the territory of other Contracting Parties

Paragraph 1 – Applying existing regulations in a spirit of liberality

Foreign population and migratory movements

The Committee notes from another source[1] that, in 1997, two million foreigners were resident in the United Kingdom, including Irish nationals (440,000), nationals of countries of the European Economic Area (400,000) and another 17,000 Europeans. It also notes that there has been a regular increase since 1994 in the annual movements of nationals of states not members of the European Union or party to the European Economic Area Agreement.

The Committee notes that in 1997, the workforce stood at 26,446,000 including 979,000 foreigners (all nationalities) i.e. less than 4% of the total.

Work permits

The United Kingdom has various categories of work permit:

– seasonal work permits valid for a maximum of three months, granted on the basis of a quota system (the current quota being 100,000). The Committee notes in this respect that this kind of permit has been issued primarily to nationals of the countries of central and eastern Europe, 40% of whom were Polish nationals;

– work permits for specific employment, valid for a period not exceeding 48 months;

– at the end of the 48-month period, foreigners holding work permits may apply for the restrictions placed on their residence to be lifted. Where such applications are approved, work permit holders obtain indefinite leave to remain in the United Kingdom which entitle them to take employment without needing to obtain work permits.

[1]WITHOL DE WENDEN C, *L'immigration en Europe*, La documentation française, 1999.

Relevant statistics

The Committee notes the statistics showing the numbers of permits granted and refused. These figures show the total numbers of permit applications made by nationals of Contracting Parties to the Charter which are not members of the European Union, namely Cyprus, Malta, Turkey and Poland. It notes the still relatively stable work permit refusal rate between 1993 and 1996 of around 20% (with a higher rate of refusal, about 30%, in 1995). It nevertheless notes a steep decline in this rate in 1997 and 1998 (9.2% and 7.4% respectively).

Conclusion

The Committee concludes that the situation of the United Kingdom is in conformity with Article 18 para. 1 of the Charter.

Paragraph 2 – Simplifying existing formalities and reducing dues and taxes

Administrative formalities

The Committee recalls that there are three kinds of work permit applications for specific employment in the United Kingdom:

– tier 1 applications (which involve a simplified procedure), a category that encompasses staff transfers within the same company, posts vital to inward investment projects in the United Kingdom and posts for which there is a shortage of workers;

– tier 2 applications, for other types of posts;

– and key worker applications.

The Committee wishes to know what administrative formalities have to be completed in respect of all these permits.

Work permits are issued by the Department for Education and Employment. Each is sent to the employer for forwarding to the future employee, who must then apply for a residence permit from the Immigration and Nationality Directorate.

Work permits are issued for a period of up to 48 months. The Committee notes from another source[1] that only business interests justify the employment of a person for such a period.

The Committee notes from the report the conditions that self-employed workers must satisfy to obtain a work permit. The Committee considers these to relate to regulations, so they come under Article 18 para. 3. It wishes the next report to give a more accurate indication of the administrative formalities required for such permits to be issued.

Extension of the permit and change of job

There is no requirement for a recruitment procedure to take place prior to tier 1 applications for extension, but employers must state what steps they have taken to fill the post with resident labour (see the definition of "resident labour" under Article 18 para. 3) in respect of tier 2 and key worker applications.

Employers wishing to take on a worker who already holds a permit must obtain the permission of the Department for Education and Employment. If the application is at tier 2, the employer must conduct a recruitment procedure.

Work and residence permits

A foreigner to whom a work permit has been granted must obtain a residence permit. Residence permits are issued by the immigration authorities on entry to British territory and have the same validity as the work permit.

Time necessary for obtaining work permits

The Committee wishes the next report to indicate the average time which elapses between submission of a work permit application and the granting of the permit. It also wishes to obtain the same information about permits issued for the exercise of a self-employed occupation.

Chancery dues and other charges

The report states that no tax is payable for the issuing of work or residence permits. Only nationals needing a visa have to pay fees for the issue of their residence permit.

[1]Internet site of the Department for Education and Employment: www.dfee.gov.uk

Conclusion

Pending receipt of the requested information, the Committee defers its conclusion.

Paragraph 3 – Liberalising regulations

Access to the national labour market

The Committee notes that skills criteria are included in the vital conditions for obtaining a work permit. Applicants must in practice meet one of these conditions: hold a recognised diploma and have two years' work experience, be a senior manager with five years' experience in a similar post, or hold highly technical qualifications and have experience of working in an appropriate field.

The Committee also notes that work permits may be issued for posts for which the aforementioned qualifications are not required, if these require specific skills and experience not immediately obtainable among the available resident workforce, which is taken to include both nationals and persons who are nationals of the member states of the European Union or of the states party to the European Economic Area Agreement or hold resident status within the meaning of the immigration legislation of 1991. The employer must demonstrate that he or she has found no candidates for the post concerned among nationals of states party to the European Economic Area Agreement. To this end, the employer must have advertised the post throughout the European Economic Area and have informed the Department for Education and Employment of the number of applications received and the number of persons selected, and must have given a detailed explanation of why no resident candidate was selected.

In its previous conclusion, the Committee noted that, in order to obtain a work permit for a self-employed occupation, a foreigner had to meet a large number of conditions, including the availability of an investment sum not less than 200,000 GBP. If the person concerned wished to continue an existing occupation, he or she had to demonstrate that the investment would result in the creation of new full-time posts. The Committee then took the view that this requirement was "unduly restrictive", and asked for the next report to state what measures had been taken, or were planned, to liberalise this regulation. The present report gives no reply on this matter.

The Committee considers that all the aforementioned criteria are evidence of restrictive regulations on the issuing of work permits (paid or self-employed workers) which do not meet the requirement for regulations to be liberalised.

Consequences of loss of job

The Committee notes that, if foreigners lose their jobs during the period of validity of their work permit, they are entitled to compensation for dismissal and to unemployment benefits, provided that they have met the contribution conditions. If an extension to their work permit beyond its initial period is refused, they have to leave the country.

The Committee notes in this context that Turkish nationals benefit from liberalised regulations under the Association Agreement between the European Union and Turkey. Turkish nationals who have been resident in the United Kingdom and no longer meet the conditions for remaining on British territory may in fact have their work permits extended.

Conclusion

The Committee considers that the situation in the United Kingdom is not in conformity with Article 18 para. 3 of the Charter as the conditions set for the employment of nationals of Contracting Parties to the Charter which are not members of the European Union are excessive.

Paragraph 4 – The right of nationals to leave the country

In the absence of any changes, the Committee concludes that the situation of the United Kingdom is in conformity with Article 18 para. 4 of the Charter.

Part II – Assessment of the position of each Contracting Party

Chapter 1 — Austria

As concerns the provisions for which a report was required in this supervision cycle,

I. the Committee concludes that Austria complies with the following provisions:

Article 7 paras. 2, 4, 7, 8, 9 and 10

Article 8 paras. 1, 2 and 3

Article 11 paras. 1 and 3

Article 14 paras. 1 and 2

Article 17

Article 18 para. 4

II. the Committee defers its conclusion with regard to the following provision:

Article 7 paras. 3 and 5

Article 8 paras. 4a and 4b

Article 11 para. 2

Article 18 paras. 1 and 2

Chapter 2 — Belgium

As concerns the provisions for which a report was required in this supervision cycle,

I. the Committee concludes that Belgium complies with the following provisions:

Article 7 paras. 1, 2, 3, 4, 6, 9 and 10

Article 8 paras. 1 and 4b

Article 11 para. 1

Article 14 paras. 1 and 2

II. the Committee defers its conclusion with regard to the following provisions:

Article 7 paras. 7 and 8

Article 8 para. 4a

Article 11 para. 2

Article 17

Article 18 paras. 1, 2, 3 and 4

III. the Committee concludes that Belgium is not fully complying with the following provisions:

Article 7 para. 5

Article 8 paras. 2 and 3

Article 11 para. 3

Chapter 3 — Denmark

As concerns the provisions for which a report was required in this supervision cycle,

I. the Committee concludes that Denmark complies with the following provisions:

Article 11 paras. 1 and 3

Article 14 paras. 1 and 2

Article 17

Article 18 para. 4

II. the Committee defers its conclusion with regard to the following provisions:

Article 8 para. 1ii

Article 11 para. 2

Article 18 paras. 1 and 2

III. the Committee concludes that Denmark is not fully complying with the following provisions:

Article 8 para. 1i

Article 18 para. 3

Chapter 4 — Finland

As concerns the provisions for which a report was required in this supervision cycle,

I. the Committee concludes that Finland complies with the following provisions:

Article 7 paras. 1, 2, 7, 8 and 10

Article 11 paras. 1, 2 and 3

Article 14 paras. 1 and 2

Article 17

Article 18 paras. 1, 3 and 4

II. the Committee defers its conclusion with regard to the following provisions:

Article 7 paras. 3, 4 and 5

Article 18 para. 2

Articles 1 and 4 of the Additional Protocol

III. the Committee concludes that Finland is not fully complying with the following provisions:

Article 8 para. 2

Chapter 5 — France

As concerns the provisions for which a report was required in this supervision cycle,

I. the Committee concludes that France complies with the following provisions:

Article 7 paras. 2, 4, 6, 7, 8, 9 and 10

Article 8 para. 1i

Article 11 paras. 1, 2 and 3

Article 14 paras. 1 and 2

Article 18 paras. 2 and 4

II. the Committee defers its conclusion with regard to the following provisions:

Article 7 para. 5

Article 8 paras. 4a and 4b

Article 18 paras. 1 and 3

III. the Committee concludes that France is not fully complying with the following provisions:

Article 7 paras. 1 and 3

Article 8 paras. 1ii, 2 and 3

Article 17

Chapter 6 — Greece

As concerns the provisions for which a report was required in this supervision cycle,

I. the Committee concludes that Greece complies with the following provisions:

Article 7 paras. 2, 4, 6, 7, 9 and 10

Article 8 paras. 1i, 3 and 4b

Article 11 para. 2

Article 14 paras. 1 and 2

Article 17

Article 18 paras. 1 and 4

II. the Committee defers its conclusion with regard to the following provisions:

Article 7 paras. 1, 3, 5 and 8

Article 8 paras. 1ii and 4a

Article 11 para. 1

III. the Committee concludes that Greece is not fully complying with the following provisions:

Article 8 para. 2

Article 11 para. 3

Article 18 paras. 2 and 3

Chapter 7 — Iceland

As concerns the provisions for which a report was required in this supervision cycle,

I. the Committee concludes that Iceland complies with the following provisions:

Article 11 paras. 1, 2 and 3

Article 14 paras. 1 and 2

Article 17

Article 18 para. 4

II. the Committee defers its conclusion with regard to the following provisions:

Article 18 paras. 1 and 2

III. the Committee concludes that Iceland is not fully complying with the following provisions:

Article 18 para. 3

Chapter 8 — Italy

As concerns the provisions for which a report was required in this supervision cycle,

I. the Committee concludes that Italy complies with the following provisions:

Article 7 paras. 6, 7, 8, 9 and 10

Article 8 paras. 1i and 4a

Article 11 para. 1

Article 14 paras. 1 and 2

Article 17

Article 18 paras. 3 and 4

II. the Committee defers its conclusion with regard to the following provisions:

Article 7 para. 5

Article 8 paras. 1ii and 2

Article 11 para. 2

Article 18 paras. 1 and 2

Article 1 of the Additional Protocol

Article 4 of the Additional Protocol

III. the Committee concludes that Italy is not fully complying with the following provisions:

Article 7 paras. 1, 2, 3 and 4

Article 8 paras. 3 and 4b

Article 11 para. 3

Chapter 9 — The Netherlands

As concerns the provisions for which a report was required in this supervision cycle,

I. the Committee concludes that The Netherlands complies with the following provisions:

Article 7 paras. 1, 2, 7, 8 and 10

Article 8 paras. 3 and 4b

Article 11 paras. 1, 2 and 3

Article 14 paras. 1 and 2

Article 17

Article 18 para. 4

Article 1 of the Additional Protocol

II. the Committee defers its conclusion with regard to the following provisions:

Article 7 paras. 4 and 9

Article 8 paras. 2 and 4a

Article 18 paras. 1 and 2

III. the Committee concludes that The Netherlands is not fully complying with the following provisions:

Article 7 paras. 3, 5 and 6

Article 8 paras. 1i and 1ii

Article 18 para. 3

Chapter 10 — Norway

As concerns the provisions for which a report was required in this supervision cycle,

I. the Committee concludes that Norway complies with the following provisions:

Article 7 paras. 2, 6, 7, 8 and 10

Article 11 paras. 1, 2 and 3

Article 14 paras. 1 and 2

Article 17

Articles 1 and 4 of the Additional Protocol

II. the Committee defers its conclusion with regard to the following provision:

Article 7 para. 5

III. the Committee concludes that Norway is not fully complying with the following provisions:

Article 7 para. 3

Chapter 11 — Poland

As concerns the provisions for which a report was required in this supervision cycle,

I. the Committee concludes that Poland complies with the following provisions:

Article 2 paras. 3 and 5

Article 3 para. 2

Article 7 paras. 2, 4, 6, 7, 8, 9 and 10

Article 8 paras. 1i and 1ii; 3 and 4b

Article 18 para. 4

II. the Committee defers its conclusion with regard to the following provisions:

Article 2 paras. 1 and 4

Article 3 paras. 1 and 3

Article 4 paras. 3 and 5

Article 8 paras. 2 and 4a

Article 9

Article 10 paras. 1 and 2

Article 11 paras. 1, 2 and 3

Article 14 para. 1

Article 15 paras. 1 and 2

Article 17

III. the Committee concludes that Poland is not fully complying with the following provisions:

Article 4 paras. 2 and 4

Chapter 12 — Portugal

As concerns the provisions for which a report was required in this supervision cycle,

I. the Committee concludes that Portugal complies with the following provisions:

Article 7 paras. 2, 3, 4, 6, 7, 9 and 10

Article 8 paras. 1ii, 2, 3 and 4b

Article 11 paras. 2 and 3

Article 14 paras. 1 and 2

Article 17

Article 18 paras. 1, 3 and 4

II. the Committee defers its conclusion with regard to the following provisions:

Article 7 para. 5

Article 8 para. 4a

Article 11 para. 1

Article 18 para. 2

III. the Committee concludes that Portugal is not fully complying with the following provisions:

Article 7 paras. 1 and 8

Article 8 para. 1i

Chapter 13 — Spain

As concerns the provisions for which a report was required in this supervision cycle,

I. the Committee concludes that Spain complies with the following provisions:

Article 7 paras. 2, 7 and 10

Article 8 paras. 1i and 3

Article 11 paras. 1 and 2

Article 17

Article 18 paras. 2, 3 and 4

II. the Committee defers its conclusion with regard to the following provisions:

Article 8 paras. 1ii and 4a

Article 11 para. 3

Article 14 paras. 1 and 2

Article 18 para. 1

III. the Committee concludes that Spain is not fully complying with the following provisions:

Article 7 paras. 1, 3, 4, 5, 6, 8 and 9

Article 8 para. 2

Chapter 14 — Sweden

As concerns the provisions for which a report was required in this supervision cycle,

I. the Committee concludes that Sweden complies with the following provisions:

Article 7 paras. 1, 2, 4, 7, 8 and 10

Article 11 paras. 1, 2 and 3

Article 14 paras. 1 and 2

Article 17

Article 18 paras. 2 and 4

Article 4 of the Additional Protocol

II. the Committee defers its conclusion with regard to the following provisions:

Article 8 para. 1ii

Article 18 para. 1

Article 1 of the Additional Protocol

III. the Committee concludes that Sweden is not fully complying with the following provisions:

Article 7 paras. 3 and 9

Article 8 paras. 1i and 3

Article 18 para. 3

Chapter 15 — the United Kingdom

As concerns the provisions for which a report was required in this supervision cycle,

I. the Committee concludes that the United Kingdom complies with the following provisions:

Article 7 paras. 2, 6, 9 and 10

Article 11 para. 2

Article 14 paras. 1 and 2

Article 18 para. 1 and 4

II. the Committee defers its conclusion with regard to the following provisions:

Article 11 paras. 1 and 3

Article 17

Article 18 para. 2

III. the Committee concludes that the United Kingdom is not fully complying with the following provisions:

Article 7 paras. 3 and 5

Article 8 para. 1i and 1ii

Article 18 para. 3

Appendix – Table showing details of acceptation of the various provisions of the European Social Charter and the 1988 Additional Protocol

Table showing details of acceptance of the provisions of the European Social Charter

■ accepted   □ not accepted

Provision of the Charter	Austria	Belgium	Cyprus	Czech Republic	Denmark	Finland	France[1]	Germany	Greece	Hungary	Iceland
Article 1 (1)	■	■	■	■	■	■	■	■	■	■	■
Article 1 (2)	■	■	■	■	■	■	■	■	■	■	■
Article 1 (3)	■	■	■	■	■	■	■	■	■	■	■
Article 1 (4)	■	■	■		■	■	■	■	■	■	■
Article 2 (1)		■	■	■		■	■	■	■	■	■
Article 2 (2)	■	■		■	■	■	■	■	■	■	
Article 2 (3)	■	■	■	■	■	■	■	■	■	■	■
Article 2 (4)	■	■		■		■	■	■	■	■	
Article 2 (5)	■	■	■	■	■	■	■	■	■	■	■
Article 3 (1)	■	■	■	■	■		■	■	■	■	■
Article 3 (2)	■	■	■	■	■		■	■	■	■	■
Article 3 (3)	■	■	■	■	■	■	■	■	■	■	■
Article 4 (1)	■	■			■		■	■	■		■
Article 4 (2)	■	■		■	■	■	■	■	■		■
Article 4 (3)	■	■		■	■	■	■	■	■		■
Article 4 (4)		■		■			■		■		■
Article 4 (5)	■	■		■		■	■	■	■		■

[1] France, Italy and Sweden are parties to the revised European Social Charter which entered into force 1 July 1999.

Ireland	Italy[1]	Luxem-bourg	Malta	Nether-lands[1]	Norway	Poland	Portugal	Slovakia	Spain	Sweden[1]	Turkey	United Kingdom

[1] As regards the Netherlands Antilles and Aruba, the Kingdom of the Netherlands considers itself bound by Articles 1, 5, 6, 16 and by Article 1 of the Additional Protocol.

Provision of the Charter	Austria	Belgium	Cyprus	Czech Republic	Denmark	Finland	France	Germany	Greece	Hungary	Iceland
Article 5	■	■	■	■	■	■	■	■		■	■
Article 6 (1)	■	■	■	■	■	■	■	■		■	■
Article 6 (2)	■	■	■	■	■	■	■	■		■	■
Article 6 (3)	■	■	■	■	■	■	■	■		■	■
Article 6 (4)		■	■	■	■	■	■	■		■	■
Article 7 (1)		■	■	■		■	■		■		
Article 7 (2)	■	■		■		■	■	■	■		
Article 7 (3)	■	■	■	■		■	■	■	■		
Article 7 (4)	■	■		■		■	■	■	■		
Article 7 (5)	■	■		■		■	■	■	■		
Article 7 (6)		■		■			■	■	■		
Article 7 (7)	■	■	■	■		■	■	■	■		
Article 7 (8)	■	■	■	■		■	■	■	■		
Article 7 (9)	■	■		■			■	■	■		
Article 7 (10)	■	■		■		■	■	■	■		
Article 8 (1)	■	■	■	■	■		■	■	■	■	
Article 8 (2)	■	■	■	■		■	■		■	■	
Article 8 (3)	■	■		■			■	■	■	■	
Article 8 (4)	■	■		■			■		■	■	

Ireland	Italy	Luxem-bourg	Malta	Nether-lands	Norway	Poland	Portugal	Slovakia	Spain	Sweden	Turkey	United Kingdom
									[1]			

[1] Spain has not been bound by sub-paragraph *b* of this provision since 5 June 1991.

Provision of the Charter	Austria	Belgium	Cyprus	Czech Republic	Denmark	Finland	France	Germany	Greece	Hungary	Iceland
Article 9	■	■	■		■	■	■	■	■	■	
Article 10 (1)	■	■			■	■	■	■	■		
Article 10 (2)	■	■			■	■	■	■	■		
Article 10 (3)	■	■			■	■	■	■	■		
Article 10 (4)	■	■			■	■	■		■		
Article 11 (1)	■	■	■	■	■	■	■	■	■	■	■
Article 11 (2)	■	■	■	■	■	■	■	■	■	■	■
Article 11 (3)	■	■	■	■	■	■	■	■	■	■	■
Article 12 (1)	■	■	■	■	■	■	■	■	■		■
Article 12 (2)	■	■	■	■	■	■	■	■	■		■
Article 12 (3)	■	■	■	■	■	■	■	■	■		■
Article 12 (4)	■	■	■	■	■	■	■	■	■		■
Article 13 (1)	■	■		■	■	■	■	■	■	■	■
Article 13 (2)	■	■		■	■	■	■	■	■	■	■
Article 13 (3)	■	■		■	■	■	■	■	■	■	■
Article 13 (4)	■	■		■	■	■	■	■	■	■	■
Article 14 (1)	■	■	■	■	■	■	■	■	■	■	■
Article 14 (2)	■	■	■	■	■	■	■	■	■	■	■

Ireland	Italy	Luxem-bourg	Malta	Nether-lands	Norway	Poland	Portugal	Slovakia	Spain	Sweden	Turkey	United Kingdom
			1									

[4] Only the provisions of paragraph 4*a* and *d* have been accepted.

Provision of the Charter	Austria	Belgium	Cyprus	Czech Republic	Denmark	Finland	France	Germany	Greece	Hungary	Iceland
Article 15 (1)	■	■	■		■	■	■	■	■		■
Article 15 (2)	■	■	■	■	■	■	■	■	■		■
Article 16	■	■		■	■	■	■	■	■	■	■
Article 17	■	■		■	■	■	■	■	■	■	■
Article 18 (1)	■	■			■	■	■	■	■		■
Article 18 (2)	■	■			■	■	■	■	■		■
Article 18 (3)		■			■	■	■	■	■		■
Article 18 (4)	■	■		■	■	■	■	■	■		■
Article 19 (1)	■	■	■			■	■	■	■		
Article 19 (2)	■	■	■			■	■	■	■		
Article 19 (3)	■	■	■			■	■	■	■		
Article 19 (4)		■	■			■	■	■	■		
Article 19 (5)	■	■	■			■	■	■	■		
Article 19 (6)	■	■	■			■	■	■	■		
Article 19 (7)		■	■			■	■	■	■		
Article 19 (8)		■	■			■	■	■	■		
Article 19 (9)	■	■	■	■		■	■	■	■		
Article 19 (10)		■	■				■	■	■		

Ireland	Italy	Luxem-bourg	Malta	Nether-lands	Norway	Poland	Portugal	Slovakia	Spain	Sweden	Turkey	United Kingdom

Table showing details of acceptance of the 1988 Additional Protocol [1]

accepted (shaded) | not accepted (blank)

Provision of the Protocol	Czech Republic	Denmark	Finland	Greece	Netherlands	Norway	Slovakia	Spain
Article 1	accepted	accepted	accepted	accepted	accepted	accepted	accepted	accepted
Article 2	accepted	accepted	accepted	accepted	accepted	accepted	accepted	accepted
Article 3	accepted	accepted	accepted	accepted	accepted	accepted	accepted	accepted
Article 4	accepted	accepted	accepted	accepted	not accepted	accepted	accepted	accepted

[5] The provisions of the 1988 Additional Protocol are contained in the revised European Social Charter: Articles 1 to 4 of the Additional Protocol correspond to Articles 20 to 23 of the revised Charter.

Sales agents for publications of the Council of Europe
Agents de vente des publications du Conseil de l'Europe

AUSTRALIA/AUSTRALIE
Hunter Publications, 58A, Gipps Street
AUS-3066 COLLINGWOOD, Victoria
Tel.: (61) 3 9417 5361
Fax: (61) 3 9419 7154
E-mail: Sales@hunter-pubs.com.au
http://www.hunter-pubs.com.au

AUSTRIA/AUTRICHE
Gerold und Co., Graben 31
A-1011 WIEN 1
Tel.: (43) 1 533 5014
Fax: (43) 1 533 5014 18
E-mail: buch@gerold.telecom.at
http://www.gerold.at

BELGIUM/BELGIQUE
La Librairie européenne SA
50, avenue A. Jonnart
B-1200 BRUXELLES 20
Tel.: (32) 2 734 0281
Fax: (32) 2 735 0860
E-mail: info@libeurop.be
http://www.libeurop.be

Jean de Lannoy
202, avenue du Roi
B-1190 BRUXELLES
Tel.: (32) 2 538 4308
Fax: (32) 2 538 0841
E-mail: jean.de.lannoy@euronet.be
http://www.jean-de-lannoy.be

CANADA
Renouf Publishing Company Limited
5369 Chemin Canotek Road
CDN-OTTAWA, Ontario, K1J 9J3
Tel.: (1) 613 745 2665
Fax: (1) 613 745 7660
E-mail: order.dept@renoufbooks.com
http://www.renoufbooks.com

CZECH REPUBLIC/RÉPUBLIQUE TCHÈQUE
USIS, Publication Service
Havelkova 22
CZ-130 00 PRAHA 3
Tel./Fax: (420) 2 2423 1114

DENMARK/DANEMARK
Munksgaard
35 Norre Sogade, PO Box 173
DK-1005 KØBENHAVN K
Tel.: (45) 7 733 3333
Fax: (45) 7 733 3377
E-mail: direct@munksgaarddirect.dk
http://www.munksgaarddirect.dk

FINLAND/FINLANDE
Akateeminen Kirjakauppa
Keskuskatu 1, PO Box 218
FIN-00381 HELSINKI
Tel.: (358) 9 121 41
Fax: (358) 9 121 4450
E-mail: akatilaus@stockmann.fi
http://www.akatilaus.akateeminen.com

FRANCE
La Documentation française
29 quai Voltaire
F-75007 PARIS
Tel.: (33) 01 40 15 71 10
Fax: (33) 01 40 15 72 30
E-mail: libparis@ladocfrancaise.gouv.fr
http://www.ladocfrancaise.gouv.fr

GERMANY/ALLEMAGNE
UNO Verlag
Proppelsdorfer Allee 55
D-53115 BONN
Tel.: (49) 2 28 94 90 231
Fax: (49) 2 28 21 74 92
E-mail: unoverlag@aol.com
http://www.uno-verlag.de

GREECE/GRÈCE
Librairie Kauffmann
Mavrokordatou 9
GR-ATHINAI 106 78
Tel.: (30) 1 38 29 283
Fax: (30) 1 38 33 967

HUNGARY/HONGRIE
Euro Info Service
Hungexpo Europa Kozpont ter 1
H-1101 BUDAPEST
Tel.: (361) 264 8270
Fax: (361) 264 8271
E-mail: euroinfo@euroinfo.hu
http://www.euroinfo.hu

ITALY/ITALIE
Libreria Commissionaria Sansoni
Via Duca di Calabria 1/1, CP 552
I-50125 FIRENZE
Tel.: (39) 556 4831
Fax: (39) 556 41257
E-mail: licosa@licosa.com
http://www.licosa.com

NETHERLANDS/PAYS-BAS
De Lindeboom Internationale Publikaties
PO Box 202, MA de Ruyterstraat 20 A
NL-7480 AE HAAKSBERGEN
Tel.: (31) 53 574 0004
Fax: (31) 53 572 9296
E-mail: lindeboo@worldonline.nl
http://home-1-worldonline.nl/~lindeboo/

NORWAY/NORVÈGE
Akademika, A/S Universitetsbokhandel
PO Box 84, Blindern
N-0314 OSLO
Tel.: (47) 22 85 30 30
Fax: (47) 23 12 24 20

POLAND/POLOGNE
Głowna Księgarnia Naukowa
im. B. Prusa
Krakowskie Przedmiescie 7
PL-00-068 WARSZAWA
Tel.: (48) 29 22 66
Fax: (48) 22 26 64 49
E-mail: inter@internews.com.pl
http://www.internews.com.pl

PORTUGAL
Livraria Portugal
Rua do Carmo, 70
P-1200 LISBOA
Tel.: (351) 13 47 49 82
Fax: (351) 13 47 02 64
E-mail: liv.portugal@mail.telepac.pt

SPAIN/ESPAGNE
Mundi-Prensa Libros SA
Castelló 37
E-28001 MADRID
Tel.: (34) 914 36 37 00
Fax: (34) 915 75 39 98
E-mail: libreria@mundiprensa.es
http://www.mundiprensa.com

SWITZERLAND/SUISSE
BERSY
Route d'Uvrier 15
CH-1958 LIVRIER/SION
Tel.: (41) 27 203 73 30
Fax: (41) 27 203 73 32
E-mail: bersy@freesurf.ch

Adeco – Van Diermen
Chemin du Lacuez 41
CH-1807 BLONAY
Tel.: (41) 21 943 26 73
Fax: (41) 21 943 36 06
E-mail: mvandier@worldcom.ch

UNITED KINGDOM/ROYAUME-UNI
TSO (formerly HMSO)
51 Nine Elms Lane
GB-LONDON SW8 5DR
Tel.: (44) 207 873 8372
Fax: (44) 207 873 8200
E-mail: customer.services@theso.co.uk
http://www.the-stationery-office.co.uk
http://www.itsofficial.net

UNITED STATES and CANADA/ ÉTATS-UNIS et CANADA
Manhattan Publishing Company
468 Albany Post Road, PO Box 850
CROTON-ON-HUDSON,
NY 10520, USA
Tel.: (1) 914 271 5194
Fax: (1) 914 271 5856
E-mail: Info@manhattanpublishing.com
http://www.manhattanpublishing.com

STRASBOURG
Librairie Kléber
Palais de l'Europe
F-67075 STRASBOURG Cedex
Fax: (33) 03 88 52 91 21

Council of Europe Publishing/Editions du Conseil de l'Europe
F-67075 Strasbourg Cedex
Tel.: (33) 03 88 41 25 81 – Fax: (33) 03 88 41 39 10 – E-mail: publishing@coe.int – Web site: http://book.coe.int